CONFLICT RESOLUTION

This book belongs to:
David Gustafson

CONFLICT
RESOLUTION

Cross-Cultural Perspectives

Edited by
KEVIN AVRUCH,
PETER W. BLACK,
and
JOSEPH A. SCIMECCA

Westport, Connecticut
London

The Library of Congress has catalogued the hardcover edition as follows:

Conflict resolution : cross-cultural perspectives / edited by Kevin
    Avruch, Peter W. Black, and Joseph A. Scimecca.
        p.   cm.—(Contributions in ethnic studies, ISSN 0196–7088 ;
    no. 28)
    Includes bibliographical references and index.
    ISBN 0–313–25796–5 (alk. paper)
        1. Intergroup relations—Cross-cultural studies   2. Conflict
    management—Cross-cultural studies.   I. Avruch, Kevin.   II. Black,
    Peter W.   III. Scimecca, Joseph A.   IV. Series.
    HM131.C74543   1991
    303.6'9—dc20   91–15991

British Library Cataloguing in Publication Data is available.

A hardcover edition of *Conflict Resolution* is available from
Greenwood Press, an imprint of Greenwood Publishing Group, Inc.
(Contributions in Ethnic Studies, Number 28; ISBN 0–313–25796–5)

Library of Congress Catalog Card Number: 91–15991
ISBN: 0–275–96442–6 (pbk.)

First published in 1991

Praeger Publishers, 88 Post Road West, Westport, CT 06881
An imprint of Greenwood Publishing Group, Inc.

Printed in the United States of America

The paper used in this book complies with the
Permanent Paper Standard issued by the National
Information Standards Organization (Z39.48–1984).

10 9 8 7 6 5 4 3 2 1

This Book is Dedicated to the
Memory of Bryant M. Wedge, 1921–1987

Contents

Foreword

Problems arise when peoples with different cultures and goals come together and interact. The modes of adjustment or conflict are various, but usually one group dominates or attempts to dominate the other. Eventually some accommodation is reached, but the process is likely to be long and, for the weaker group, painful. No one scholarly discipline monopolizes the research necessary to comprehend these intergroup relations. The emerging analysis, consequently, is inevitably of interest to historians, social scientists, psychologists, and psychiatrists.

In the majority of chapters in this anthology, case studies reveal how specific non-Western, nonindustrial societies resolve or fail to resolve their own internal conflicts. Sometimes such conflicts can be productive and "harmony" may or may not be the ideal to be achieved. The authors derive cultural principles that transcend the specific conflicts they describe in detail. They report new, empirical data in their analyses and interpretations.

In addition, the view is expressed that such cross-cultural perspectives may not be neglected and are truly essential to comprehend or resolve conflicts in Western societies that, as is glaringly evident, are ending this century with a gargantuan incidence of conflicts. When efforts are made, as they must be, to resolve conflicts between members of ethnic groups who reside in the same society or in different societies, their expectations, interactions, and eventual acceptance or rejection of proposed resolutions are likely to be markedly affected by their cultural backgrounds as well as by their own unique ways of behaving and assessing current problems. A brief historical account is offered that suggests that detached, academic researchers have sought, although not impressively or successfully, to resolve conflicts of various sorts.

In general terms social scientists and others are deliberately or inadvertently challenged to improve some of their cherished categories, such as culture, conflict, and even reality.

This book is appropriately dedicated to the memory of Bryant M. Wedge, a psychiatrist who extended his craft into managerial and international situations. Those of us who knew him appreciated, too, his ability to express himself clearly without resorting to jargon and neologisms. The editors by and large have followed his example and offer a volume worthy of him.

LEONARD W. DOOB

CONFLICT RESOLUTION

1

Introduction: Culture and Conflict Resolution

Kevin Avruch

BENVENISTI'S COMPLAINT

Meron Benvenisti is a Jewish Israeli, a *sabra* (one born in Israel), and a recognized scholar of the Crusader period. His father is a Sephardi—a speaker of Ladino, a dialect of Castilian Spanish laced with Judeo-Arabic, spoken in the late fifteenth century, when both Jews and Muslims were expelled from Catholic Spain. His mother is an Ashkenazi—a Lithuanian speaker of Yiddish, a dialect of High German laced with Hebrew, Aramaic, and Slavic. Benvenisti is no stranger, then, to the nuances of culture. In the 1970s he served under Teddy Kollek as a deputy mayor of Jerusalem, with special responsibilities over East Jerusalem and its Arab inhabitants. By the early 1980s, due in part to his public pronouncements on behalf of Arab rights and his public pessimism about the future of Arab-Jewish relations, he was out of public office and forced into the semiretirement of a scholar's life. But he did not return to the study of the Crusades. He has since devoted himself to studies of contemporary Israel, to Jewish policies on the West Bank, to the implications these carry for the Israeli-Palestinian conflict.

In a political memoir called *Conflicts and Contradictions* Benvenisti writes with some exasperation of dealings with conflict "resolvers...who believe that communal conflicts are like a chessboard where one can think up the best arrangement of chess pieces and move them all at once" (1986:118). Such "frustrated peacemakers," as he calls them, even go so far as to organize themselves into a new academic specialty. Benvenisti recalls a particular encounter with them:

I became extremely aware of the discipline called "conflict resolution," especially of the branch specializing in producing manuals for resolving conflicts in easy steps. One winter not long ago I participated in a workshop for resolving the Israeli-Palestinian conflict held at a distinguished American university. Our workshop was squeezed between similar workshops dealing with the "northern Ireland conflict" and the "Cyprus conflict." My frustration grew slowly until at a formal dinner I had one glass too many. I stood up and said to the organizer, a "resolver" par excellence, "I wonder if you know who we are at all. For all you care, we can be Zimbabweans, Basques, Arabs, Jews, Catholics, Protestants, Greeks, Turks. To you we are just guinea pigs to be tested, or at best to be engineered." To his credit, I hasten to add, he stood up and, with tears in his eyes, said, "Thank you, I needed that." (1986:118–19)

CONFLICT RESOLUTION: A NEW "CLINICAL" DISCIPLINE?

In one sense the purpose of this volume is to offer the beginnings of a response to "Benvenisti's complaint": to move beyond a tearful acknowledgment and take culture seriously in the emerging field of scholarly and political concerns called "conflict resolution." The response proposed by this collection is modest. For one thing, we chose not to leap to the level of nation-state conflicts in the global arena. Culture does have a role to play in our understanding of international security, of conflict resolution in the so-called state system (see Rubinstein and Foster 1988), but our goal is to underline its relevance to interpersonal, community, and institutional conflicts. In addition, two of the chapters step back and view this development from a larger perspective. Joseph Scimecca focuses on the beginnings and incipient professionalization of the new field in the United States. Laura Nader critically considers this emergence as a larger cultural construction—a problem in the sociology, or political economy, of knowledge.

More generally the impetus for this volume, which deals with aspects of a cultural approach to understanding conflict and conflict resolution, comes from the work of all three editors in the Center (now Institute) for Conflict Analysis and Resolution at George Mason University. Established in 1980 largely through efforts of the late social psychiatrist Bryant Wedge, the center in 1982 became the first institution of higher education in the United States to offer a professional postgraduate degree in conflict management—thus helping to proclaim the new discipline that so discomfited Benvenisti. In 1988 it admitted its first class of doctoral students into the first Ph.D. program in conflict analysis and resolution in the world.

From its inception the center brought together a multidisciplinary group of social scientists oriented strongly toward the development of both "theory" and "practice" in conflict resolution. Wedge himself was

oriented toward practical applications. Perhaps because of his background in medicine, the reigning metaphor for this part of our endeavor
became "clinical." In the earliest M.S. curriculum Wedge stressed the
mastery of conflict management "process"—training, intervention, and
technique—over leisurely theorizing and introspection. On one level
Wedge understood that conflict was inevitable, not always bad, and often
an engine of desirable social change. But as an engaged and committed
social activist, he also saw conflict in the nuclear age as dangerous and
pathological. Social conflict that escalates into violence he called the result
of "narcissistic rage," a pathology of the self suffered and acted out by
a group or nation (Wedge 1986). If, to carry the clinical metaphor further, pervasive unmanaged conflict was a sort of endemic and pandemic
social pathology, then the costs of epidemic outbreaks—individual,
group, mass, and state violence in the nuclear age—were far too high
to contemplate passively from the sidelines.

The clinical metaphor that guided our endeavors had several consequences, some of them unintended. While it did galvanize a number of
faculty and attract activist graduate students—one of the intended consequences—it also helped mask some real problems in reconciling conflict
resolution "theory" (whose development we saw as both necessary and
imminent) and "practice." Practice appeared to be much further developed than theory. After all, long before George Mason University came
on the scene, there were practitioners of the art—the several arts—of
conflict resolution, conflict management, conflict regulation, or conflict
intervention, to cite some of the terms used. There were mediators,
arbitrators, and adjudicators of one sort or another. There were diplomats, arms-reduction negotiators, management-labor relations specialists, divorce mediators, family therapists, even, arguably, lawyers in
at least some of their guises and practices.

At certain levels of professional accomplishment, all of these individuals could claim to have mastered some area of practice—but by following what sorts of "theory"? Theoreticians generalize, abstract, model,
and propose overarching explanations of, say, negotiations. They offer
principles and prescriptions. At their most immodest, such theoreticians
may speak of the "science" of negotiations. Practitioners (say, in labor
relations) in contrast tend to rely on years of master apprenticing, sea-
soning, experience, "feel," and intuition. When they come to teach their
apprentices they are more apt to offer descriptions of the world rather
than prescriptions for it. They might speak of the "art" of negotiations
or of their craft, rather than of a "science" (Raiffa 1982).

In the field of conflict resolution no less than in medicine, the tension
between art and science, practice and theory, is a basic one. Sometimes
theory suggests a new practice—a new therapy or drug, to pursue the
medical analogy. But just as often, it seems, practice continues despite

inadequate theory, or no theory, or just plain wrong theory. For example, physicians know the powerful analgesic effects of salicylic acid, and have used it clinically, for a long time, without understanding much or any of the neurology or biochemistry that makes it work. Again, in some instances physicians use leeches today (to remove microbloodclots post-surgically, for example), and physicians used them two centuries ago (to remove evil spirits or humours). The theory behind the use was different in each case (and modern medicine proclaims the latter one just plain wrong), although superficially the practice looks the same.

A clinical orientation can mask problems of the relation between theory and practice because very often it is practice that "drives" theory. (As it must. We will use a drug that we know works before we understand how or why it works. Alternatively, we can think we know why it works and be wrong, and this will have no effect on its actual efficacy, since actual efficacy is independent of our theories of efficacy.) Theory follows practice, in this case, or one can say that practice dominates theory. The implication of this, of course, is that *where* practice is situated *there* will theory be derived.

In medicine, perhaps, such distinctions may be moot. A broken leg is a broken leg in Papua New Guinea or Stockholm, and aspirin is an effective analgesic in both places. But the same cannot be said of a broken marriage, a broken friendship, or a broken promise. Marriages, friendships, and promises, among many other things, are constituted not by the panspecies biology of *Homo sapiens sapiens*, but by culture. However unproblematic the clinical orientation may be for medicine, the same cannot be said for such an orientation in conflict resolution. In this emerging field, most of the practice we know about is in the West and situated in special portions of it: in industrial or postindustrial societies, in bureaucratically organized states with formal judiciaries backed by coercive structures, in relations between organized labor and management, between corporations, between diplomats, among elites, among the middle classes, among the essentially empowered. In this case the warning, *where practice is situated there is theory derived*, raises a particular set of problems. Some of them are variants on Benvenisti's complaint, that an assumed universal practice dismisses situated differences. These problems, once again, point to culture.

A CULTURAL APPROACH TO
CONFLICT RESOLUTION

Consider, for example, a theory of negotiation derived from white middle-class American practice. Among other things such a theory prescribes (and as it happens, delimits) the role of affect (emotions) in the process of negotiation. Partly because it deals with affect, such a theory also describes a concept of the person—self and other—as negotiator. Such a person is expected to remain calm, to think logically, and to calculate rationally. But is this conception universally valid? Thomas Kochman (1981:40) holds that black and white Americans approach negotiation, and specifically the issue of "emotionality," very differently:

In general, whites take a view of the negotiating procedure that is markedly different from the view taken by blacks. Though blacks regard whites as devious in insisting that emotions be left in front of the meeting-room door, whites think that blacks are being devious by insisting on bringing those emotions into the room. [Whites believe that] If the meeting is to be successful, the black's anger and hostility will be allayed by the results of the meeting. . . . Blacks simply do not see things that way. To leave their emotions aside is not their responsibility; it is the whites' responsibility to provide them first with a reason to do so.

With respect to affect, two very different sorts of "persons" confront one another in black/white negotiations. In one sense both persons are conceptually coequal. Both are based on "folk" models of personhood, drawn from black and white American culture, respectively. But in an important sense they are not at all coequal. White society dominates black, and therefore the white "folk" model represents the standard (of "proper" behavior and "acceptable" personhood) by which the other is judged. A cultural difference is thus reduced to a matter of "ethnicity." Ethnics are always placed on the periphery. (The only "folk" model becomes the "black folk" model.) Kochman links these different senses of the person with the larger problems of power and domination: "The requirement to behave calmly, rationally, unemotionally, and logically when negotiating is looked upon by blacks as a *political requirement*—and to accede to it in advance is considered a *political defeat*" (1981:40, emphasis added).

The "politics of personhood" establishes the hegemony of one conception of it over others. As the proper and acceptable negotiator is evaluated, so too is the process of negotiation. This means that the white theory of negotiation is not simply one theory among a number of alternatives; it becomes theory for negotiation in general. The discourse of such a theory, which, conceptually speaking, is but one folk model among many, gets reified and elevated to the status of—if not science then—an expert system. Thus conflict resolution as a new discipline may join other expert systems, such as jurisprudence, homeopathic medicine, or industrial psychology. Distancing themselves from their roots in the commonsense knowledge and belief systems of the folk, they are all characterized by a self-consciousness that sets them and their experts apart, and points to the engineered dimension of such systems where specialists codify, systematize, and administer. They create rules and compile rule-books. They privilege a particular discourse.

The thrust of much recent work in the sociology of law, and especially critical legal studies (Beirne and Quinney 1982; Kairys 1982; Critical Legal Studies Symposium 1984), has been to assert that a privileged discourse is not necessarily a veridical or even a relevant one. Sally Merry (1986, 1990), for example, has demonstrated the multiplicity of what she calls "legal ideologies" existing between the "courthouse elites" and the working class in American culture. Sally Merry and Susan Silbey (1984) explain the apparent unattractiveness of many alternative dispute resolution (ADR) media (court-ordered mediation, for example), and the subsequent low rates of voluntary usage to all the middle class, as due to the fact that the basic assumptions about the person—as rational, strategic, maximizing, and the like—built into those media have more to do with the worldview of the jurists and social scientists who designed them, than with those for whom they are intended. Merry criticizes the ADR movement as a whole for ignoring the "interactive relationship between dispute resolution and cultural practice" (1987:2060), and thus isolating disputes from the very social and cultural contexts that render them meaningful. The ADR movement, as Nader and Scimecca's contributions to this volume make clear, is where the new discipline of conflict resolution has attached itself (some lawyers say limpet-like) to the older one of law (Adler 1987).

There are nevertheless important differences in the conception of the person and of human nature in law and conflict resolution. The newness and social science bias of conflict resolution, as compared to law, give it a pragmatic and technocratic gloss that law may avoid. Nevertheless the folk conceptions of the person—and of a human nature that is presumed to animate such a person—that we encountered in Kochman's description of white American culture are the very ones that have been elevated to become the axioms of contemporary conflict resolution theory.

The essential axiom assumed by conflict resolution theory has to do with rationality. In the theory "calm," "rational," and "logical" (and the important one we may gloss as "maximizing") are not just person-descriptors, as in any folk psychology, but rather person-predicates. In its starkest form in conflict resolution studies this model comes to us in the mathematical theory of games (von Neumann and Morgenstern 1944; Rapoport 1960). With slightly fuzzier edges it comes to us in the bargaining theories of economists. Rationality and maximization are conserved, although some of the mathematical strictures are loosened (Gulliver 1979:36–51). And, often refracted by social psychologists, it comes to us in a slew of semipopular theorizing about conflict resolution, most notably in *Getting to Yes* by Roger Fisher and William Ury (1981). Conflict resolution or problem solving, as they prefer, comes to resemble a sort of archeology in which one lays bare overlying strata ("positions") to get at underlying ones ("interests"). Elsewhere Kevin Avruch and Peter W.

Black (1990) have explored some of the implications for conflict reso-lution theory of these and related metaphors, ones that flow from "stra-tigraphic" conceptions of human nature and the person. But for our purposes here, and in keeping with the points raised by Kochman on black/white conflicts, let us return to the more specific problem of emotions.

Emotions, in Fisher and Ury's world, comprise something that one must "get past" (by allowing to "ventilate," for example) in order to get to underlying layers of interests. This, of course, is how one gets to the underlying stratum of rationality, where "efficient" problem solving is possible (Raiffa 1982:139). Separate the person from the problem, they advise. This is as much to say that one ought to separate the person from emotions. Such a prescription assumes a human nature—and a resulting conception of the person—in which the two, person and emo-tions, are in fact separable. Notice that we have returned to the "folk model" of the person that, according to Kochman, middle-class white Americans bring with them to meetings with black Americans. (There emotions can be "left in front of the meeting-room door.") But by the time Kochman's (ethnographic) description ends up as Fisher and Ury's (practice-situated) prescription, the folk model has been promoted in rank—enshrined in an expert's system. Because there was no self-reflexive consideration of the prescription's cultural (class and ethnic) provenance, its promotion occurred totally unself-consciously. Situated in such a practice, the folk model is enshrined, and derived, as theory.

THE CULTURE OF CONFLICT RESOLUTION: POWER AND PRAXIS

There are in fact at least two ways in which the assumption that "per-son" and "emotions" are easily separable is problematic. Both involve the cultural construction of personhood, but the first focuses our atten-tion explicitly on power. It flows from Kochman's ethnography and can be found in his remark that the separation of emotions—"leaving them at the door"—is for the blacks a *political* act. Blacks may understand the white conception of personhood-without-affect but choose not to accede to it. Middle-class blacks may even share this conception and still hold off on acceding to it prematurely in negotiations, for political reasons. Such "tactical uses of passion," to borrow F. G. Bailey's (1983) phrase, may occur as self-consciously rhetorical devices. They often occur as well, as Kochman's example illustrates, in situations of gross inequalities of power among contestants.

In this volume Bailey's chapter (Chapter 4) pursues the first—rhetor-ical and persuasive—use of emotions and personhood, while Laura Na-der (Chapter 3) considers the role of power. Bailey explores his theme by seeing personhood as constructed in terms of culturally constituted presentations of self called "masks." Masks are worn to convince others to accept certain definitions of situations, called "caricatures." Such masks and caricatures arise particularly in situations of conflict. They comprise, indeed, the resources that actors bring to conflicts in order to "manage" them. Bailey's sense of "conflict management" is adversarial and highly conflictual. Management is conflict carried on under a rhetorical banner that calls it its opposite. In this view "peacemakers" are those who can restrain antagonists by imposing their definition of the situation on them. Conflict managers, Bailey writes, are also contestants for power.

Although Bailey has focused his analysis on the microsociology of conflict, this message is also Nader's. The so-called harmony model of law that undergirds ADR (and arguably the entire emergent field of conflict resolution) is very much linked in Nader's analysis to issues of control and autonomy. She compares the "confrontational decade" of the 1960s in the United States, with its concern for justice and rights, with the "harmonious" 1970s and 1980s, with its antilitigious cry, "Don't be negative!" ADR is part of a set of "management techniques" (here echoing Bailey's sense of management), including education and some forms of therapy and therapeutic communities, that all function finally to suppress criticism. In a metaphor that surpasses Bailey's invocation of mere persuasion, and vividly characterizes the political agenda behind ADR and conflict resolution as social movements, Nader calls the harmony model a "cultural soma" that the powerful may use to anesthetize the disempowered. (She also shows that it can be used the other way, "antihegemonically," as the Zapotec do.)

Power, authority, and conflict "management" techniques are also the concerns of Kamil Kozan's study of interpersonal conflict styles among Jordanian managers, educators, and bureaucrats (Chapter 5). Kozan's analysis rests on the "dual-concern" model of conflict resolution as developed by R. R. Blake and J. S. Mouton (1964) and refined by K. Thomas (1976; see also Pruitt and Rubin 1986:28–35). Because a relatively large research literature exists in organizational theory and behavior studies (largely out of American business schools) about American managers and their conflict resolution styles, Kozan is able to compare the Jordanian profile with the (generic) American one.

Focusing on the issues of authority relations between the parties and the topic of their dispute, Kozan finds that, compared to Americans, Jordanians are extrasensitive on matters concerning personal habits, and managers will often "accommodate" subordinates. In fact, there are very low levels of "forcing" down the hierarchy, despite a public image of authoritarianism and centralized decision making. Decisions by superiors must be "sold" to subordinates, not imposed. Power, writes Kozan, is certainly sought and protected but not forcefully used to achieve organizational objectives. This leads to a situation of "ritualistic formalism," one where centralization is only apparent, not effective. Nevertheless, as Kozan learns when he delves further into his case-study material, while authority might be ritualistic with respect to formal organizational goals (the "business of the organization"), so that compromise and accommodation are the favored conflict resolution styles, this is certainly not the case when it comes to the assertion of personal power. In a neat comparison to Bailey's deans and provosts, Kozan describes a university president who may not always ensure that policy decisions are being implemented throughout the university, but has total control over who gets into university housing. To explain this apparent paradox—personal power is sought after but forcing is avoided—Kozan explores dimensions of Jordanian and Arab culture.

THE CULTURE OF CONFLICT RESOLUTION: MORAL COMMUNITIES AND MORAL ECONOMIES

In one approach to personhood, emotions, and conflict, culture enters the picture as a resource capable of mediating disequal power relations—"masking" them in both Bailey and Nader's senses. There is a second approach to culture and conflict, one that also takes us into considerations of personhood (self and others) and emotions. But here culture is not only a mediating resource; it is fully constitutive. Here, for example, culture may imply a radically different conception of personhood—one where person and emotions, say, are not a priori separable (Lutz 1988:91–92), or one where the "Western-inflected" conception of the self/person, wherein the autonomous self is clearly demarcated from other autonomous persons, is not parsed the same way (Shweder and Bourne 1984:193–95). In these cases we may presume first that emotions are not available for tactical uses similar to those with which blacks bedevil whites. (This is not to say they are never available for tactical uses!) We may also presume that some whole notions of what conflict (and thus conflict resolution) is about—autonomous, individualistic, calculating, and ruthless self-maximizers pursuing their goals in rationalist and utilitarian universes—are in for serious recastings.

Merry has written—mainly to remind certain jurists, proponents of ADR, and inveterate behaviorists—that disputing "is cultural behavior, informed by participants' moral views about how to fight, the meaning participants attach to going to court, social practices that indicate when and how to escalate disputes to a public forum, and participants' notions of rights and entitlements. Parties to a dispute operate within systems of meaning.... The normative framework shapes the way people conceptualize problems, the ways they pursue them, and the kinds of solutions they look for" (1987:2063). Such a view, in this volume, finds clear expression in Peter Just's analysis of conflict resolution and dispute settlement among the Dou Donggo of Indonesia (Chapter 6).

Just argues that conflict resolution processes must be understood in their larger context, particularly in terms of what he calls the "moral economy" of the society. Such a moral economy is itself based on underlying and culturally constituted assumptions about the nature of human nature, the individual, social behavior, and social order itself, all of which have a moral valence. Building on earlier work on the sociology of Dou Donggo law and evidentiary procedures (Just 1986), he describes two disputes, one resulting in "mediation," the other in "adjudication," in rich detail. With his focus on conflict resolution as aiming to restore "appropriate" social relations in relatively closed (although by no means hermetically sealed) "moral communities," Just echoes the findings of the classic studies of the anthropology of law and dispute resolution (Gluckman 1955; Gibbs 1963; Nader 1964). These studies understood conflict resolution in small-scale, multistranded social systems from within the larger functionalist paradigm of system maintenance (Gluckman's "peace in the feud" idea), equilibrium (Nader's notion of "making a balance"), and individual adaptation (Gibbs' equation of conflict resolution and therapy; see on this last point White's and Shook and Kwan's chapters in this volume). But Just also goes beyond the functionalist program precisely as he directs our attention to the Dou Donggo's constitution of their life-worlds: *their* understandings of human nature, of appropriate aggression, of the "persons" of mediators and adjudicators, of the deep-seated moral assumptions about the equality of husbands and wives in a "successful" marriage, and so on. (He also surpasses the classic functionalist paradigm in his careful and insightful discussions of Dou Donggo political and jural encapsulation in the Indonesian state, changing calculi of "success" for men and women, and the monetarization of the local economy, among other things.)

Although starting from the Durkheimian language of moral communities and social relations, Just brings us back again to considering the cultural constructions of human nature and personhood—self and others—as crucial to our understanding of Dou Donggo conflict resolution theory and practice.

This attention to the "folks'" own understandings of conflict and ways to manage it is at the center of Peter Black's analysis (Chapter 7). Black is interested in uncovering the "cultural logic" that Tobians themselves use when faced with conflict and the need to manage or resolve it. He takes us into the middle of the drama of an attempted murder that occurred during his fieldwork on the island. At the same time as he describes the Tobian responses to, and understandings of, the unfolding events, he contrasts his own. The variance in these responses and understandings is what brings on the "surprise" of his title. His own understandings of what constitutes a "proper" investigation of an attempted murder—great attention paid to the question of motive, for example— or his astonishment at the utterly anticlimactic and indecisive way in which the magistrate's meeting-of-inquiry ended, are used by Black as the wedge into the Tobians' world. This world—like all such worlds-of-meaning, our own included—rests on diverse sets of "cultural presuppositions" that people use to frame and reframe "narratives." The narratives often use events of the past (in this case an attempted murder that occurred three decades before) to make sensible those of the present—and thus to provide prescriptions for the future. These narratives are themselves often subject to negotiation in their telling and retelling. Their verisimilitude nevertheless resides ultimately in shared "common sense." What is a person really like? How do you teach a child? Why should one try to murder another? This kind of knowledge is of course what Tobians refer to naturally (but never quite artlessly) in their management of conflictual situations. Black concludes by emphasizing that it is to this taken-for-granted and commonsense view of things and persons that any cultural outsider (perhaps conflict intervenor) must attend.

THE CULTURE OF CONFLICT RESOLUTION: ETHNOCONFLICT THEORY AND PRAXIS

Conflicts are, John Paul Lederach writes (Chapter 8), in every sense of the word, "cultural" events. Like all cultural events, they are constituted largely by the taken-for-granted, commonsense understandings that people have about their world, including themselves and the other people who inhabit it. Such common sense includes knowledge about what is right and wrong, how to proceed, whom to turn to, when, where, and with what expectations. For analytical purposes Lederach divides his enquiry into two parts. The first deals with how people—Costa Ricans and Nicaraguan refugees in Costa Rica in particular—define, understand, and make sense of conflict and disputes. The second concerns their techniques for resolving disputes (including the use of third parties). He subsumes both parts under the rubric (following "ethnomethodology" as used by sociologists, or "ethnoscience" by anthropologists) "ethno-conflictology." There is some sense in keeping them separate. Avruch and Black (1991) deal with people's understandings of conflict and disputes in terms of "ethnoconflict theory" (*their* theory). People's techniques, processes, or practices for resolving or managing conflicts are addressed by means of "ethnopraxis." Giving these concepts separate labels and keeping them apart analytically allows us explicitly to tack back and forth between theory and practice, as this issue was raised earlier.

Earlier, the issue was raised in the context of conflict resolution as an emerging "clinical" discipline. Since clinical practice was relatively far along (although fragmented in many different arenas) and theory making relatively immature, the clinical character of the discipline led to a situation where, in an unrecognized way, practice could dominate or lead theory. Thus, where practice is situated (in the West) there will theory be derived. The chapters in this volume where the connections between ethnoconflict theories and ethnopraxes are richly explored demonstrate that this view must be refocused. In a sense, we must reverse figure and ground, since these chapters all begin with a call to understand the Costa Rican's, Santa Isabelan's, Tobian's, Dou Donggan's, or Hawaiian's phenomenology of and common sense about conflict, before exploring their respective praxes—techniques and processes—of resolution. Thus the maxim that guides these chapters, sensitive as they are to the cultural construction of conflict resolution, is the one that starts with (ethno) theory, rather than practice. Where theories (about self and others, about affect, about conflict, about right and wrong, etc.) are situated, there will practices be derived.

Both Lederach and Geoffrey White (Chapter 9) stick very close to language and the discourse of conflict—"conflict talk" in Lederach's words, "productive metaphors" in White's—in their respective analyses. Both point to the special importance of conceptions of personhood in the structuring of conflict and conflict resolution. Both warn against assuming that the "person" in Costa Rica or Santa Isabela is to be parsed in the Western mode—as an existential isolate, a highly individuated and autonomous actor. Lederach speaks of a "holistic," socially networked conception of the person. White describes the Solomon Islander as an individual embedded in a matrix of social relations. Neither the highly abstracted legal persona of Western jurisprudence, nor the rational calculator of game theory, nor the presumed "really real" inner self of Western psychotherapy, are appropriate categories of analysis.

In both Costa Rica and Santa Isabel, the root metaphors for conflict and conflict resolution have to do with "entanglements" and "disentanglements." These similarities aside, an interesting difference emerges in the way in which the Costa Ricans and Santa Isabelans approach the problem of disentangling entanglements. We can see the difference precisely because of the close attention both Lederach and White give to the respective phenomenologies of conflict and conflict-talk in their Costa Rican and Solomon Island contexts.

For the Costa Ricans, the underlying understandings of conflict and conflict resolution are cognitive and navigational in nature. One is trapped "inside" a conflict and one tries to "get out." Crucial to getting out is the first and foundational step: to *ubicarse*, which is the way one gets one's bearings, locates, and situates oneself in the larger "net" of social relations. If this self-orientation is successful, one can then *platicar*, "talk" or "dialogue," in order to *arreglar*, "fix," or "arrange" or "manage" an exit, a way out (*salidar*). The entrance of a third party (*tercero*) in these Central American interpersonal conflicts is both natural and constant, Lederach writes. The *tercero* connects people to people, and keeps the "net" integral.

In Santa Isabel, the underlying metaphors are not cognitive or navigational in nature, but affective and rhetorically suasive (but compare White's therapeutic sense of rhetoric with Bailey's more draconic and power-based one). In formal "disentangling sessions" (a formality echoed in Hawaii's revival of *ho'oponopono*) Santa Isabelans repair social relations by using emotions—"sadness," "shame," and "anger," in their English glosses—to construct, fill in, and set up, as White puts it, social scenarios in which conflict events are structured and made explainable and resolvable. He calls such sessions exercises in "moral negotiation," echoing Just's depiction of Dou Donggo moral economy and conflict resolution (but compare White's description of a Santa Isabelan's rhetoric of emotions with Just's Dou Donggo's rather more muscular rhetoric of threat and aggression). What is at stake in these sessions is the constitution of intersubjective social reality. The processes of negotiation, the ongoing and self-renewing disentanglings, matter more than the specific outcomes, decisions or "end-products."

This concern with process qua process takes us also very close to the heart of E. Victoria Shook and Leonard K. Kwan's chapter on *ho'oponopono* in contemporary Hawaii (Chapter 10). Like Lederach and White, Shook and Kwan are sensitive to the emic dimensions of conflict in native Hawaiian culture. Conflict is seen as a sort of disturbance or "blocked pathway" in the channels of "flowing affect" by which persons are connected. Citing Karen Ito (1985), they assert that the channel or "conduit" metaphor is found in the Hawaiian notion of *hukihuki*, literally "pull, pull." Colloquially, Hawaiians will say of such blocked relationships that they are "all jam up!" They may also invoke the image of *hihia*, an "entanglement"—an image we have already encountered. *Ho'oponopono* means, in this sense, a "setting to right." Focused on interpersonal, and especially family, relationships, it utilizes a third party (*haku*) as a facilitator. Often a respected elder, the *haku* is known to the parties, but is not usually directly involved in the conflict at hand.

Like White, Lederach, and Black, Shook and Kwan ground their analysis first in a discussion of indigenous ethnoconflict theory. The theory itself is an elucidation of local concepts of personhood (self and other) and cosmology. Their analysis of *ho'oponopono* as ethnopraxis, summarized in a flow chart of the process, can then highlight and contextualize the salient parts—prayer, discussion, confession, apology, forgiveness, and release—in terms of the ethnoconflict theory whence they emerge. Shook and Kwan conclude their chapter with some cautions about making too facile equivalences between, say, *ho'oponopono* and negotiation: there is not one, they state. Indeed, even the translation of *haku* as "facilitator" is one they mistrust.

Ho'oponopono fits very well the conflict-resolution-as-therapy model that James Gibbs (1963) described for the Kpelle moot, and that White alludes to in his discussion of disentangling sessions on Santa Isabel. Today it is used as well in extrafamilial settings, by ministers in their pastoral work, by social workers, and even in penology. Many of these settings are explicitly therapeutic. Although *ho'oponopono* is conceived of as part of "traditional," old native Hawaiian culture, its use fell off in the nineteenth century due to the influence of Christian missionaries. A version of it was revived, principally by Mary Kawena Pūku'i, and through her various publications and demonstration workshops in it, her version has become in recent years the model for contemporary practitioners.

In this sense *ho'oponopono* is very much a self-consciously constructed process of conflict resolution, although it claims to represent not the expert system of a newly emerging discipline (the issue that began this chapter), but rather the revival of "genuine" folk Hawaiian culture. Not quite a social movement, perhaps, in Peter Adler's (1987) sense as discussed by Scimecca in this volume, *ho'oponopono* emerges here as yet another example of an "invention of tradition" (Hobsbawm and Ranger 1983), and thus more of an ethnic marker in Fredrik Barth's (1969) terms. It is a product of "authentic" native Hawaiian "wisdom" in a multiethnic setting, one in which, moreover, native Hawaiians are disadvantaged with respect to the other ethnic groups. One is reminded here, too, of Nader's discussion of how the Zapotecs use their "harmony model" as part of their self-assertion and struggle against hegemonically dominant groups.

CULTURE AND CONFLICT RESOLUTION: SOME CONCLUDING REMARKS

Several contributors to this volume end their chapters by addressing explicitly the issue of cross-cultural conflict resolution—of "outsiders" to the culture acting as third parties, facilitators, or mediators of one sort or another. And all of them urge caution (if not outright pessimism) about the productive possibilities of such intervention. Such concerns and cautions respond directly, if not completely, to the key problem in cross-cultural conflict resolution that I termed, at the outset of this introductory chapter, "Benvenisti's complaint."

Attention to Benvenisti's complaint means that we adopt first the perspective on conflict resolution that all of these chapters demonstrate: the necessity to place conflict and conflict resolution processes in a larger sociocultural context and not isolate them from the encompassing worlds-of-meaning in which, in onging ways, they remain embedded. In particular, attention must be paid to the native's understandings of human nature and personhood (self and others)—and affect—as the starting points of our enquiries. We begin with ethnotheories and link them to ethnopraxes. While saying we must pay attention to things psychological, however, it is not our intention to psychologize the study of conflict resolution, nor promote a sort of reductionism. Ethnopsychologies, including ethnotheories of conflict, are themselves cultural and social constructions. They are not removed from the myriad effects of power, class, ethnicity, and colonialism—from, that is, the flow of history (Avruch and Black 1991). Rather, they are in part determined by such flows. The same can of course be said of ethnopraxes. Whatever their "pristine" form in some ur-authentic past (cf. *ho'oponopono*), native ethnopraxes have been incorporated (not always voluntarily) into centralized nation-state legal institutions. They may get supplemented or supplanted by the ethnopraxes of the more powerful "center"—the old imperial metropole or the new capital. For example, Just, Black, and White each describe situations where the village must always look over its shoulder, as it were, to the city. In Just's case the village successfully keeps a dispute away from central authorities; in Black's the authorities arrive by boat long after the problem has been "managed" by those in the community; and in White's case the dispute is based largely on the fact that some in the village proceeded to plead their case to the center, and so violated some essential understandings about how that moral community ought to work.

Finally, paying attention to Benvenisti's complaint means that in the face of presuming easy universal truths for processes of conflict resolution—"negotiation looks the same everywhere"—our response should be studied agnosticism. At this stage in our collective knowledge about conflict resolution in other cultures, such agnosticism represents both humility as well as a spur to further, empirical, research. In this spirit this volume is a contribution toward our understanding of this important, but still very much emergent, field.

REFERENCES

Adler, Peter. 1987. Is ADR a Social Movement? *Negotiation Journal* 3:59–71.
Avruch, Kevin, and Peter W. Black. 1990. Ideas of Human Nature in Contemporary Conflict Resolution Theory. *Negotiation Journal* 6:221–228.
———. 1991. The Culture Question and Conflict Resolution. *Peace and Change* 16:22–45.
Bailey, F. G. 1983. *The Tactical Uses of Passion*. Ithaca: Cornell University Press.

Barth, Fredrik. 1969. Introduction. In *Ethnic Groups and Boundaries*, ed. F. Barth. Boston: Little, Brown.

Beirne, Piers, and Richard Quinney, eds. 1982. *Marxism and Law*. New York: Wiley.

Benvenisti, Meron. 1986. *Conflicts and Contradictions*. New York: Villard Books/ Random House.

Blake, R. R., and J. S. Mouton. 1964. *The Managerial Grid*. Houston: Gulf.

Critical Legal Studies Symposium. 1984. *Stanford Law Review* 36(1–2).

Fisher, Roger, and William Ury. 1981. *Getting to Yes*. Boston: Houghton Mifflin.

Gibbs, James. 1963. The Kpelle Moot. *Africa* 33:1–10.

Gluckman, Max. 1955. *The Judicial Process among the Barotse of Northern Rhodesia*. Manchester: Manchester University Press.

Gulliver, P. H. 1979. *Disputes and Negotiations: A Cross-Cultural Perspective*. Orlando: Academic.

Hobsbawm, Eric, and Terence Ranger, eds. 1983. *The Invention of Tradition*. Cambridge: Cambridge University Press.

Ito, Karen. 1985. Affective Bonds: Hawaiian Interrelationships of Self. In *Person, Self and Experience: Exploring Pacific Ethnopsychologies*, eds. G. White and J. Kirkpatrick. Berkeley: University of California Press.

Just, Peter. 1986. Let the Evidence Fit the Crime: Evidence, Law, and "Sociological Truth" among the Dou Donggo. *American Ethnologist* 13:43–61.

Kairys, David. ed. 1982. *The Politics of Law: A Progressive Critique*. New York: Pantheon.

Kochman, Thomas. 1981. *Black and White Styles in Conflict*. Chicago: University of Chicago Press.

Lutz, Catherine. 1988. *Unnatural Emotions: Everyday Sentiments on a Micronesian Atoll and Their Challenge to Western Theory*. Chicago: University of Chicago Press.

Merry, Sally. 1986. Everyday Understandings of the Law in Working-Class America. *American Ethnologist* 11:253–70.

———. 1987. Disputing Without Culture. *Harvard Law Review* 100:2057–73.

———. 1990. *Getting Justice and Getting Even*. Chicago: University of Chicago Press.

Merry, Sally, and Susan Silbey. 1984. What Do Plaintiffs Want? Reexamining the Concept of Dispute. *Justice System Journal* 9:151–78.

Nader, Laura. 1964. An Analysis of Zapotec Law Cases. *Ethnology* 3:404–19.

Von Neumann, J., and O. Morgenstern. 1944. *Theory of Games and Economic Behavior*. Princeton: Princeton University Press.

Pruitt, D., and J. Rubin. 1986. *Social Conflict: Escalation, Stalemate, and Settlement*. New York: Random House.

Raiffa, Howard. 1982. *The Art and Science of Negotiation*. Cambridge: Harvard University Press.

Rapoport, Anatol. 1960. *Fights, Games and Debates*. Ann Arbor: University of Michigan Press.

Rubinstein, Robert, and Mary LeCron Foster, eds. 1988. *The Social Dynamics of Peace and Conflict: Culture in International Security*. Boulder: Westview.

Shweder, Richard, and Edmund Bourne. 1984. Does the Concept of the Person

Vary Cross-Culturally? In *Culture Theory: Essays in Mind, Self, and Emotion,* eds. R. Shweder and R. LeVine. Cambridge: Cambridge University Press.

Thomas, K. 1976. Conflict and Conflict Management. In *Handbook of Organizational and Industrial Psychology,* ed. M. Dunnette. Chicago: Rand McNally.

Wedge, Bryant. 1986. Psychology of the Self in Social Conflict. In *International Conflict Resolution: Theory and Practice,* eds. E. Azar and J. Burton. Boulder: Lynne Rienner.

2

Conflict Resolution in the United States: The Emergence of a Profession?

Joseph A. Scimecca

A *Fortune 500* company hires specialists to deal with disputes between employees and customers. The State Department's Center for the Study of Foreign Affairs holds a number of symposia and workshops that bring together diplomats who have been active in recent international negotiations and academicians who have studied these negotiations in an attempt to formulate techniques that can be taught to American foreign service officers. A Catholic bishop is summoned as a mediator when Cuban-American prisoners begin to riot. Neutral third parties are called in to help resolve community housing disputes in the Midwest. Thousands of couples, instead of retaining a divorce lawyer, seek out mediators who help facilitate the process whereby the couples work out the conditions of the divorce on their own. Environmentalists and executives of a company accused of polluting a stream meet to resolve their differences at a university-run mediation center in the Southeast. All of these examples are part of a new way of dealing with conflict.

These new approaches to conflict are usually referred to by the general term "conflict resolution." Something whose roots can be traced to four (sometimes separate, sometimes intertwining) movements, all of which began in the mid-1960s and early 1970s: (1) new developments in organizational relations; (2) the introduction of the "problem-solving workshop" in international relations; (3) a redirection of religious figures from activist work in peace-related endeavors to an emphasis upon "peacemaking"; and (4) the criticism of lawyers and the court system by the general public that resulted in what is known as alternative dispute resolution (ADR).

These four movements, which comprise the major divisions in the new field of conflict resolution,[1] are all part of a more encompassing phenomenon in recent American history—the realization that the bureaucratization of the modern world has resulted in extreme depersonalization. This realization resulted in the questioning of legitimate authority characteristic of the 1960s and early 1970s in America. Thus, the emergence of the field of conflict resolution must be seen in the context of the larger framework of social and cultural change in American society.

In the United States, as in all industrialized societies, legitimacy is based on authority embodied in the legal system, bureaucratic administration, and centralization. Indeed, we live in a society characterized by the rationalization of law, centralization and concentration within industry, and the subsequent extension of state intervention to previously private human actions.

Like the civil rights movement, the women's liberation movement, the anti-Vietnam War movement, and the questioning of every major institutional order in the 1960s, conflict resolution was born in a time of questioning whether traditional legal authority served the needs of people or supported a status quo that reinforced social and political inequality. The 1960s ushered in a time of change and conflict. It was perceived by an active and vocal, if not large, part of the population that change was good, and the conflict that often produced the change was also a positive thing and not something to be avoided.

Each of the four movements in conflict resolution, in their own unique way, represents a challenge to traditional authority, a part of this new way of looking at change and conflict. In the area of organizational relations this took the form of a questioning of top-down, centralized decision making and the role conflict played in organizations. In international relations, the "power paradigm" (the view that there are severe limitations to political reform because human beings are power-seeking creatures by nature and must be controlled by strong government action)[2] was challenged via the notion that human beings seek to fulfill their basic needs rather than always seeking power and material interests. In certain religious organizations this took the form of an emphasis upon the religious community's ability to deal with its own disputes rather than resorting to the secular legal system, and the expanding of these procedures to the international arena. Finally, the growth of alternative dispute resolution (ADR) represented a reaction against the rationalization of law in the form of common law, and a reemergence of a distrust of lawyers who were seen as being in the service of elites who perpetuated a legal system that produced unequal justice.

We will look at the emergence of conflict resolution in the United States by focusing upon the four movements that have shaped it, and then try to answer a fundamental question: *Do the conflict intervenors who claim to practice conflict resolution constitute a profession?* As William Goode (1961:307) puts it, "Spokesmen for almost every white-collar job have asserted that they are professional." Conflict resolution is no exception and this question needs to be addressed if we are to understand the recent and future development of conflict resolution in the United States.

PATHS TO THE EMERGENCE OF CONFLICT RESOLUTION

Organizational Relations

Most classical organizational and industrial theorists (Mooney and Reiley 1939; Taylor 1911/1947) saw organizations as closed systems, assuming that conflict was disruptive and detrimental to the organization's functioning. Of the early theorists only Mary Parker Follet (1940) recognized the possible constructive possibilities for conflict within organizations. She wrote (1940:30–31) that instead of condemning conflict

we should set it to work for us. Why not? What does the mechanical engineer do with friction? Of course his chief job is to eliminate friction, but it is true that he also capitalizes friction. The transmission of power by belts depends on friction between the belt and the pulley. The friction between the driving wheel of the locomotive and the track is necessary to haul the train. All polishing is done by friction. The music of the violin we get by friction. We left the savage state when we discovered fire by friction. We talk of friction of mind on mind as a good thing. . . . We have to know when to try to eliminate friction and when to capitalize it, when to see what work we can make it do.

Follet recommended cooperative problem solving rather than suppression as a preferred conflict management tool (Alban 1987).

It was not until the mid-1950s that the transition took place to what S. P. Robbins (1974) refers to as the behavioralist's school of organizational behavior, where conflict was viewed as an inevitable and integral aspect of productive organizations. Much of this new view of conflict is attributable to sociologist Lewis Coser, whose *Functions of Social Conflict* (1956) introduced the German social philosopher Georg Simmel (1858–1918) to the American social science and organizational behavior literature.

The implementation of nonsuppressive techniques of handling conflicts lagged about a decade behind this new look at conflict. Not until the mid-1960s was the resolution of conflict in organizations and industry thought of in anything but the traditional way—by forms of power bargaining and negotiation, where both parties to the conflict or dispute tried to gain as much as they could while giving up as little as possible. But, then, social scientists and management consultants began to point to the need for some type of cooperative interaction between concerned parties, something they believed would lead to increased productivity. This represented a real break from the authoritarian model of management and along with it came the realization that stable solutions to labor-management problems required some type of accommodation to the needs of both sides. Zero-sum solutions, where one party gains at the expense of the other, were seen as ineffective and inefficient. If short-term settlements, and not long-term resolutions, were the only result, then the same problems would surface at the next bargaining session. Indeed, oftentimes, the subsequent bargaining sessions became more bitter as the party that saw itself as losing in the previous round of bargaining now sought to make up for its losses and win even more than its adversary had previously won. For those who were studying this process of the escalation of conflict, the logical next step was to call for decisions that would be made as a result of cooperation among the parties concerned.

In particular, R. R. Blake, H. A. Shepard, and J. S. Mouton (1964) began to formalize a new approach to conflict as they described divergent assumptions under which conflict occurs. They pointed to five ways of dealing with conflict. The first is withdrawal. A second way is to try and smooth over the differences that are seen as the basis of the dispute. Third, one or more parties to a conflict may force a win-or-lose resolution. The fourth way is the most commonly used approach, that of compromise. These four ways, however, are problematic, in that, with the possible exception of total withdrawal, the conflict will usually reoccur. In order to resolve conflicts so that they will not reoccur Blake, Shepard, and Mouton advocated a fifth way, the use of a problem-solving attitude, similar to what had been called for by Follet.

According to Barbara Alban (1987:30), Blake, Shepard, and Mouton looked at conflict theory as it existed and developed models for applying it to organizational settings. In so doing they blended what they considered to be the most useful aspects of these theories and an entire literature sprung up describing research based on their approach (see Argyris 1970; Bazerman and Lewicki 1983; Brown 1988; Robbins 1974; Simkin 1971). The work of Blake, Shepard, and Mouton also led to the use of the mediator (a neutral third party who is not empowered to render a decision but only assists the disputants in reaching a negotiated agreement).

In short, the introduction of problem solving and mediators into organizational behavior represented a questioning of the traditional approaches to dealing with conflict, approaches based on a hierarchical and centralized model of bureaucracy that not only defined "legitimate authority" in the industrial world, but in the society at large as well. It must be noted that although the insights that came from the conflict

resolution pioneers in the organizational relations area made some head-
way in industry, there was little change in labor-management bargaining
as evidenced by the fact that most collective bargaining still proceeds
much the same as it did twenty years ago.[3]

The Problem-Solving Workshop in International Relations

The rudimentary processes of conflict resolution begun in organizational relations spread beyond this field in the mid- and late 1960s, in
the form of the problem-solving workshop, to the international arena.
The underlying idea of the problem-solving workshop is to bring together representatives of the conflicting parties in a relatively isolated
setting away from diplomatic protocol and publicity—preferably an academic setting—where they can engage in face-to-face interaction under
the guidance of social scientists knowledgeable about conflict theory (Kelman and Cohen 1979:289).

The development of the problem-solving workshop as an attempt to
resolve international conflicts was predicated on the belief that such
conventional methods of dealing with international conflicts as international law, alliances, and deterrence had not only failed to fashion
peaceful resolutions of conflicts but by imposing losses on the vanquished
had produced a spiraling effect that led to further conflicts and wars
(Hill 1982; Light 1984).

Three different groups—the London group of John Burton and his
associates (Burton 1969, 1972, 1982; de Reuck 1974; Mitchell 1973), the
Yale group of Leonard Doob and his associates (Doob 1970, 1971, 1974,
1976; Doob and Foltz 1973, 1974; Doob and Stevens 1969; Walton 1970),
and the Harvard group of Herbert Kelman and his associates (Cohen
et al. 1977; Kelman 1970, 1972, 1979; Kelman and Cohen 1976, 1979)—
are generally credited with introducing the problem-solving workshop
into the international conflict arena.

In the mid-1960s, under the leadership of Burton, a former Australian
foreign secretary and a participant in the 1945 UN Charter Conference,
academics at the Centre for the Analysis of Conflict at the University of
London advocated a whole new process of resolving international conflicts. Based on the work of Blake, Shepard, and Mouton (1964), the
London group's approach required a neutral and skilled third party,
which they defined as a panel of facilitators who would help the disputing
parties arrive at a mutually agreed upon solution to their conflict. Burton
and his colleagues are credited with actually instituting the first "international problem-solving workshop," which they labeled "Controlled
Communication Workshops" (Burton 1969). The term "controlled communication" referred to the role played by the panel of facilitators, who
were there to insure that a dialogue free of traditional, zero-sum power

bargaining and negotiation could take place. It was the primary job of
the facilitators to make sure that acceptable outcomes would evolve from
the meetings.

The "controlled communication" workshop took place in 1965, when
Burton, with the approval of Prime Minister Harold Wilson, invited
nonofficial, but highly placed representatives from Indonesia, Malaysia,
and Singapore, countries that were then involved in a continuous violent
conflict. These governments had previously refused an invitation by
Wilson to meet. The panel of facilitators consisted of ten scholars.[4] The
workshop lasted over a week, with some additional follow-up by the
Centre.

The Centre for Conflict Analysis continued its research into conflict
resolution and the use of problem-solving workshops, and in 1966, when
the United Nations official in charge of the Cyprus negotiations, Nobel
Peace Prize winner Ralph Bunche, could not persuade the Greek and
Turkish Cypriots to meet together, the Centre asked the conflicting
parties to meet and they did so. Once again, the panel was composed
of ten scholars.

The Greek and Cypriot representatives requested further meetings
but it was felt at the time that this would interfere with UN procedures.
Although no positive conflict resolution results came out of this workshop, it was still considered to be successful in that valuable research on
conflict processes was accumulated (Burton 1969).

Also in the mid-1960s, Leonard Doob of Yale University (independently of what was occurring in England) had begun to consider the use
of sensitivity training as an aid for resolving conflicts. In 1969, Doob
and his Yale associates scheduled the "Fermeda workshop" (named after
the Fermeda Hotel in which it took place) in South Tyrol, Italy, to deal
with the border disputes among the nations in the Horn of Africa—
Ethiopia, Kenya, and Somalia. None of the representatives of the Horn
of Africa nations was an official government representative. The Ethi-
opian and Kenyan representatives were leading academicians in their
respective countries, and the Somalian representatives came from the
fields of education and law but did include some government officials.

The results of this workshop were mixed. No solution to the conflict
was achieved, but gains were seen in the understanding of the others'
views, new openness toward innovative ideas for solutions, and insights
into the process itself. Eleven months later, in July 1970, a follow-up
workshop was held with thirteen of the original eighteen participants.
Most of the participants agreed that the original workshop had had a
positive impact even though the dispute had not been settled (Hill
1982:123).

Doob and his associates then turned to the conflict in Northern Ireland, and arranged for a workshop to be held in Stirling, Scotland. This

workshop was attended by fifty-six Protestant and Catholic residents of Belfast who met with a team of American social scientists. Here again, the results were mixed. Doob and Foltz (1973, 1974) argued that positive attitudes emerged from the workshop, but G. H. Boehringer and colleagues (1974) claimed that the potential costs of such a workshop in an ongoing violent conflict outweighed the possible benefits.

Herbert Kelman, who was a participant in the Burton group's Cyprus workshop, with his associates at Harvard, attempted to integrate Burton's approach with that of Doob's. Concentrating on the Middle East, Kelman held that Burton's approach was essentially a research one, which emphasized the transfer of changes in the participants in the policy realm, whereas Doob stressed a learning workshop with an emphasis upon creating conditions for change in those who participated (Hill 1982:125). Kelman's workshops attempt to incorporate both of these aspects. For example, Kelman places greater emphasis on the analysis of group processes than does Burton, and makes a sharper distinction than does Doob between interpersonal and intergroup processes. Kelman's main objective is to treat the interaction between the individual participants as a reflection of the relationships between the groups they represent (Kelman and Cohen 1979:291).

Although Kelman has led a problem-solving workshop that focused on the India–Pakistan–Bangladesh conflict (Cohen and Kelman 1979), over the years he has concentrated on conflicts in the Middle East, in particular the Israeli-Palestinian problem.

As with the London group and the Yale group, the results of Kelman's workshops have been mixed. Although much research has been accumulated and individual participants of the workshops have come to see the other side's position more clearly, the Israeli-Palestinian problem still remains one of the world's most volatile conflicts.

It is obvious, then, that none of the above three groups can claim great success with their problem-solving workshops. Nevertheless, the introduction of this approach was, and is, still seen as an alternative to traditional means of dealing with international conflicts. As such, it has provided a major impetus for the growth of conflict resolution in the United States.

Religion and Peacemaking

The role of religious leaders in the conflict resolution movement is obvious. The pope mediated an agreement in 1984 between Chile and Argentina concerning the Beagle Channel; the All-Africa Council of Churches and the World Council of Churches were instrumental in the talks that stopped the fighting in the civil war in Sudan in 1972; Quakers were mediators in the Nigerian civil war from 1967 to 1970, and attempted conciliation between the two Germanies after World War II and in the India-Pakistani War of 1965; Anglican envoy Terry Waite, before he himself was taken hostage in Lebanon, negotiated the release of missionaries in Libya in 1985. As Cynthia Sampson (1987:4) reminds us, however, "A distinction must be made from the beginning between the work of religious figures as third parties in conflict resolution—an activity referred to as 'peacemaking'—and the more activist work of religious figures for various peace-related causes." For the purposes of this brief history we are only interested in Sampson's first category, that of the religious figure as third party intervenor or "peacemaker," and even more specifically how this has been institutionalized in religious organizations.

We will concentrate on two groups—the Quakers and the Mennonites—using them as exemplars of the role religion has played in the development of conflict resolution. More than any other religious groups, these two are further along in the institutionalization of conflict resolution as part of their religious mission.

The Quakers have had a long tradition of trying to resolve disputes without resorting to the legal system. According to Arthur A. Whiting (1988:11–12), this tradition manifests itself in

a sense of belonging to one community, unified in its purpose, without the need for different communities to be governed by one universal legal system. Instead, it was permissible and, in fact, desirable to be governed by private systems of dispute settlement that were tailored to the specific needs of the community rather than for the individual. This was desirable because the needs of the individual were identified with the needs of the community in which the individual lived, and law was designed to protect this community and so to protect the individual.

The Quakers had used mediation and arbitration in Europe and simply brought this practice with them to America (Odiorne 1956). In Pennsylvania, where the Quakers settled in large numbers, alternatives to the law were the norm. "While English standards governed the practice of law and the operation of the courts, the major legal system was the extra-official system of the Quakers" (Odiorne 1956:164–65).

Although none of the dispute-resolving procedures used by the Quakers were compulsory or binding, nevertheless, they did have highly evolved sets of procedures. When a dispute occurred, the party who felt wronged spoke with the other party in hopes of resolving their differences. If no agreement was reached, the two parties would pick a third party to act as a mediator. If the decision of the third party was rejected the matter was brought before the town meeting—not so much as to determine the rights of the disputing parties, but to determine the reasons for the impasse (Whiting 1988:13).

The influence of the Quakers has perhaps been most visible at the international level. In particular, Adam Curle (1971, 1986) is the most well known and successful of Quaker international mediators, and is considered to be a pioneer in the field of international conflict resolution. An important contribution of Curle (1986) is his distinction between "nonofficial mediation" and "official mediation." The difference between the two approaches relates to the degree of impartiality of the two types of mediator. The official mediator may represent powers that are acting in their own interests, whereas the unofficial mediator is genuinely impartial and seeks only the reduction of suffering caused by the conflict (Sampson 1987).

Curle and other Quaker mediators stress reconciliation (the bringing of the parties toward a peaceful means of resolving their differences) among disputants in a given conflict. This is similar to the procedures used by Quakers in domestic disputes (described above) with the obvious difference being that there is no international equivalent of the town meeting.

Given their history of pacifism and humanitarianism and the emphasis upon "consensus decision making," the Quakers are often afforded trust and legitimacy that politically or economically motivated groups may not receive. For example, most Quaker interventions in conflicts have been preceded by various kinds of humanitarian aid programs in the region in question or, in many instances, by the first-hand experience of key national leaders in Quaker international conferences (Sampson 1987:4).

The Quakers practice what C. H. Yarrow (1968:165) calls "balanced partiality." This represents an attempt on the part of the mediator to be a sympathetic listener and is manifested through putting oneself in each of the other party's place. The Quaker theology of powerlessness, of sharing or relinquishing power, rather than acquisition of power enables them to offer a nonthreatening presence to the parties in a conflict (Sampson 1987). It should be noted, too, that although the Quakers are most known for the use of conflict resolution in the international arena, they have also been instrumental in introducing conflict resolution at the local level, in particular, in the educational system. The Friends' establishment of the Children's Creative Response to Non-Violence directly led to other projects in the schools, such as the use of Kid-Meds (children who mediated conflicts on the playgrounds) and New York City's School Mediator Alternative Resolution Program (SMART), which has become a model for conflict resolution programs in American high schools.

Although the Mennonite Church, like such other peace churches as the Church of the Brethren, has had a long history of engagement in causes of peace, its institutional entrance into the conflict resolution field can be traced to a series of talks given by Methodist minister John Adams

and Methodist layperson and college professor James Laue to a Mennonite audience at Bethel College in 1976. Inspired in part by Adams
and Laue, the Mennonites agreed in 1977 to establish an agency mandated to respond in practical ways to conflict (Kraybill 1989:6).

According to Ron Kraybill (1989:6), who headed the first Mennonite
Conciliation Service (MCS), in the beginning

everything in sight seemed green. Mennonites had strong interest in the "min-
istry of reconciliation," but little skill or experience. There was no "field" of
dispute resolution, only a few scattered agencies and individuals; the American
Arbitration Association; Paul Wahrhaftig of a soon-to-be-terminated mediation
project of the American Friends Service Committee; the Institute for Mediation
and Conflict Resolution in New York; Laue, Adams and assorted others.

MCS cultivated various relationships within the religious community.
For example, they helped the Christian Legal Society, a national association of evangelical lawyers, establish local Christian Conciliation Services (CCS). This service of the CCS offers mediation to Christians as
well as seminars on biblical peace making to local churches. Given the
conservative politics of the Christian Legal Society, few of its members
would have been interested in discussing international peace alternatives,
but their concern with disputes within the church and among church-
goers was a selling point for establishing CCS.

At present, the MCS has over a dozen chapters that provide mediation
training and services in the United States. These regional groups work
with various conflicts, ranging from local church conflicts to international
conflicts (Kraybill 1989). The MCS thus provides mediation services to
its own Mennonite constituents as well as training individuals to be
"peacemakers."

One of the conflicts in which the Mennonites have offered mediation
services is reported in this volume by John Paul Lederach, who succeeded
Ron Kraybill as head of the MCS. Lederach's conflict intervention was
based on the Mennonite practice of establishing a presence in a local
area over a long period of time before entering into the dispute.

Although the above brief history makes no claims to being exhaustive,
it does point up the importance of religious organizations in the development of the field of conflict resolution, in particular, their emphasis
upon providing alternatives to both power bargaining among nations
and traditional notions of secular common law.

Alternative Dispute Resolution

Parallel to what was occurring in the 1960s and 1970s in organizational
relations, international problem-solving workshops, and religious peace-

making, alternative dispute resolution (ADR), arose, in varying degrees, as a pragmatic response to the critical tenor of the times. Unfortunately, although it has had an impact in the legal field, ADR has been defined in a number of ways, some of which are contradictory and others of which are logically inconsistent. For example, the Ad Hoc Panel on Dispute Resolution and Public Policy assembled by the National Institute of Dispute Resolution in 1981 defined alternative dispute resolution "to include all methods, practices, and techniques, formal and informal, within and outside the courts that are used to resolve disputes." Unfortunately, such a definition is so all-encompassing that it provides no distinction between traditional and alternative methods of dispute resolution.

Because the panel looked at ADR as encompassing all of the major processes that are now being used to deal with disputes (Administrative Conference of the United States 1987:36–38), it listed the following as the most important ADR processes:

1. *Adjudication.* Includes both judicial and administrative hearings, where parties can be compelled to participate.

2. *Arbitration.* Widely used in labor-management disputes, where a neutral third party renders a decision after hearing arguments and reviewing evidence.

3. *Court-Annexed Arbitration.* Judges refer civil suits to arbitrators who render prompt, nonbinding decisions. The option is available to return to court if a party or both parties are not satisfied with the decision.

4. *Conciliation.* An informal process in which the third party tries to bring the disputants to agreement by lowering tensions, improving communications, interpreting issues, exploring potential solutions, and in general trying to bring about some sort of negotiated settlement.

5. *Facilitation.* Where the facilitator functions as a neutral process expert to help parties reach mutually accepted agreements. The facilitator avoids making any substantive contributions.

6. *Med-Arb.* A third party is authorized by the disputants to serve first as a mediator and then as an arbitrator empowered to decide any issues should mediation not bring about a satisfactory settlement.

7. *Mediation.* A structured process in which the mediator (a neutral third party) assists the disputants to reach a negotiated settlement of their dispute. The mediator is not empowered to render a decision.

8. *Mini-Trial.* A privately developed method used to bring about a negotiated settlement in lieu of corporate litigation. Attorneys present their cases before managers with authority to settle; most often a neutral advisor is present (usually a retired judge or another lawyer).

9. *Negotiation.* A process where two parties bargain with each other.

10. *Ombudsman.* A third party employed by the institution to handle the grievances of its employees and constituents. The ombudsman can either be

empowered to take action directly or to bring suggestions to those in decision-making positions in the institution.

If the panel's definition of what constitutes ADR is accepted then there can be no "alternative" dispute resolution because every conceivable dispute resolution technique is encompassed by the panel's definition. Perhaps with this in mind, Adler (1987:59), rather than defining ADR, inventories what he considers to be its major practices. He begins with the three most important ones: arbitration, mediation, and fact finding. He goes on to say that a fuller and more complete "inventory of ADR methods would include (in no particular priority): fact-finders without recommending authority; voluntary mediation; mandated mediation; therapeutic mediation; Med-Arb; contractual, final offer and court-ordered arbitration; mini- and summary jury trials, negotiated investment strategies; policy dialogues; and the use of special masters and referees appointed by judges for purposes of settlement, fact-finding, or arbitration" (Adler 1987:59–60).

Although Adler's inventory is more discriminating than the Ad Hoc Panel's definition, it is also too broad, and includes both coercive and noncoercive processes. In the interests of clarity, then let us define ADR to include only those alternatives to the legal system that use a third party intervenor in a noncoercive manner. With this stated, let us look at how the ADR movement grew in the United States.

A major official impetus for the growth of ADR was a 1976 American Bar Association-sponsored National Conference on the Causes of Popular Dissatisfaction with the Administration of Justice. The conference concluded that alternative forms of dispute resolution, in particular mediation and arbitration, would ease congested courts, reduce settlement time, and minimize costs. The development of "neighborhood justice centers" (which practiced mediation) and multidoor courthouse programs (which directed disputants to the most appropriate dispute-resolving mechanism: litigation, mediation, or arbitration) were encouraged.

This recommendation fit in nicely with the sentiment of the time concerning the judicial system. The 1960s had witnessed an attack on the courts for their bias in dealing with the lower class and minorities, and their failure to redress inequalities in society. Furthermore, the antilawyer sentiment that characterized much of the 1980s was just beginning.

The creation of neighborhood justice centers (NJC) or community mediation centers (CMC) was congruent with antielitist sentiments, and NJCs and CMCs played an important part in the growth of ADR. One of the first such centers, the San Francisco Community Boards, was founded by Raymond Shonholtz, a former attorney for the California

Rural Legal Aid program. This became a model program for neighborhood self-governance. Shonholtz (1987) was also instrumental in establishing the National Association for Community Justice in 1985, which consisted of hundreds of local mediation centers.

Christine B. Harrington and Sally E. Merry (1988:507–9) see community mediation as developing along three ideological lines: delivery of dispute resolution services; social transformation; and personal growth and development. The delivery of dispute resolution services arose as a possible reallocation of judicial resources—the courts were simply too congested to function efficiently. The emphasis upon social transformation involved talk of community empowerment through self-governance and decentralized judicial decision making. Those who saw personal growth and development as an end believed that mediation offers a more humane response to individual needs than does the courts.

PROFESSIONALISM

Are those individuals who are practicing in the field of conflict resolution "professionals"? Although there are numerous definitions of professionalism (see Carr-Saunders and Wilson 1933; Friedson 1970; Moore 1970), three criteria are found in just about all of the accepted definitions and by consensus are considered to be the most important determinants of professional status: (1) acceptance by the general public; (2) a service orientation; and (3) prolonged specialized training in a body of abstract knowledge. How does conflict resolution fare in relation to these three important defining variables?

Acceptance by the General Public

Evidence for the acceptance of conflict intervention in the United States is mixed. Although there is some movement toward collaborative problem solving in organizations (see Peters and Waterman 1982; Ouchi 1981; Gilley et al. 1986), the norm still seems to be hierarchical decision making, and conflict is still usually seen as something to be avoided. Although mediation has been a formal part of the institutionalized framework of labor relations from the time labor unions came into prominence in the late nineteenth century (Kolb 1983:2), with the possible exception of the Federal Mediation and Conciliation Service (FMCS) established in 1913, mediation has had little impact outside of limited government or public policy conflicts.

Although the international problem-solving workshop has been adopted by the Foreign Service Institute of the United States as one means of training diplomats and foreign service officers, it would be foolish to argue that the U.S. government in its negotiations with foreign powers operates in anything other than the power-politics mode.

Religious peacemaking interventions seem to be growing particularly at the local levels, with the Quakers and the Mennonites expanding their services. At the international level, however, the results are mixed at best. Anglican Terry Waite was himself taken hostage, and although there are successes as reported in this volume by John Paul Lederach, priests are still being murdered in Latin America.

Finally, although the 1970s and 1980s witnessed the growth of both court-affiliated and independent mediation centers, as well as the growing number of workshops and seminars dealing with such conflict resolution topics as negotiation and mediation, survey data show that the public oftentimes prefers traditional legal means of resolving disputes (Hofrichter 1987).

A Service Orientation

Here, too, the evidence is mixed. On the surface, conflict resolution seems to meet the service orientation test. Both the international problem-solving workshops and the emphasis upon peacemaking by religious practitioners point to the service orientation. When we look closely at the use of conflict resolution techniques in organizations and in the ADR movement, however, certain questions can be raised. For example, although the emphasis is upon resolving conflicts so that work and interactions can proceed smoothly in organizations, there is little or no focus upon the conditions that produced the conflict in the first place. Oftentimes conflicts are dealt with by facilitating the individual's adjustment to the conditions of the workplace, conditions that ultimately may be harmful to the individual or may only produce short-term solutions at the expense of long-term resolutions (Scimecca 1991).

As for the ADR movement, a major criticism is that ADR has lost sight of its original purpose: its concern for the poor, for all those who did not have access to the law (Harrington and Merry 1988). In Laura Nader's (this volume) view the prime focus of ADR is organizational expansion, and the carving out of profitable jobs for new "professionals." Along these lines it can be argued that the American Bar Association's interest in ADR has less to do with providing alternatives to the law than with opening up new sources of revenue for lawyers.

Prolonged Specialized Training in a Body of Abstract Knowledge

As with the two other criteria for professionalism, the evidence is mixed concerning specialized training in a body of abstract knowledge.

A number of universities have institutionalized conflict resolution programs. In May 1984, George Mason University awarded the first graduate degrees in conflict management in the United States; in the fall of
1988 it began the first Ph.D. in conflict analysis and resolution.[5] The
University of Colorado has a specialty in conflict resolution within its
Ph.D. program in sociology; and Syracuse University offers a conflict
and peace studies specialty under its doctorate in social science. Nevertheless, there are still far too many workshops and training sessions that
claim to teach the techniques of conflict resolution in anywhere from
twelve to forty hours.

Furthermore, the field of conflict resolution lacks a theoretical base
that can undergird its practice. And although there are many comprehensive theories of conflict, theories of conflict resolution are few and
far between. Indeed it can be argued that conflict resolution theories
can be divided into two categories: game theoretical frameworks and
human needs theory. While this excludes a whole history of conflict
theory, namely, the Marxist and Weberian frameworks, they are not
theories of conflict resolution and as such have not played any real role
in the development of conflict resolution. As Avruch and Black (1989:1–
2) say, "The current state of conflict resolution theory and practice reflects the diverse backgrounds of those who have been drawn to it." We
can go even farther and argue that state of theory is even worse than
Avruch and Black state, given that game theory and human needs theory
are at present quite flawed.

Game theory uses assumptions of perfect information (that is, every
party perfectly understands everyone else's possible actions), and therein
lies its most basic weakness as a theory. Conditions of perfect information
rarely if ever exist. Game theory also assumes that the parties or players,
in the end, cooperate—their actions are in accordance with some agreed
upon plan. This, in turn, assumes communication between them, and
also a mechanism for enforcing the agreements they reach. Players may
jockey for relative position, but they end up working together toward a
rational and mutually efficient goal (Schellenberg 1982:188). Such assumptions do not take into consideration that deep-seated conflicts are
often irrational, nor does the assumption of an essential vacuum consider
the role that culture and social structure (read power) play in conflicts.

Human needs theory fares no better. Although this approach has been
a part of social science for some time, indeed has provided the foundation
for the "Goals, Processes, and the Indicators of Development" (GPID)
project of the United Nations University, which resulted in a major
edited publication, *Human Needs* (Lederer 1980), it is John Burton who
is most often associated with human needs theory of conflict resolution.

Burton's theory has been criticized for its emphasis upon genetic de-
terminism and its subsequent failure to take culture and social institu-

tions into consideration (Scimecca 1990). Avruch and Black (1987:91) ask, "Where do these needs come from? And why these and not others?" Christopher Mitchell (1990) raises the question of whether some needs are more important than others. Although Burton originally saw these needs as genetically based, in a response to Avruch and Black (Burton and Sandole 1987:97), he modifies his position somewhat by accepting the thesis of Robert Boyd and Peter Richerson (1986) that humans have a "dual inheritance system," one cultural and the other genetic. What is important "is that universal patterns of behavior exist" (Burton and Sandole 1987:97). Although this represents a movement from a pure genetically determined position, it still places Burton in the sociobiologist camp and does not answer the question of where needs come from, or whether some are more important than others; nor does it resolve the dilemma of ascertaining just how much culture influences human needs, dual inheritance system not withstanding. Finally, Burton (1987, 1990a) sees power as irrelevant, claiming that it has no role in problem solving or conflict resolution processes. Conflict resolution as envisioned by Burton is a purely analytical process. Power becomes a "nonvariable" when the parties to a conflict, with the help of a facilitation team engage in analytical problem solving. Although Burton's assumption about power in the resolution process raises interesting possibilities, at best, that is all it is: an assumption with no empirical support. To speak of conflict and conflict resolution without speaking of power, even in a workshop setting, seems naive.

Burton to his credit has been one of the few scholars in the field of conflict resolution to call for a conflict resolution process that is derived from a theory of conflict. In the end, however, he violates his own assumptions and makes a leap of faith when he relegates power to irrelevance in his conflict resolution process. Without a theory of conflict resolution the field is left with a number of processes that are dependent upon the idiosyncratic expertise of the individual practitioners. Nowhere is this more clearly seen than in ADR.

ADR has simply become a number of different processes. Indeed, this is why "dispute" as a term is employed rather than "conflict." The justification for its use and the processes employed are based more in the legal tradition and in the experience of the individual practitioner than in any theoretical framework. As a consequence there is an emphasis on process, unsupported by articulated insights into the generic nature of different disputes. ADR as practiced represents an emphasis upon the *how* without any real theoretical justification for *when* and *why* to use the techniques.

Although conflict resolution has had a tremendous growth in the United States in the past quarter of a century, and despite the claims of its

practitioners that it has achieved the status of a profession, professionalism still eludes the field. The acceptance by the general public is mixed,
as is the evidence that conflict resolution meets the service orientation
test of a profession. It is the third criterion—that of a prolonged specialized training in a body of abstract knowledge—that seems to be the
most problematic at the present time. Conflict resolution simply does
not have a theoretical base to undergird its practice, and until it does,
even if it meets the first two criteria, it still will not be a profession. At
best, conflict resolution will be a number of various movements lumped
under a common title. Such a theoretical framework must take such
variables as culture and power into consideration, something that is just
now being addressed. This volume represents a step toward this goal—
that of exploring the role of culture in conflict resolution.

NOTES

1. I would include such areas as environmental conflict resolution and divorce
mediation as part of the ADR movement.

2. For an excellent introduction to and summary of the "power paradigm"
in international relations theory, see Dougherty and Pfaltzgraff 1981:84–127.

3. Although one can only speculate as to why this is so, my interpretation is
that the animosity built up over years of power bargaining has precluded any
substantial changes in this area.

4. Roger Fisher, who would later coauthor, with William Ury, *Getting to Yes*
(1981), the most popular book in the field of conflict resolution, was one of three
American scholars among the ten facilitators.

5. In June 1991, Diane LeResche was awarded the first Ph.D. in conflict
analysis and resolution by George Mason University.

REFERENCES

Adler, Peter S. 1987. Is ADR a Social Movement? *Negotiation Journal* 3:59–66.
Administrative Conference of the United States. 1987. *Sourcebook: Federal Agency
Use of Alternative Means of Dispute Resolution* (Office of the Chairman).
Washington, D.C.
Alban, Barbara. 1987. The Evolution of Intraorganizational Conflict Manage-
ment: A Synoptic Review. Unpublished paper, George Washington Uni-
versity, Department of Management.
Argyris, Chris. 1970. *Intervention Theory and Method: A Behavioral Science View*.
Reading, Mass.: Addison-Wesley.
Avruch, Kevin, and Peter Black. 1987. A "Generic" Theory of Conflict Reso-
lution: A Critique. *Negotiation Journal* 3:87–96, 99–100.
———. 1989. The Concept of the Person in Contemporary Conflict Resolution.
Paper presented at the First Conference on Current Thinking and Research in Psychological Anthropology, Society for Psychological Anthropology, San Diego, Calif.

36   CONFLICT RESOLUTION

Bazerman, Max H., and R. Lewicki eds. 1983. *Negotiating in Organizations*. Beverly Hills, Calif.: Sage.
Blake, R. R., H. A. Shepard, and J. S. Mouton. 1964. *Managing Intergroup Conflict in Industry*. Houston, Tex.: Gulf.
Boehringer, G. H., J. Bayley, V. Zeroulis, and K. Boehringer. 1974. Stirling: The Destructive Application of Group Techniques to a Conflict. *Journal of Conflict Resolution* 18(2):257–75.
Boyd, Robert and Peter J. Richerson. 1986. *Culture and The Evolutionary Process*. Chicago: University of Chicago Press.
Brown, L. D. 1988. *Managing Conflicts of Organizational Interfaces*. Reading, Mass.: Addison-Wesley.
Burton, John W. 1969. *Communication and Conflict: The Use of Controlled Communication in International Relations*. London: Macmillan.
———. 1972. *World Society*. London: Cambridge University Press.
———. 1979. *Deviance, Terrorism and War*. New York: St. Martin's.
———. 1987. *Resolving Deep-Rooted Conflict: A Handbook*. Lanham, Md.: University Press of America.
———. 1990a. *Conflict: Resolution and Provention*. New York: St. Martin's.
———. 1990b. Introduction. In *Conflict: Human Needs Theory*, ed. John Burton. New York: St. Martin's.
Burton, John W. and Dennis J. D. Sandole. 1987. "Expanding the Debate on Conflict Resolution." *Negotiation Journal*. 3:1:97–99.
Carr-Saunders, A. M., and P. A. Wilson. 1933. *The Professions*. Oxford: Clarendon.
Cohen, S. P., H. Kelman, F. D. Miller, and B. L. Smith. 1977. Evolving Intergroup Techniques for Conflict Resolution: An Israeli-Palestinian Pilot Workshop. *Journal of Social Issues* 33(1):165–88.
Coser, Lewis. 1956. *The Functions of Social Conflict*. New York: Free.
Curle, Adam. 1971. *Making Peace*. London: Tavistock.
———. 1986. *In the Middle: Non-Official Mediation in Violent Situations*. New York: St. Martin's.
de Reuck, Anthony. 1974. Controlled Communication: Rationale and Dynamics. *Human Context* 6(1):64–80.
Doob, Leonard. 1971. The Impact of the Fermeda Workshop on the Conflicts in the Horn of Africa. *International Journal of Group Tensions* 1(1):91–101.
———. 1974. A Cyprus Workshop: An Exercise in Intervention Methodology. *Journal of Social Psychology* 94:161–78.
———. 1976. A Cyprus Workshop: Intervention Methodology during a Continuing Crisis. *Journal of Social Psychology* 98:143–44.
Doob, Leonard, ed. 1970. *Resolving Conflicts in Africa: The Fermeda Workshop*. New Haven: Yale University Press.
Doob, Leonard, and William Foltz. 1973. The Belfast Workshop: The Application of a Group Technique to a Destructive Conflict. *Journal of Conflict Resolution* 17(4):237–56.
———. 1974. The Impact of a Workshop upon Grass-Roots Leaders in Belfast. *Journal of Conflict Resolution* 18(2):237–56.
Doob, Leonard, and Robert Stevens. 1969. The Fermeda Workshop: Different

Approach to Border Conflicts in Africa. *Journal of Psychology* 73(2):249–66.

Dougherty, James E., and Robert K. Pfaltzgraff, Jr. 1981. *Contending Theories of International Relations: A Comprehensive Survey.* 2d ed. New York: Harper and Row.

Fisher, Roger, and William Ury. 1981. *Getting to Yes.* Boston: Houghton Mifflin.

Fisher, Ronald J. 1983. Third Party Consultation as a Method of Intergroup Conflict Resolution: A Review of Studies. *Journal of Conflict Resolution* 27(2):301–34.

Follet, Mary Parker. 1940. *The Collected Papers of Mary Parker Follet*, eds. Henry C. Metcalf and Lyndall Urwick. New York: Harper and Brothers.

Friedson, Elliot. 1970. *Profession of Medicine.* New York: Dodd and Mead.

Gilley, J. Wade, Kenneth A. Fulmer, and Sally J. Reithlingschoefer. 1986. *Searching for Academic Excellence.* New York: Macmillan.

Goode, William. 1961. The Librarian: From Occupation to Profession. *Library Quarterly* 31(4):306–18.

Harrington, Christine B., and Sally Engle Merry. 1988. Ideological Production: The Making of Community Mediation. *Law and Society Review* 22(4):501–27.

Hill, Barbara J. 1982. An Analysis of Conflict Resolution Techniques: From Problem-Solving to Theory. *Journal of Conflict Resolution* 26(1):109–38.

Hofrichter, Richard. 1987. *Neighborhood Justice in Capitalist Society.* Westport, Conn.: Greenwood.

Kelman, Herbert. 1972. The Problem-Solving Workshop in Conflict Resolution. In *Communication in International Politics*, ed. Richard L. Merritt. Urbana: University of Illinois Press.

———. 1979. "An Interactional Approach to Conflict Resolution and Its Application to the Israeli-Palestinian Relations. *International Interactions* 6(2):99–122.

Kelman, Herbert. 1970. The Role of the Individual in International Relations: Some Conceptual and Methodological Considerations. *Journal of International Affairs* 24(1):1–17.

Kelman, Herbert, and Stephen Cohen. 1976. The Problem-Solving Workshop: A Social-Psychological Contribution to the Resolution of International Conflicts. *Journal of Peace Research* 13:79–90.

———. 1979. Resolution of International Conflict: An Interactional Approach. In *The Social Psychology of Intergroup Relations*, eds. S. Worchel and W. G. Austin. Monterey, Calif.: Brooks/Cole.

Kolb, Deborah. 1983. *The Mediators.* Cambridge, Mass.: MIT.

Kraybill, Ron. 1989. Reflections on a Decade: Mediating Peace. *Conciliation Quarterly* Winter:6–7.

Laue, James. 1987. The Emergence and Institutionalization of Third Party Roles in Conflict. In *Conflict Management and Problem Solving: Interpersonal to International Applications*, eds. Dennis J. D. Sandole and Ingrid Staroste-Sandole. London: Frances Pinter.

Lederer, Katrin, ed. 1980. *Human Needs: A Contribution to the Debate.* Cambridge, Mass.: Oegeschlager, Gunn and Hain.

LeResche, Diane. 1991. Procedural Justice, of, by, and for American Ethnic

Groups: A Comparison of Interpersonal Conflict Resolution Procedures Used by Korean-Americans and American Community Mediation Centers with Procedural Justice Theories. Unpublished diss., George Mason University, Fairfax, Va.

Light, Margot. 1984. Problem-Solving Workshops: The Role of Scholarship in Conflict Resolution. In *Conflict in World Society: A New Perspective on International Relations*, ed. Michael Banks. New York: St. Martin's.

Mitchell, Christopher. 1973. Conflict Resolution and Controlled Communication. *Journal of Peace Research* 10:123–32.

——. 1990. Necessitous Man and Conflict Resolution: More Questions about Basic Human Needs Theory. In *Conflict: Human Needs Theory*, ed. John Burton. New York: St. Martin's.

Mooney, J. D., and A. C. Reiley. 1939. *The Principles of Organization*. New York: Harper Brothers.

Moore, Wilbert E. 1970. *The Profession: Rules and Roles*. New York: Russell Sage.

Odiorne, George S. 1956. Arbitration and Mediation among the Early Quakers. *Arbitration Journal* 9:161–66.

Ouchi, William G. 1981. *Theory Z*. New York: Avon.

Pepinski, Harold, and Richard Quinney, eds. 1991. *Criminology and Peacemaking*. Bloomington, Ind.: University of Indiana Press.

Peters, Thomas J. and Robert H. Waters, Jr. 1982. *In Search Of Excellence*. New York: Harper & Row.

Robbins, S. P. 1974. *Managing Organizational Conflicts*. Englewood Cliffs, N.J.: Prentice-Hall.

Sampson, Cynthia. 1987. A Study of the International Conciliation Work of Religious Figures. Harvard University Program on Negotiation, *Working Paper Series 87–86*. Cambridge, Mass.

Sandole, Dennis J. D., and Ingrid Staroste-Sandole, eds. 1987. *Conflict Management and Problem Solving: Interpersonal to International Applications*. London: Frances Pinter.

Schellenberg, Thomas. 1982. *The Science of Conflict*. New York: Oxford University Press.

Scimecca, Joseph A. 1990. Self-Reflexivity and Freedom: Toward a Prescriptive Theory of Conflict Resolution. In *Conflict: Human Needs Theory*, ed. John Burton. New York: St. Martin's.

——. 1991. "Conflict Resolution and a Critique of Alternative Dispute Resolution." In Harold Pepinski and Richard Quinney, eds. *Criminology as Peacemaking*. Bloomington, IN: University of Indiana Press.

Shonholtz, Raymond. 1987. The Citizen's Role in Justice: Building a Primary Justice and Prevention System at the Neighborhood Level. *Annals of the American Academy of Political and Social Sciences* 494:42–53.

Simkin, W. 1971. *Mediation and the Dynamics of Collective Bargaining*. Washington, D.C.: Bureau of National Affairs.

Taylor, Frederick W. 1911/1947. *Scientific Management*. New York: Harper and Brothers.

Walton, Richard E. 1970. A Problem-Solving Workshop on Border Conflicts in Eastern Africa. *Journal of Applied Behavioral Science* 6(4):453–89.

Whiting, Arthur A. 1988. The Use of Mediation as a Dispute Resolution Tool:

An Historical and Scientific Examination of the Role and Process of Mediation. Unpublished diss., Syracuse University, Syracuse, N.Y.

Yarrow, C. H. 1968. *Quaker Experiences in International Conciliation.* New Haven: Yale University Press.

3

Harmony Models and the Construction of Law

Laura Nader

The movement between harmony and confrontational or adversarial law models has been documented by historians for a number of societies. There are also a number of instances where within a single society the differential use of both of these models has been described. This chapter indicates where such shifts have taken place and outlines what a theory of harmony might look like. Social science theories generated in the West reflect the belief that conflict is bad and in need of explanation, while its opposite is valued behavior that needs no explanation. An extreme example would be the felt need to explain war rather than peace, or the felt need to do something about disputes rather than their absence. It follows then that this chapter is a critique of a social science bias stemming from the culture of the observers, while also an attempt to cut through this bias in order to scrutinize the purposes attached to harmony models of law.

Assumptions deeply held among anthropologists stemming from their cultural upbringing suggest a strong attachment to harmony models (as with Christians more generally). The configurationalists were interested in discovering the themes or values that hold a culture together and distinguish it from others. The linguist Edward Sapir (1924) referred to consistent, harmonious, balanced cultures as "genuine" rather than "spurious." Intercultural variation and contradictions were often ignored, smoothed over, or attributed to too rapid culture change. For the users of an equilibrium model, conflict was discord, its opposite order or harmony, and the model for studying community was a consensual one. Indeed, Max Gluckman (1959) even found "Peace in the Feud." R. Dahrendorf (1967) noted that the functionalists' stress on common values and equilibrium may have stemmed from a concern with normative behavior or a nostalgia for synthesis indicating that the negative and positive valuations assigned to both conflict and harmony may be seen as products of a particular construction to which Western or European social scientists belong. Thus while theories of conflict abound (Nader 1968), theories explaining harmony models of law are mainly subsumed under ideas of mini-max in game theory, or embedded in equilibrium theory.

Finally, although folk models indicate otherwise there is no hard evidence to support the notion that either conflict or harmony law models are inherently more "genuine" or more "spurious" or somehow better or worse than the other. Indeed, there is good evidence in the instances that follow of harmony models of law being used for purposes of pacification and for purposes of maintaining autonomy.

THE POLITICAL ECONOMY OF LEGAL MODELS

In sixteenth-century Castile, the medieval tradition that allowed a magistrate to base decisions not on the law, but on personal estimation of what was correct, was altered to a more formal legal system whereby litigants could win (Kagan 1981:22–23). R. Kagan writes that lawsuits were thought to be at odds with Christian belief in which compromise was the ideal and preferred means of ending disputes. With rapid demographic, social, legal, and political changes following the Spanish incursions into the New World, the courts came to be linked to an increase in adversarial legal behavior and presumably to a decline in religious fervor. The adversary process and a confrontation style were henceforth used as a political and economic legal strategy, but the compromise, harmony model was exported to the New World where it took root. The colonial policy established by the Spanish Crown in the sixteenth century still influences Mexican Indian village courts. The Crown underwrote the legal identity of each Indian community, and although the officers of the Crown retained the privilege of judging major crimes, the Indian sector of society was granted autonomy to administer the law. An examination of village social organization and the working of village law courts among the mountain Zapotec of Talea de Castro in Oaxaca, Mexico, reveals the heritage of Spanish colonial power and the uses of harmony legal models as control and/or pacification techniques and at the same time as political strategies (Nader 1990).

Interestingly, the Talean concern for harmony does not make them less litigious; it makes them more litigious because "you should not take authority into your own hands." In cases of violence, it is not the fighting that is central but the reasons for fighting. Taleans are not so much concerned with violence as the escalation of violence. In analyzing the data it becomes apparent that managing the contradictions between violence and harmony, between balance and controversy is an act of politics as well as one of law and justice. In male-female cases harmony is pursued and the village official waxes eloquent on harmony and on the importance of role and obligation. Cross-sex violence has little potential to escalate and thus such cases activate the village authority as conciliator. The frequency of cross-sex violence with its associated conciliation gives the courts their predominantly conciliatory slant. On the other hand, same-sex violence evokes accusatory and threatening styles more along the lines of adjudication. Harmony models accommodate both styles when the final purpose is control.

The use of conciliation and harmony models of law was widespread beyond Indian Mexico, as was the belief that litigation was to be avoided at almost all costs. In a book describing legal models in collision David Langum (1987) carefully documents the clash of legal traditions for the Mexican California frontier between 1821 and 1846. Amidst his references to sources illuminating the Mexican tradition he mentions that "In 1820 a Mexican lawyer, Juan M. Barquera, wrote a manual of procedures and law for the guidance of alcaldes, almost none of whom had formal legal training.... Alcaldes, he said are 'citizens chosen as fathers of the country.' ... They should 'work assiduously for the interior harmony of society' " (133). Langum describes the application of a paternalistic process by which the breach in community is healed.

On the other hand, the Anglo-American ex-patriates who came to Mexican California held a different set of ideas about a system that looked for certainty, and abhorred the particularistic manner of the Mexican harmony model. Much as in Spain of the sixteenth century, the spirit of individualism and acquisitiveness accompanied a growth in litigation with adversaries and clear win/lose decisions.

The collision between harmony models of law and conflict models was also present in seventeenth- and eighteenth-century Protestant New England villages and the more urbanized areas. Villages strove to maintain harmonious internal relations in order to remain independent from the influence of the Boston colony leaders (Lockridge 1970; Zuckerman 1970). In these villages legal models were to "serve the common interest at the expense of competing individual claims" (Auerbach 1983:16). Yet, with the rise of economic and social stratification, industrialization, commerce and trade, increased immigration, and declining church membership, the conflict model legal tradition, in which adversaries sparred, replaced the counter-tradition expressed in mediation and arbitration.

Within a longer time frame the oscillations between harmony model and conflict model dispute handling are more obvious. J. Auerbach (1983) argues for the appearance of harmony models (alternatives to courts) over a 350-year period in American history, and in the process

pinpoints the post-Civil War period as a time when the state began to
organize alternative dispute settlement processes in order to allay fears
of class warfare and racial discord. A century later there appears a similar
pattern. During the 1960s in the United States adversarial law was highly
valued as a means of attaining civil rights and civil remedies in issues of
race, sex, consumer problems, environmental questions. During the
1970s and 1980s, a variety of bedfellows with mixed motives marshaled
their allies and moved with surprising speed to introduce a policy embodying harmony ideology in the form of alternative dispute resolution
(ADR), and over a ten-year period translated that ideology into action
and institution building (Nader and Singer 1976; Abel 1982; Tomasic
and Feeley 1982). The history of that exchange of a conflict model for
a harmony model does not indicate that harmony ideology is benign;
on the contrary harmony ideology of the 1970s and 1980s is a powerful
form of direct and indirect control (Nader 1989a, 1989b).

The point of calling attention to the use of harmony or adversarial
models in both the Spanish-Mexican and Anglo-American legal traditions is not so much to describe the workings of these systems as to
explain why fluctuations in legal ideologies associated with a tolerance
for controversy or a search for harmony surface from time to time and
with what consequence. In examining the consequences of harmony
models of law in particular we come to understand their meaning in
different circumstances.

THE SPREAD OF HARMONY LAW MODELS

In order to examine the notion that harmony models of law are linked
to both control and autonomy, we need to examine the ethnographic
record and consider the spread of European Christianity and colonialism
as a possible source of harmony models that anthropologists sometimes
attribute to "the natives." For the Zapotec the harmony style and associated ideologies were recently used as tools for restricting the encroach-
ment of external, superordinate power, a component of a political
ideology that is counter-hegemonic. But the question of origin is another.
Was this local law constructed as a result of the diffusion of ideas of
harmony and its opposite by means of political and religious colonialism?
The theoretical issues raised by a comparative examination pivot around
the origin, use, and consequences of concepts of harmony. From the
outset the limitations of the evidence should be acknowledged; it ranges
from implicit connections between religious missionizing and disputing
processes allowing for inference, to explicit connection of the role of
Christian missionaries in disputing processes.

The detailed example of the Talean Zapotec who have been colonized
and missionized for over four hundred years together with the com-

parative evidence that I have culled suggest the need for a theory of cultural control that merges harmony and conflict as part of the same control system. Harmony and conflict are not antithetical as previous theories of conflict have suggested. From the outset we need to firmly fix in our minds that there is nothing wrong or right with either conflict or harmony behavior per se. It is the uses and the consequences of behavior that are of interest. The idea of a neutrally valued harmony or conflict is difficult for Westerners to grasp unless we understand from the start that a morality about harmony and conflict is just as much a construction as is the construction of a social organization that mirrors the ideology of either. Harmony may be used to suppress peoples by socializing them toward conformity in colonial contexts, or the idea of harmony may be used to resist external control. In what follows we concentrate on harmony models that operate as control or as pacification in the colonial and missionizing contexts.

In 1963, James Gibbs observed a model of harmony while studying what he thought of as the therapeutic processes of conciliatory dispute settlement used by the Kpelle of Liberia in Africa. Before him S. Nadel (1947), Gluckman (1955), P. Bohannan (1957), I. Shapera (1959), P. Gulliver (1963), and others had noted the influence of models of conciliation or reasonableness among the African peoples they had studied. All of these anthropologists make brief mention of the colonial government and missionary influence in passing. For example, Gluckman mentioned that the Lozi had absorbed the beliefs and ideology of Christianity although few were practicing Christians. He notes (Gluckman 1955:157) that "Litigious consensus breaks down when judges and litigants have different norms as where a Catholic husband might deny the kuta's power to divorce his wife." He refers to the break-up of the homogeneity of Lozi society further in "The Case of the Watchtower Pacifists," indicating how Christian sect values enter into the Barotse courts. Nadel (1947) paints the broader picture when he writes:

Christianity—the rigid, orthodox persuasion of missions—is an uncompromisingly alien creed. It cannot be satisfied with underlining the universal moral tenets—the evilness of murder, respect for property or marital rights. It ignores traditional marital rights in preaching monogamy; it breaks up the family system; it bans dances as bad, or beer-drinking as immoral, and thus denies vital features of social integration. It aims at changes so radical that they demand themselves the protection of ad hoc created laws rather than lend strength to a slowly emerging new morality. (p. 512)

There are differing constellations in the examples from Africa that indicate the double impact of Christian missions and colonial courts on African law and the consequent ubiquitousness of harmony ideology. In a recent analysis of the African documents Martin Chanock (1987) draws our attention to the idealization of African dispute processes that has evolved from the colonial situation as "a way of settling personal disputes and conflicts of interest by trying to find a solution acceptable to both parties . . . the antithesis of settlement by compromise is settlement by reference to abstract principles" (p. 5). Chanock goes on to note that legal writers concurred with the view of anthropologists:

> African law was a system of keeping the balance . . . geared . . . not to decisions imposed but to acceptable solutions. In the traditional African community there was no polarization of needs, of taste, or of values, and once the facts were established, "the same solutions will appeal to all and ways to achieve them will seem obvious" . . . the feeling of balance will be something spontaneous and self-evident. (p. 6)

In Chanock's brilliant exposition of the myths and images of African customary law, the processes of reconciliation and the egalitarianism of precolonial societies are contrasted with the stark historical realities. For example, among the Chew it seems clear that the precolonial period was a time of harsh punishment for sorcery, theft, adultery, and the like—a contrast to later notions that Chewa judicial institutions functioned to remove hatred by patient examination and persuasion. Chanock also quotes Canter on the Lenje of Zambia, noting the contradiction in values that the Lenje offer when speaking of reconciliation, that is, harmony with force. Chanock observes that maintaining harmony with force loses its egalitarian warmth.

For our purposes the data that Chanock brings together on the missionary presence in Africa from the 1830s onward is revealing of the original connection among local law, the presence of Christian missions, and the spread of harmony models. Chanock uses the term "missionary justice" to call attention to the fact that from the early 1860s missionaries were heavily involved in the settlement of disputes according to a Victorian interpretation of the biblical law they had brought with them and that they generally fit with English procedures as they knew them. Chanock mentions several early missions that were notorious for their zeal and violent punishments. He notes that these early excesses in punishment led to a change in policies, but that the missions continued to be active as conciliators in disputes. Although there were regional variation and differences among mission groups, mission justice suffered from contradiction. Missionaries found it difficult to respect the separation of religion from law, a separation that is so much a part of the Western system. They found this separation especially difficult to maintain in relation to the law of marriage and divorce, which they saw through the lens of mid-Victorian Christian law. Indeed, some missionaries promulgated the Ten Commandments as the law of God, and according to Chanock, the missionaries were glad to be peacemakers and hand down Christian judgment while the colonial courts evolved the whole into something we call customary law, which emphasized conciliation and compromise operating on the principles of Christian harmony ideology.

Chanock's work is rich on the origin, use, and modern-day consequences of harmony ideology. From the point of view of local law, compromise is the politics of adjustment. But more important, compromise becomes a politics of survival when indigenous communities are trying to restore a lost social solidarity as they learn to cope with threats from more powerful outside societies. In postcolonial time community courts became places where people engaged in discourses that established and reinforced common beliefs and values, discourses that were conscious political strategies for places where indirect rule and relative local autonomy were imposed by the colonials. Groups that support harmony often share the belief that the forces of disorder lie outside of their group (Greenhouse 1986). In fact, it is the recognition of external threat that sometimes mobilizes religious-based beliefs. African peoples used harmony at different points in their contact experiences—when war and raiding were being routed, when sophisticated African native courts were dealing with colonization of the governing and missionizing kind, or when agriculturalists sought to protect their communal lands from developers.

Recent fieldwork in Swaziland provides the clearest formulation of the uses of harmony over the politics of land. Swaziland has been described as a unique case of the "triumph of indigenous authority and a substantial subordination and/or containment of alien legal norms" (Takiramboudde 1983). In *The Politics of Harmony* (1988) Laurel Rose describes how harmony ideology is used at different points in the disputing process, predominantly by the chiefs. Commoners and new elites are challenging old formulations about land, and chiefs' uses of harmony rhetoric are said to be a strategy of indigenous hierarchical control. Harmony rhetoric is found in the speeches made at customary legal proceedings and national meetings and rituals.

Swazi statements about harmony suggest its multidimensional nature: unity, consensus, cooperation, compliance, passivity, and docility. And while all Swazis define harmony as social unity and cultural integrity the manner of its use in disputing claims differs by class. Rose reports that the traditional elites use harmony ideologies to legitimate their administrative roles and validate the continuance of the traditional land tenure system. The new elites use harmony to legitimate their positions, and while they may create an illusion of unity that accords with their individual land class interests, they often are responsible for internal social conflict. Both traditional and new elites use harmony ideologies to justify control. Swazi commoners strategically respond to harmony ideologies in presenting their case by abiding by the principles of harmony ideologies. Commoners resist harmony rhetoric when they feel that the social good has been violated or when they, as individuals, will suffer severe consequences. Harmony models of law are not benign in Swaziland or elsewhere.

The notion that harmony models of law are not necessarily benign gains strength from scattered materials found in ethnographic data of a more recent period on the Pacific. Anthropologists are increasingly including the missionary in the ethnographic work on contemporary peoples, unlike an earlier time when missionaries were thought to be peripheral to the real objectives of anthropological research (Beidelman 1974; Shapiro 1981). Ethnographers in the field for a short time might have problems documenting an influence that takes place over a long period of time and in people's minds. Edward Schieffelin (1981) was able to penetrate the language of the evangelical process as it relates to the use of harmony models as thought controls and specifically as the new thought changes patterns of handling disputes.

Schieffelin illustrates how the church motivated the Kaluli of New Guinea to accept Christianity. He points to the key symbol of Judgment Day and the second coming of Jesus Christ as used by the pastors, some of which paralleled and confirmed elements in the Kaluli's own mythological and religious tradition. The idea of Judgment Day not only made sense to the Kaluli as revenge, but it altered their relations to each other. Traditionally the regulation of conduct between individuals was a matter to be settled by those involved, guided by the canons of reciprocity and sanctioned by the threat of retaliation or revenge. With Judgment Day, one's conduct toward others is no longer a matter between two persons but between an individual and God: "The fundamental direction of moral reciprocity was moved from the horizontal place between people to the vertical between man and God mediated by pastor and church organization" (Schieffelin 1981:155).

Pastors used the rhetoric of Judgment Day to undercut the traditional means of social harmony or social solidarity in order to install new ones. They suggested for example, that if one killed a pig, it should not be given to just one other person, but distributed to everybody. This destroys the meaning of prestation. In traditional times the unreciprocated gift or unavenged wrong provided the urgency for protagonists to take a step to attain resolution. Judgment Day is replacing this process, not between individuals, but in general. Although Schieffelin does not deal directly with justice the transformation of social relations also apparently transformed the Kaluli sense of justice, repressing the urgency for resolution of conflict through reciprocation or compensation. But the main contribution of Schieffelin's report is related to the function of rhetoric as "the vehicle by which the message is rendered into a social construction upon reality" (p. 156).

George Westermark's work (1986, 1987) on the Agarabi village of the Highlands of Papua New Guinea provides an example of such mission-izing working in the courts. The Agarabis were the earliest converts to Adventism in the Highlands. Perceiving themselves as followers of the true Christian faith, Adventists employed several church-related activi-ties in their dispute management, such as the oath taken on the Bible, communion service, confession rituals, and church elder intervention. Westermark observes that Adventists use fillage courts as often as non-Adventists, even though the courts emphasize their adjudication rather than their mediation component. But Adventists, explains Westermark, use courts to extract a sympathetic hearing for Adventist beliefs. In time, these beliefs are given precedence by equating Adventist rules with the laws of the government. Westermark concludes that judicial hearings are utilized even though church officials disparage them: "Adventists . . . believe that court proceedings do not encourage a proper Christian attitude of conciliation" (1986: 142). Yet, dispute outcomes are shaped by the Adventist desire for group harmony and religious merit. In spite of the view that the court is a dangerous weapon, the courts are used actively and in Westermark's view are a forum for proselytizing.

Earlier published works on New Guinea also mention the spread of harmony ideology in relation to law and pacification more generally. Marie Reay (1974:219–20) notes that the spread of Christianity intro-duced a new style of court hearing among the peoples she studied. Councillors would rebuke people who spoke angrily, saying that anger belonged to Satan. They prayed that people's anger would "die." More emphasis was placed on the restoration of friendly relations than upon the allocation of compensation. Reay also notes that missions played an important role in pacifying warlike clans and in prohibiting violence in interpersonal relations.

Ann Chowning (1974:152–53) questions the emphasis that anthro-pologists have sometimes placed on restoring peace and harmony in disturbed social relations. In some Melanesian societies there is a tol-erance of and even enjoyment of quarreling—provided it does not lead to killing within the community. Some people do not feel the need to live in harmony. On the same point A. L. Epstein (1974:32) remarks that living in amity is a social value to which different societies attach different weight. One can feel the power of the missions and their role in spreading the harmony ideal into arenas of dispute handling in these anthropological observations.

In other parts of the Pacific the presence of missions is well into its second century. Wesleyan missionaries arrived in Tonga in 1826 to begin the process of Westernizing indigenous institutions. Recent ethnographic work (Marcus 1979) describes the litigation of disputes in court as an alternative mode of conflict management among the Tongans of Polynesia for whom social avoidance and ready conciliation are more characteristic. The Tongans frequently use the European-derived court system, but Marcus notes, through the use of lawyers are able to resume friendly relations following litigation. It would be useful to know what the missionaries have been teaching the Tongans about the morality of disputing. Morman missionaries presently in Tonga represent a church that has been very vocal on what they think of courts and litigious behavior. Brigham Young did not mince words when describing courts as "a cage of unclean birds, a den and kitchen of the devil, prepared for hell" (in Dredge 1979:199). The introduction of Western forms of government and the dismantling of the former system of social stratification that Marcus describes occurred simultaneously with the introduction of Christian beliefs. The contradictory elements that Marcus notes may be the contradictions of Western courts and Western Christianity respectively symbolized by controversy and harmony. The ideas he records about when and how to get angry, how to ask forgiveness, and how to express residual resentment are reminiscent of the Georgia Baptists so well described by Carol Greenhouse (1986).

The most powerful force in introducing and spreading harmony ideologies need not be the Christian missionaries. Note, for example, the state-sponsored legal informalism in parts of the Indian subcontinent in the nineteenth and twentieth centuries. The "state" in the guise of the Company Raj, Imperial India, or modern India has promoted "arbitration" and "compromise," an ideal most persistently expressed as *panchayat* justice. The history of the rise and spread of the idea of *panchayat* justice is still being written, but it is generally conceded that its political intent is and has been pacification, a quieting of the population. Following the tradition of indirect rule the British East India Company courts in rural south India decentralized the reorganized local self-government using the institutional forms of *panchayats* (Meschievitz and Galanter 1982). A brief summary of state introduction of harmony rhetoric into U.S. legal models is an example that is more recent and closer to home.

CHRISTIAN LIFE, SOCIAL HARMONY, AND LEGAL CULTURE

In a 1640 case quoted in Auerbach (1983:23–25), Mrs. Hibbens quarreled with Mr. Crabtree about his fee for carpentry work. The final disagreement was not over wages, however, but over the unbrotherly manner in which Mrs. Hibbens pursued her disagreement. She did not deal with Mr. Crabtree face to face. Mrs. Hibbens was accused of not dealing with her workers in a Christian way; finally she was expelled from the church. Communal harmony was threatened and Mrs. Hibbens was silenced. There was conflict in early New England, but the people did not think it well to resolve conflict through law; in fact the society could not tolerate legal conflict. Auerbach puts it this way (1983:22): "Litigation was perceived as a form of self-aggrandizement contrary to the best interests of the community. It was also un-Christian: law, in the words of one minister was 'a heart without affection, a mind without passion.' " Conflict was either suppressed or dealt with through mediation. The choice was between enforced harmony or open schism.

The same threads found in Auerbach's early New England are operative today among Southern Baptists of Hopewell, Georgia. In Carol Greenhouse's *Praying for Justice* (1986), the people of Hopewell are characterized by law avoidance or law aversion. Greenhouse reconstructs the link between the Christian life and social harmony. She speaks of the shadow of conflict in a past that generates or motivates a studied harmony, and of present-day Hopwellian struggles for harmony as a sign of commitment to Jesus and fear of community disintegration. Studied harmony is the effort to reduce the rate of conflict. In Greenhouse's rendition of Hopewell beliefs, harmony is the twin of justice. And while harmony is valued as the measure of human worth, Greenhouse says, "harmony has a somewhat negative cast, in that its meaning has more to do with the silencing of disputes than with the absence of disagreement" (1986:197). This silencing of disputes that accompanies the harmony model has not received adequate attention except by those promoting rights by means of adversarial behavior.

This history of legal cultures in the United States is the history of conditions under which dispute settlement preferences are "shifting commitments" (Auerbach 1983). These shifting commitments usually involve a change from legal models based on harmony to those characterized by adversarial models. Of course, no period is characterized by a single model. For example, it is fair to say that a prominent feature of legal culture in the 1960s was its adversarial mode. The adversarial legal model was used in the pursuit of justice, to deal with concerns of right and wrong. The 1960s have been remembered as confrontative, a time when many social groups felt encouraged to come forward with their agendas: civil rights, consumer rights, environmental rights, women's rights, American Indian rights. The decade has been described as a time of rights explosion.

The early 1970s was characterized by harmony rhetoric. The concerns were not with justice, but with harmony and efficiency. Harmony law models usually emphasize programs that support nonjudicial means for dispute handling. The alternative dispute resolution movement (known as ADR) came into being. Law schools shifted their training in the adversarial methods and began to include training in alternative dispute resolution mechanisms. The concern with harmony was accompanied by the silencing of disputes; Americans were told that they were too litigious. The production of harmony, the movement against the contentious, the movement to control the disenfranchised, and the loss of concern with rights created a model of law that was intolerant of conflict, its causes, and its expression. An intolerance for strife seeks to rid the society of those who complain—"love it, or leave it"—and by various means attempts to create consensus, homogeneity, and agreement. The harmony model of the 1970s and 1980s is a kind of cultural soma that tranquilizes potential plaintiffs who increasingly agree to consent to treatment by means of mediation or who are told "Don't be negative." The rationalization for how well harmony works was often sought in the anthropological literature. The Kpelle of Liberia (Gibbs 1963) who have a moot court procedure, a therapeutic model to settle family problems (although in reality the Kpelle litigated many of their disputes), and the Zapotec of Mexico (Nader 1969) who followed a mini-max model as an ideal (give-a-little, get-a-little) rather than zero-sum game solutions (while they also litigated a good deal) were used as examples of how American justice could become "more civilized."

The Roscoe Pound Conference, "Perspectives on Justice in the Future," held in St. Paul, Minnesota, in 1976 was a turning point indicating a cultural shift with ramifications far beyond the law. A way of thinking about the structural problems of inequality, about social relations more generally, and about solutions to these problems by cultural means was dramatized. The solution that emerged was a procedural reform whereby the harmony model would come to replace the adversarial model in law. The rhetoric at the conference extolled the virtues of alternative disputing mechanisms governed by harmony and efficiency: the courts were overcrowded. American lawyers and the American people were too litigious; new tribunals were needed to divert cases generated by the regulated welfare state. Alternative dispute agencies were described as being agencies of settlement or reconciliation, and people who stood in the way of such procedural reforms were said to suffer from "status quoism."

In the years following the conference the public was immersed in alternative dispute resolution rhetoric. The language was formulaic (Bloch 1975); generalizations were repeated without grounding, authority and danger were invoked, and values were presented as facts (Nader 1989a). Because of his authoritative position as Chief Justice, Warren Burger carried considerable weight in setting the tone of the language that characterized the speeches and writings of the movement. Burger warned that adversarial modes of conflict resolution were tearing society apart and that alternative fora were more civilized (1982a). He claimed that Americans are inherently litigious. He argued that lawyers should serve as "healers of human conflicts" (1982b:7) where plaintiffs are patients needing treatment, and claimed that training a lawyer as adversarial is anachronistic. Burger again warned that the loads on the courts were too great.

The framework of the harmony ideology is beginning to take hold, while the rhetoric and origins of the ideology go unquestioned. Most lawyers are not doing work that carries them anywhere near a courtroom context. There is no evidence for saying that Americans rely primarily on the adversary process for resolving all their disputes; Americans negotiate primarily and only rarely move to third party handlers (Nader 1980). Further, Burger's argument that Americans are becoming increasingly litigious does not stand the test of numbers (Galanter 1983). In spite of evidence to the contrary, the chief justice proceeded relentlessly with his solution, privatization of law, which meant taking a large volume of private conflicts out of the courts and into the channels of arbitration, mediation, and conciliation (1985).

The theory of harmony that undergirds the alternative dispute resolution movement conceptualizes harmony behavior as the keystone of community. Harmony, the same theory explains, causes the country to be more productive, more innovative, and more entrepreneurial (Cannon 1986). The harmony theorists believe that litigation causes loss of community, destroys trust and cooperation, and leads to problem solving based on emotion rather than on rationality and efficiency. Alternative dispute resolution is also seen as essential to democracy because the parties are afforded the opportunity to deal with the real issues rather than to be entrapped in lawyers' rhetoric. Embedded in this harmony theory is a belief that individual assertion of rights is evil. The harmony theorists are constructing a social order that exercises injunctions against conflict and even against voicing disputes.

Some critics have described the alternative movement as antilegal, antirights, and antijustice in the sense of an absolute justice orientation. It is preferable to talk about its consequences in terms of the view of conflict that is carried by mediation forums of the 1980s (Rothschild 1986). The harmony theorists see conflict as dysfunctional and threatening to the social order, a phenomenon to be diffused. This notion of conflict presumes societal consensus about rights and values, which leads to the operation of mediation forums that have no explicit standards of justice. Furthermore the ideology of mediation is visualized as a process that brings people together; disputes are reshaped as communication problems rather than conflicts over values. Unequal power does not enter the paradigm, and disputes about facts and legal rights are transformed into disputes about feelings and relationships. Rothschild observes that the harmony model is one where conflict is personalized, and where social problems become localized in the realm of emotion. Indeed, alternative dispute resolution such as mediation leaves no written record and no legacy as do the courts whose recorded cases allow us to understand the etiology of injury and prevention.

Harmony theory predicts that consensus will build community, state, and business. The premise is that everyone shares (or ought to share) the same goals. In harmony discourse, the talk of rights and remedies is absent, while rhetoric about mythical litigation explosions becomes a way to explain American business failure, the high cost of insurance, and more. In the minds of some analysts alternative dispute arrangements represent a relatively new type of political domination. Harmony ideology serves to control confrontational politics; it also controls or suppresses criticism. The institutionalization of harmony models operates as an informal state embedded in the practices of everyday life, and intertwined with educational institutions, therapy communities, and management techniques more generally.

THE ROLE OF CULTURE IN DISPUTE RESOLUTION

Ambiguities surrounding the study of the cultural components of law have been plentiful even among anthropologists in whose discipline culture plays a central role. When the anthropologist of an earlier day set out to understand other cultures, culture was a concept used to describe shared traditions passed from one generation to another, and the products of that shared tradition. We can no longer speak about culture solely as the organic notion of the early anthropologists. Theorists today speak about hegemonic culture, which is constructed at a point and moves out as control of others by their own "consent." By hegemony Gramsci meant (Boggs in Greer 1982) "the permeation throughout civil society—including a whole range of structures and activities like trade unions, schools, the churches, and the family—of an entire system of values, attitudes, beliefs, morality, etc. that is in one way or another supportive of the established order and the class interests that dominate it" (305). Ideas such as harmony, confrontational politics, or efficiency may originate locally, spread, or be imposed, recombined, and used to control or to resist control, and result in distributing power by means of remedy generated.

Over the past decades anthropologists of law and legal historians have observed that with the development of colonialism harmony models replaced feuds and wars, and with the development of nation-states the harmony model, so commonly associated with communities under colonialism, was being replaced by the adversary model (Nader and Todd 1978; Abel 1979). In Japan between 1922 and 1942 formal conciliation was used as a substitute for trials (Haley 1982). In the old nation-states the situation appeared to be moving in the opposite direction. Vilhelm

Aubert (1969) reported that Norway had moved toward the harmony model and away from the adversarial one with the development of the welfare state. A decade later the harmony model was also center stage in the United States. Such observations indicate that cultural values underlying disputing processes change over time and circumstance and that they are profoundly political.

In addition, we learn from ethnography that harmony and controversy have different meanings to different people and classes. Sally Merry (1982) has made a similar point in relation to mediation. The key difference between harmony ideologies revolves around harmony as a means or goal. For the Zapotec disputing may be a means to harmony and autonomy. For Southern Baptists (Greenhouse 1986) harmony is both the means and the goal and is phrased in opposition to conflict. For the Shia Moslems in Lebanon (Nader 1965) conflict is part of the struggle in life, normative behavior. For those spearheading commercial or colonialist politics harmony is an ideology of pacification and a way to civilize populations, a tool to create different cultural forms.

Social scientists who have looked at cultural components of dispute resolution without drawing distinctions between levels of activity find it difficult to develop a theory of harmony that is greater than particular dispute resolution styles. In my essay "Styles and Court Procedure: To Make the Balance" (1969), I contrasted the harmony model in disputing processes with a zero-sum game model in terms of the impact on individual litigants. The analysis was set in the paradigm of particular cases, and the meaning of harmony or zero-sum models for the construction of law and the social order was implied: the impact for individuals was writ large for the wider social order. I missed the meaning of harmony as an internal accommodation to conquest and domination. In *The Behavior of Law* (1976), Donald Black analyzed four styles of social control: penal, compensatory, therapeutic, and conciliatory. Black sees the outline of these styles and their concomitant mechanisms as useful distinctions in describing the characteristics of social control. Black describes the conciliatory style as having a standard of harmony and a solution through resolution. As applied to the Zapotec, the Hopewellians, and the legal reform movement we find that conciliation, harmony, and resolution have quite different meanings in each place. We need to distinguish between clusters of beliefs and their consequences. From the evidence at hand, conciliation, harmony, and resolution have such different consequences as to merit different labels: harmony that leads to autonomy is different than harmony that leads to control or pacification; conciliation may lead to conflict as well as to resolution, and harmony as well as to justice. Disputing processes cannot be explained as a reflection of some predetermined set of social conditions; rather they reflect the processes of cultural construction that may be a response to demand, a product of ruling interests, or a result of class conflict. Harmony as a general conception for life should be scrutinized in relation to the construction of law much as conflict has been scrutinized in relation to the development of law.

There are no political or ideological institutions that are not also agencies of control. Antonio Gramsci's idea of hegemony is useful in forcing us to look at the institutions through which dominant belief systems are transmitted. Concepts like the informal state help us to visualize the motivation of organizations and professions who seek control through cultural pacification. But the struggle from pacification or the struggle for freedom and autonomy may better utilize concepts such as class or community.

Carol Greenhouse (1986) suggests the negative valuation of conflict in the Baptist community of Hopewell and the contemporary equation of Christianity and harmony began during the years between the first white settlement in the country and the Civil War. Law avoidance, law aversion, and the importance of consensus and harmony were as important for community survival in Hopewell as among the Zapotec Indians, although the Zapotec litigate to achieve harmony while the people of Hopewell avoid litigation. Greenhouse reconstructs the way in which local Baptists built their ethic from elements available in the culture at large and so developed "a strategy that transformed conflict so effectively that it no longer threatened the local church's survival but instead essentially guaranteed it" (p. 183). Chief Justice Burger and his colleagues built a reform ethos out of elements that were available in the culture at large, developing a strategy that transformed the confrontational politics of the 1960s and 1970s. Harmony models thus serve to suppress and to pacify populations.

We have given theoretical recognition to conflict because it is exemplified in behavior. Harmony on the other hand is housed in the realm of ideas. Any social scientist seeking a theory of harmony will recognize that the morality of disputing processes is now everywhere heavily influenced by ideas of a religious nature. Law and religion may have been separated in Western legal systems at least ideally, but in the greater part of the real world they are not separable. A new range of questions regarding the role of culture in disputing processes is imperative. In pursuing the role of culture in dispute resolution we increasingly articulate the position of the anthropologist so as to avoid being enmeshed in our own cultural grids, in our own dispute resolution preferences.

REFERENCES

Abel, R. L. 1979. Western Courts in Non-Western Settings: Patterns Used in Colonial and Neo-Colonial Africa. In *The Imposition of Law*, eds. S. Burman and B. Harrel-Bond. New York: Academic.

———. 1982. *The Politics of Informal Justice*, vol. 1, *The American Experience*; vol. 2, *Comparative Studies*. New York: Academic.

Aubert, V. 1969. Law as a Way of Resolving Conflicts: The Case Industrialized Society. In *Law in Culture and Society*, ed. L. Nader. Chicago: Aldine.

Auerbach, J. 1983. *Justice Without Law?* New York: Oxford University Press.

Beidelman, T. 1974. Social Theory and the Study of Christian Missions. *Africa* 44(3):235–249.

Black, D. 1976. *The Behavior of Law*. New York: Academic.

Bloch, M. 1975. *Political Language and Oratory in Traditional Society*. London and New York: Academic.

Bohannan, P. 1957. *Justice and Judgement among the Tiv*. London: Oxford University Press for the International African Institute.

Burger, W. E. 1979. Keynote Address. In *Perspectives on Justice in the Proceedings of the National Conference on the Causes of Popular Dissatisfaction with the Administration of Justice*, eds. A. L. Levin and R. R. Wheeler. St. Paul, Minn.: West.

———. 1982a. Isn't There a Better Way? Annual Report on the State of the Judiciary. Remarks of Warren E. Burger, Chief Justice of the United States at the Midyear Meeting, American Bar Association, Chicago, Ill., Jan. 24.

———. 1982b. Remarks of Warren E. Burger, Chief Justice of the United States at New York University and the Institute of Judicial Administration, New York City, Nov. 18.

———. 1985a. Remarks of Warren E. Burger, Chief Justice of the United States at the American Law Institute, Washington, D.C., May 14.

———. 1985b. Remarks of Warren E. Burger, Chief Justice of the United States at the Twin Cities Advisory Council of the American Arbitration Association, et al. Luncheon, St. Paul, Minn., Aug. 21.

———. 1985c. Year-End Report on the Judiciary by Warren E. Burger, Chief Justice of the United States.

Cannon, M. 1986. Contentious and Burdensome Litigation, A Need for Alternatives. *Phi Kappa Phi Journal*: 10–12.

Chanock, M. 1987. *Law, Custom, and Social Order: The Colonial Experience in Malawi and Zambia*. Cambridge: Cambridge University Press.

Chowning, A. 1974. Disputing in Two West New Britain Societies: Similarities and Differences. In *Contention and Dispute*, ed. A. L. Epstein. Canberra: Australian National University Press.

Dahrendorf, R. 1967. *Society and Democracy in Germany*. New York: W. W. Norton.

Dredge, C. P. 1979. Dispute Settlement in the Mormon Community: The Operation of Ecclesiastical Courts in Utah. In *Access to Justice*, vol. 4, *Anthropological Perspective*, ed. K.-F. Koch. Milan: Dott. A. Giuffre Editore.

Epstein, A. L., ed. 1974. *Contention and Dispute: Aspects of Law and Social Control in Melanesia*. Canberra: Australian National University Press.

Galanter, M. 1983. Reading the Landscape of Disputes: What We Know and Don't Know (and Think We Know) about Our Allegedly Contentious and Litigious Society. *UCLA Law Review* 31:4.

Gibbs, J. 1963. The Kpelle Moot: A Therapeutic Model for the Informal Settlement of Disputes. *Africa* 33:1–11.

Gluckman, M. 1955. *The Judicial Process among the Barotse of Northern Rhodesia.* Manchester: Manchester University Press.

———. 1959. *Custom and Conflict in Africa.* Glencoe, Ill.: Free.

Greenhouse, C. 1986. *Praying for Justice: Faith, Order and Community in an American Town.* Ithaca, N.Y.: Cornell University Press.

Greer, E., ed. 1982. Legal Hegemony. In *The Politics of Law: A Progressive Critique,* ed. D. Kairys. New York: Pantheon.

Gulliver, P. 1963. *Social Control in an African Society: A Study of the Arusha, Agricultural Masai of Northern Tanganyika.* Boston: Boston University Press.

Haley, J. O. 1982. The Politics of Informal Justice: The Japanese Experience, 1922–1942. In *The Politics of Informal Justice,* vol. 2, ed. R. L. Abel. New York: Academic.

Kagan, R. 1981. *Lawsuits and Litigants in Castile, 1500–1700.* Chapel Hill: University of North Carolina Press.

Langum, D. 1987. *Law and Community on the Mexican California Frontier: Anglo American Expatriates and the Clash of Legal Traditions, 1821–1846.* Norman and London: University of Oklahoma Press.

Lockridge, K. 1970. *A New England Town: The First Hundred Years.* New York: W. W. Norton and Company.

Marcus, G. 1979. Litigation, Interpersonal Conflict, and Noble Succession Disputes in Friendly Islands. In *Access to Justice,* vol. 4, *Anthropological Perspectives,* ed. K.-F. Kock. Milan: Dott. A. Giuffre Editore.

Merry, S. E. 1982. The Social Organization of Mediation in Nonindustrial Societies: Implications for Informal Community Justice in America. In *The Politics of Informal Justice,* ed. R. L. Abel. New York: Academic.

Meschievitz, C. S., and M. Galanter. 1982. In Search of Nyaya Panchayats: The Politics of a Moribund Institution. In *The Politics of Informal Justice,* ed. R. L. Abel. New York: Academic.

Nadel, S. 1947. *The Nuba.* London: Oxford University Press.

Nader, L. 1965. Choices in Legal Procedure: Shia Moslem and Mexican Zapotec. In *American Anthropologist,* vol. 167.

———. 1968. Conflict: Anthropological Aspects. In *International Encyclopedia of the Social Sciences,* 3:236–42.

———. 1969. Styles of Court Procedure: To Make the Balance. In *Law in Culture and Society,* ed. L. Nader. Hawthorne, N.Y.: Aldine.

———, ed. 1980. *No Access to Law—Alternatives to American Judicial System.* New York: Academic.

———. 1989a. The Crown, the Colonists and the Course of Village Law. In *History and Power in the Study of Law,* eds. J. Starr and J. Collier. Ithaca, N.Y.: Cornell University Press.

———. 1989b. Review of Praying for Justice, Faith, Order and Community in an American Town by Carol J. Greenhouse. In *Law and Society Review,* January.

———. 1990. Harmony Ideology: Justice and Control in a Mountain Zapotec Village. Stanford: Stanford University Press.

Nader, L., and L. R. Singer. 1976. Dispute Resolution . . . What are the Choices? In *California State Bar Journal* 51(4).

Nader, L., and H. Todd, eds., 1978. *The Disputing Process: Law in Ten Societies.* New York: Columbia University Press.

Reay, M. 1974. Changing Conventions of Dispute Settlement in Minjarea. In *Contentions and Dispute: Aspects of Law and Social Control in Melanesia,* ed. A. L. Epstein. Canberra: Australian National University Press.

Rose, L. 1988. The Politics of Harmony: Land Dispute Strategies in Swaziland. Unpublished Ph.D. diss., Department of Anthropology, University of California, Berkeley. (In press, Cambridge University Press.)

Rothschild, J. 1986. Mediation as Social Control. Unpublished Ph.D. diss. Department of Sociology, University of California, Berkeley.

Sapir, E. 1924. Culture, Genuine and Spurious. *American Journal of Sociology* 29:401–29.

Scheiffelin, E. L. 1981. Evangelical Rhetoric and the Transformation of Traditional Culture in Papua New Guinea. *Comparative Studies in Society and History* 23(1):150–57.

Shapera, I. 1959. *A Handbook of Tswana Law and Custom.* New York: Oxford University Press.

Shapiro, J. 1981. Ideologies of Catholic Missionary Practice in a Postcolonial Era. *Comparative Studies in Society and History* 23(1):130–49.

Takirambudde, P. 1983. External Law and Social Structure in an African Context: An Essay about Normative Imposition and Survival in Swaziland. *Comparative and International Law Journal of Southern Africa* 16:209–228.

Tomasic, R., and M. Feeley. 1982. *Neighborhood Justice: Assessment of an Emergent Idea.* New York: Longman.

Westermark, G. 1986. Court Is an Arrow: Legal Pluralism in Papua New Guinea. *Ethnology* 25(2):131–49.

———. 1987. Church Law, Court Law, Competing Forums in a Highlands Village. In *Anthropology in the High Valleys: Essays on the New Guinea Highlands in Honor of Kenneth E. Rad.* Novato, Calif.: Chandler and Sharp.

Zuckerman, M. 1970. *Peaceable Kingdoms: New England Towns in the Eighteenth Century.* New York: Alfred A. Knopf.

4

Tertius Luctans: Idiocosm, Caricature, and Mask[1]

F. G. Bailey

CULTURE AS A WEAPON

This essay considers a way in which the concept "culture" might be used to understand conflict management in formal organizations. More generally, it describes a process of simplification which occurs when culture is used as a guide for action.

Culture is a collection of constructs about the way the world is, about the way people are, and about the way both should be. These constructs take the form of both beliefs and values. Any particular collection is identified by the people who hold it (Cheyenne culture, Israeli culture, and so on) or by the institutions or settings in which it is found. This identification can be carried progressively downwards (from the general to the particular), for example in a series that runs from the culture of universities—of university officials—of deans—of science deans—of science deans in Third World countries—of science deans in India—of Dean Mukherji. The final level is the culture of an individual, a total set of personal constructs. The array of cultural knowledge at the disposal of any particular individual is an idiocosm.[2]

The process of simplification that translates culture into action selects out of the whole idiocosm two kinds of product: one is a caricature and the other is a mask. A caricature emphasizes select features of a person or an object or a situation so as to excite in the viewer a particular attitude. A mask is a mode of presenting oneself in a manner thought likely to persuade particular people in particular settings to accept a particular caricature.

I will argue that the concept of cultural difference is necessary for understanding conflict. As between peoples or institutions or individuals there will surely be shared items, but the postulate of cultural difference means that no two sets of cultural constructs will contain the identical selection of items. A model of conflict management that ignores cultural differences and bases itself on universal human features, whether psychobiological or situational, will provide such general explanations for behavior that they will be of little practical use.

Certainly there are situational generalizations about conflict that are valid in all cultures. For example, conflict everywhere arises out of scarcity: two or more parties strive for something that only one can have. But what is scarce necessarily depends upon what is desired, and that varies from one culture to another. Power is necessarily scarce everywhere, because it can be exerted only when someone is deprived of power. But what constitutes an exercise of power is differently defined by different people. In short, we cannot understand what goes on in human interactions, unless we know, so far as that is possible, what is in the minds of the actors. Part of what is in their minds is their culture, and in the context of conflict we should try to understand that culture, doing so at the very specific level of the idiocosm.

A culture, in one of its aspects, is a set of imperfectly shared beliefs and values that guide conduct. The sharing is incomplete, individuals having their own personal selection in the form of their idiocosm. In that way they make their own culture, but they do not make it entirely as they wish. There are two constraints. First, culture is thrust on them by others, and in that sense exists above and beyond any individual. It is therefore true—if somewhat vacuous—to say that items in an idiocosm cannot be generated de novo. An idiocosm is a selection from what is available; novelty comes from the selection and not from the items selected. Second, since culture is a guide for conduct in a world that can move independently of culture, if cultural rules are to remain effective they must be adapted to changing circumstances.

But there is rarely any immediate test of what is effective, because the very definition of failure, let alone of its causes, is itself a construct, an interpretation, a part of culture, and therefore open to argument. Culture is only in the end a guide for conduct. In the beginning culture constitutes a weapon for contestants who seek to impose on one another definitions of what is going on, what should be going on, what is proper, what is honorable, what is advantageous, who is good, who is evil, who is dangerous, who is useful, who is treacherous, who can be trusted, and so on. Only when one definition has prevailed (through victory or through compromise), can it become a guide for conduct.

To think of conflict management as no more than "peacemaking" is to miss half the reality and most of the fun. Peacemakers succeed to the extent that they exert control by restraining (or even eliminating) antagonists. They take away power, and in doing so become antagonists.

Conflict management is a type of combative behavior. This is the principle of *tertius luctans*, the third man as contestant.

Conflict managers are contestants for power even when their aim is to limit conflict. The claim to be "above the fray" is in itself, of course, an advertisement of power. They are still "managing conflict," even when their intervention causes its escalation. In a formal sense a referee stands above a contest in the same way that the rules of the game stand above the game; indeed, the rules are the source of authority. Referees sometimes exercise power by giving covert support to one or the other contestant. But there is another way in which every referee, even when truly neutral, inevitably exercises power. Since political strife, including that inside formal organizations, is only imperfectly governed by rules, referees (and other would-be managers of conflict) have no choice but to bring the generality of rules down to the particularity of actual contests. In doing so they make manipulative definitions of the situation and impose these definitions on the contestants, if their intervention is to be successful. In short, the strategy of conflict management is of necessity also a strategy of conflict.

In this essay cultural definitions of conflict will be inferred from the statements of three individuals, each powerful in his respective institution. Since all three institutions are universities, where the medium of instruction is English, they have certain cultural features in common; this permits comparison. But the differences among the three individuals are striking enough to see three distinct idiocosms of conflict out of which come three distinct caricatures of the place of conflict in institutional life and of the masks appropriate for its management.

The justified sinners, whose confessions I will present, are two vice-chancellors and a dean.[3] Each of their discourses has its own construction of the nature of conflict in a university. Each discourse defines the essential character of the institution, explains the origins of conflict, and suggests, explicitly or implicitly, a strategy for its management.

THE DEAN

The dean wore two masks. The outer mask was that of a good bureaucrat, for whom conflict indicated a regrettable failure in bureaucratic design. Not far beneath was another persona who regarded conflict as not only inevitable, but even enjoyable. He also had an explicit strategy for its management.

His institution had been elevated, during the academic boom of the 1950s, from local college to university. When I interviewed him in the late 1970s, there was still a frontier atmosphere about the campus and the dean had in him an element of the pioneer. He was very much his own man. He exuded energy; a doer, abrupt, direct, and an aggressive talker. His appointment as dean was for life, but he maintained an active research career (in industrial relations) and saw himself as a practical scholar involved in administration because he found it enjoyable. He had charge of the Faculty of Social Studies, which included departments of sociology, economics, politics, administration, and several others.

He presented a very clear image of himself. Part of the image was a wholly unsentimental concern for getting things right. He voiced a hard-headed regret ("not much to be done about it now") for having hired second-raters during the rapid expansion. Since they now had tenure, more able younger people could be appointed only on time-limited contracts. "Things might have been better managed," he said. Of course at the time the money had to be spent and the appointments made, and it would be silly to look around for someone to blame. The regret seemed not so much for the loss of intellectual excellence as for our human incapacity to run affairs in a rational manner.

But the dean in fact did set a high value on intellectual excellence, on knowledge and its advancement. He stressed his own engagement with research. He was annoyed when he found himself, as dean, lumped in the category of "they" (that is, the administration). He insisted that the best university administrators were also distinguished scholars (a proposition I doubt). A high academic reputation, he said, is evidence of a clear mind, and to exercise power effectively, minds must be clear. He also had firm ideas about teaching: the design of a course must be primarily the responsibility not of committees but of the instructor.

This respect for academic matters partly explains his conduct at departmental meetings. He attended meetings in all departments in his faculty as of right. But, he insisted, he went as an observer, to find out what people thought and to coordinate the interests of different departments. He also went to supply information. This was badly needed: "They haven't the faintest bloody idea of how the place works." He did not go to meetings, he made clear to everyone, to influence decisions: he believed in decentralization. Academic matters in a department should be its exclusive responsibility. His conduct was also a demonstration of trust in departmental heads. He took care, he said, not to undercut their authority and discouraged individuals from coming directly to him, without first taking their problems to the departmental head.

The entire image, up to this point, is consistent. As dean he stood aloof from academic concerns (but always ready to help with information). He respected the integrity of academic disciplines and trusted his heads of departments to conduct affairs in a rational manner. Thus he exemplifies certain bureaucratic virtues. Bureaucracies are by design specialized as to task, and roles in them are hierarchically organized. Furthermore the powers of any office are strictly defined. This is a world (supposedly) of firm boundaries, maintained by keeping records, observing precedent, elaborating rules, and paying close attention to detail, a place not for leaders but for managers. Tight boundaries and careful analytical forethought are designed to make everything predictable, in other words, a world without conflict.

But this is only the top side of the dean's image. Since his colleagues did not have "the faintest bloody idea of how the place works" he sometimes decided to "bias the situation." If a decision came down from on high that neither he nor the teachers liked (for example, extending the time for withdrawal from courses), it had to be implemented. But he would let everyone know how its practice could be sabotaged. There were other times when, tiring of some prolonged defense of something he did not like (for example, using university letterhead for certain kinds of questionnaire), he made plain the adverse consequences, sometimes inventing penalties that he knew would never be exacted. These two instances of "extrabureaucratic" behavior were, I suspect, no less a part of his public image (among his colleagues) than was his concern for rational administration and academic pursuits. They knew that he resorted to dirty tricks, sometimes for their benefit and sometimes to get his way over them. This capacity to play politician attracted adjectives like "tough," "astute," and "effective."

He was well aware of the link between power and information. At the time he was in the "doghouse," because he had "leaked" information about a discussion of higher councils, going prematurely public, embarrassing senior administrators and preventing them from making what they considered the rational decision. Likewise, when making new appointments, he told me, it was certainly wise to consult others, but to do so discreetly. He sounded out public opinion by talking to individuals or listening to gossip in that highly unofficial place, the coffee room. This, he explained, eliminated pressure groups, because those of like opinion did not know of one another's existence, or even if they did they were without a public forum.

He described his own superior, the director of the institution, as an astute man who enjoyed playing the elder statesman in a "find-the-consensus, above-the-rabble, will-of-the-meeting, have-no-power-myself" style. He went on:

Also he's clean. He's clean to the point of being crazy. The council wanted to buy him a house: he refused. The council wanted to buy him a Mercedes: he refused. He travels economy class: once going to some meetings he wanted to talk to a member of council and to me, both of us being in the first class because other people were buying the tickets. The director paid the difference out of his own pocket. He's crazy. It makes it damned hard for the rest of us to get anything for ourselves. It isn't just the image of being "above all this": he really is.

This was said in a tone of rueful admiration. But he added that the director maintained his organizational innocence only by keeping himself quite apart from the university's internal politics. Those who had to run the place from the inside could not realistically aspire to such elevated standards.

The dean was no elder statesman, by no means "above all this"; he enjoyed a fight. "I like the job. I once tried just teaching and research and I was bored stiff: no excitement, no fights. You need to get into fights from time to time." But he also knew it was a mistake to let fighting become an end in itself, rather than an occasional and enjoyable muscle-toning exercise. The deans, he said, made this mistake in the early days; now they presented a united front to the higher administration, even though they might "fight like cats" among themselves.

He liked the bureaucratic restraints built into allocation procedures. Formulas were absolutely necessary: for example, his university distributed resources among departments on the basis of student numbers. A percentage was retained for distribution through debate, so that some element of carrot-and-stick remained, but the great virtue of the system meant that even a department whose head was detested by everyone was not penalized. He drew a vivid picture of a neighboring university in which one department had suffered for years because its permanent head had a bad case of collegial halitosis.

Even the ordinary academic, whose institutional common sense he thought ludicrously underdeveloped, in time realized the emotional and practical costs of prolonged fighting over resources. His faculty (social sciences) had a small discretionary fund. Its distribution, by common consent, lay entirely in his hands. From time to time he amused himself by suggesting that his colleagues might prefer to allocate these monies themselves—good democratic procedure—and he watched with pleasure their nervous reluctance to enter into what they knew would be a zero-sum game: if someone got more, someone else got less and, "with six departments where do you bloody well begin? They want me to do it, and so long as I am not wildly out of line, they are happy to go along with it. They gripe, of course, but they don't want to do it themselves. They confront me, but not each other: and they quiet down when I tell them get on with it themselves." Then followed a characteristic aside: "I take some off the top for my own office. It's shown in the figures, but it's so small in comparison to the total, that they hardly notice—fortunately."

The dean has a quite unbureaucratic tolerance for inconsistency. The disbursement of ad hoc monies within his faculty remains centralized (in his hands), but that of similar funds among faculties had been decentralized. A formula provides each faculty with its share, and then members of that faculty decide how to make the allocation among themselves. The result is that, for example, a sociologist from one faculty might meet a colleague from a different faculty at the same conference and learn that they were getting different expense allowances. Then there would be an outcry to have the funds centralized again. Of course, the dean remarked, it was not fair, but if you have some decentralization it keeps the dingbats happy and lets them think they are running the place.

The dean, finally, had a contempt for what he called "rhetoric":

There's too much bloody rhetoric. If a guy has a good reason for doing something, he gives it. If he doesn't have a good reason he talks about educational excellence and such things. I am totally cynical. Institutions like this are organized anarchies. They do not have goals; or they don't know what they are; or they have a lot of goals at different levels. Drop a hat and someone will give you a speech about goals, but like any other institution the institutional goal here is first to expand, and if that can't be done at least to stay in business.

THE VICE-CHANCELLORS

The dean was not given to sermonizing. But a man in power finds it hard to escape calls to the pulpit, and, not long before I interviewed him, he had given a keynote address on the subject of higher education. He told his audience to face facts and realize that academic institutions were no different from any others and they had best learn how to cope with the politics inevitable in an academic jungle.

Normative addresses are not usually that down-to-earth, and those given by the vice-chancellors certainly were not. They sermonized abundantly. One man presided over a well-established institution of high renown in a rich country (Vice-Chancellor High). The other university was newly established, located in a poor region, and beset with many difficulties. Its head we will call Vice-Chancellor Low.[4]

High, in one address, had this to say:

Let me say that I believe it is proper that a vice-chancellor should dilate from time to time on those great issues which universities, taken in the broad, stand for in our society. We represent, after all, an accumulated tradition which goes back in our culture for six centuries and more. For all the proper—and improper—criticisms of what we do, I doubt if it is anywhere seriously suggested that it should now be dispensed with. I may well speak on these matters some time: there are times and occasions when as university people it behooves us to express the faith that is in us.

From time to time, in the course of the address, he returns to celebrate our vocation:

On this score I want to remark that as I have gone around departments I have become rather concerned that the new calls in recent years upon an academic's time have not always been satisfactorily allowed for. It is wholly right that variety, dedication and innovation should be among the hallmarks of our teaching. There is much to be said too for the new assessment procedures; as there is for the democratization of departmental government. But these things sometimes seem to trench upon the development of scholarly and scientific expertise and en-quiry—upon what is usually called "research"—to an altogether undue extent. We cannot, I believe, overlook the fact that as academics we have obligations to probe vigorously at the frontiers of knowledge and understanding—as well, periodically, to make our insights known to others through publication.

High opens the address with a point that he describes as "quite fundamental."

It is, I believe, essential to bear constantly in mind that at its core the work of the university consists of a large number of people quietly going about their academic business. For academic staff and students this means that in a myriad of ways they are either busily engaged in laboratories, amid a great multiplicity of technical aids; or are going to the library to find a book or an article; or are reading, writing, talking, listening, poring over the data they have collected, thinking—all to the end that they may seek out for themselves knowledge and understanding, so that when the appropriate moments arrive, they may either employ this in the cause of further understanding, and/or so put their insights into words that these can be effectively passed on to others.

He then lists the activities of those who make the scholarly endeavor possible by "writing letters, picking up telephones, participating in meet-ings." Third, there are others who type, pay bills, check inventories, look after the buildings, and so forth.

These words convey the magnitude of the enterprise (and therefore minister to the sense of importance of those employed in it). High stresses responsibility, the dependence of everyone on everyone else, and the unity of purpose within an apparent diversity. He also talks about his own role, as head of the institution. Listing those few departments (out of about eighty) he, as vice-chancellor, had not yet visited, he says, "I hope . . . that before very long one of our number at least will have been in every department on this campus, and gleaned some inklings of its business."

One more selection comes from an address High made a year later:

It is not easy to strike a balance here. I do not think it serves the university well to cry "wolf" prematurely. I have not thought that one could properly talk hitherto of the university being "damaged," let alone of its efforts being "destroyed," by the financial constraints under which we are living. What has happened is that various activities have been curbed, reduced, postponed, and that a number of very proper hopes have been gravely disappointed. I am speaking here in general terms. I am all too well aware that in particular cases the correct statement is that certain individuals' careers have been very directly blighted.

I now present extracts from the same kind of address by Vice-Chancellor Low.

Unless we display a true sense of discipline and responsibility, the goodwill which we gain through some of our activities can very easily be lost through unthinking actions and selfishness. In most places it is the sensational which makes the news and hits the headlines. The good work, quietly and patiently undertaken is not fodder for the media whose staple diet is crisis, unrest, and dissent. I must ask all staff and students to remember that their personal, individual actions often get attributed to the institution and sometimes these can seriously tarnish and damage much of what we seek to build. While I do not wish to erect a bureaucratic framework or to limit the freedom enjoyed by any of us, I cannot, because of the responsibility entrusted to me permit an untidy system to gain roots. [...] Some of our benefactors have got to the stage where they will take no more buffeting and I cannot, in all honesty say, I disagree with them. Some of our clients and our masters, are not exactly enamored either with those occasional outbursts on the part of a few, which in the guise of academic freedom, cover a multitude of sins!

Those remarks occur near the end of the address. The same theme appears near the beginning:

Colleagues and friends, I am convinced that there is a consensus on our general objectives—on where we wish to go. Inevitably, there are many routes which could be taken, different forms of transport that can be used and we even have a choice of traveling companions [...] These matters can be discussed—they need to be discussed and hopefully will be seriously examined and assessed. But there comes a time, even in academe, when decisions have to be taken. Once this is done, it behooves all concerned—all the voyagers—to cooperate fully [...] This is not to imply that we should worship at the shrine of conventionalism and that there is no room here for dissent but it does mean that those whose radicalism is centered only on disruption and destruction are less welcome as fellow travelers—passengers or crew! I recall also those who shout the loudest, about colonialism and imperialism—who inveigh against divide and rule but who themselves "guru like," establish constituencies among us—and insidiously condition us to look for skeletons in cupboards where there are none. They can more readily destroy than create; they can divide, but cannot rule. [...] True leadership also requires the ability to follow.

A year later Low delivers an even more explicit message:

Let me make it absolutely clear that when your actions put the university's reputation and its standing at risk, I will be obliged to take appropriate action. I am not prepared to put into jeopardy those advances that have been so painstakingly gained merely to satisfy bravado and personal popularity, which appears to be placed higher in the scale of values, than the institution's welfare.

By the following year, Low felt it necessary to swing the pendulum back, at least a little. It was still necessary to exercise strong control over the "tiny minority" whose behavior "might be described as extreme," but it was also necessary to remember that universities had a responsibility to the world of scholarship:

I have my own doubts as to whether what I say will necessarily make any difference to the institution, but I will say it just the same. [...] In an institution of this kind, when you are attempting to push it outwards, to get it better recognized and accepted [...], to improve teaching standards and to make sure that those who are coming in get the best courses they can have, it is tremendously important to retain what is essential in the nature of a university, and that is its commitment to scholarship.

The embattled Vice-Chancellor Low ended his address with the announcement that he had accepted an invitation to continue his task for two more years. He added, somewhat sadly, that he realized that the news would "be received with mixed feelings." He also said:

Colleagues, I felt I should speak to you frankly. It is an addiction of mine. We have a saying at home: "If you have got anything to say, do not put any water in your mouth before you say it." I have said my piece. I am tremendously grateful for the measure of support and encouragement which I have had over the last two years. And it has been considerable. I hope that the pockets of indifference or obstruction within the university will disappear. If they do not, we may have to remove them, but we shall not give up.

WHAT IS AN INSTITUTION?

The above discourses share certain definitions, because all three institutions are engaged in tertiary education and research. All three have the same *dramatis personae*: scholars and teachers (variously known as "faculty" or "staff"); students (of whom we hear little); the administration (the vice-chancellor, registrars, bursars, deans, department heads, and their staffs); and a world outside that pays for the institution and—to varying degrees—holds it accountable. That much is common to the three discourses. It answers the question of what the components and functions of a university are. But so far nothing has been said about how things work.

Once that question is asked, the three definitions diverge, the dean going in one direction and the vice-chancellors in another.

The dean sees his institution as an agglomeration of different and usually antagonistic interests: faculty against administration; deans fighting each other; departments in competition; individual scholars looking to their own interests, whether scholarly or otherwise. There is an inevitable tension between order and disorder, competition being carried on through the "organized anarchy" of politics and restrained, to some extent, by institutional rules. The institution is, in the last resort, a set of routines and procedures on the one hand, and on the other hand an arena: if it runs well, then most people get some of what they want, no one goes undeservedly to the wall, and the goals of scholarship and research are served without too much time and energy wasted on pointless altercation.

Behind this institutional construct is a more abstract assumption about human nature. The dean is rational in several senses of that word. He believes in calculation. He knows that right thinking will find the means to reach the goal. Even if you live to regret a decision, because it was the wrong one—like the hasty hiring of second-raters—that merely shows mistakes can be made; it does not mean there could be any other sensible way of making decisions. He knows there is no rational way of selecting an ultimate value, because by definition rational justification can only be made for means and not for ends. It is surely this awareness that makes him contemptuous of "rhetoric"—vacuous talk about values like "educational excellence." Values not in the ultimate category—in other words, plain interests or interests masquerading as values—can be handled rationally, because most of his colleagues, although stupid, ill-informed, and easily manipulated, are at least rational in the manner assumed by rational choice theorists. Whatever they say about the public good (that is, about the institution) they are primarily concerned for themselves. Essentially they are free riders. They are happy to let other people run the collectivity, even dole out scarce resources: "They gripe, of course, but they don't want to do it themselves." The ultimately rational people are those few like himself whose self-interest is enlightened to the point of entering into coalitions for mutual benefit. Finally, the dean is rational in the sense that he has little room for sentiment or for emotions, which, he thinks, inhibit the use of reason. He enjoys a good fight, but that has more to do with exercising skill than with venting hostility. Combative he certainly is, but not hostile. Also he has a fundamental contempt for most of his colleagues, but he stops far short of hatred. When compared with Vice-Chancellor Low, he is quite free from rancor.

The two vice-chancellors, like the dean, respect scholarship, but the view they share of institutions is very different from his. For them a university is not (or in Low's case, should not be) an arena, a set of rules and strategies by which a power game is played. A university is a corporation, but more than a corporation. It is more even than a community of scholars, a treasure-house of values and a seat of intellectual accomplishments. A university, they seem to say, is a living entity, an organism, which can be served, saved, made great, damaged, or destroyed. A university must be intrinsically valued: it is an end in itself.

These are holistic notions: in the institution all individuals become one, and so vanish. The dean's world, by contrast, is full of individuals, usually elbowing each other out of the way. Vice-Chancellor High, it is true, does call attention to the componential aspects of his university. He hopes to visit all the departments, so that "at least one of us will have been in every department." He lists many different activities—reading, writing, talking, analyzing data, working in laboratories or libraries, picking up telephones, attending meetings, typing letters, maintaining the buildings, and so forth. But all these separate and distinct items are identified only to assert their unquestionable unity, to celebrate effortless cooperation in the service of the institution and its goal of making intelligible "those great issues which universities, taken in the broad, stand for in our society." In that majestic phrase the small individualities that make up the dean's world are rendered faceless: the collectivity is all.

That outlook leaves little room for rationality in any of the senses exemplified by the dean. Such a statement would, of course, outrage both vice-chancellors, who preside over universities, which by definition are citadels of reason. But reason is not sufficient; indeed, it is sometimes unnecessary. Vice-Chancellor High is perfectly explicit about this: "There are times and occasions when as university people it behooves us to express the faith that is in us." This is not, whatever High might claim, a faith in reason. The dean's world does run on right reasoning; for the vice-chancellors their world runs on right feeling. Right feeling means giving a proper importance to the institution not as a provider of services but as a recipient of service. This sentiment is a necessary part of their solution for all distributional problems. To value the collectivity is by definition to be altruistic and thus, in one simple step, to solve the problem of scarce resources; those who have the right feeling are more intent on giving than on getting.

The natural mode in which the members of a university interact is cooperation and consensus. There are no opposed interests; in the end everyone's well-being converges in the well-being of the institution itself. Only one kind of contest is permissible, because it benefits the institution: orderly rational debate intended to uncover the correct solution to a problem. This is very far removed from the dean's "fighting like cats." In fact a debate is not a struggle at all, for by definition one's "opponent" in a dialectical encounter is not an enemy to be eliminated but a comrade in the quest for truth. It follows that anyone in a university who conducts himself antagonistically is misbehaving. Such a definition obviously lays preemptive claim to the moral high ground.

THE ORIGINS OF CONFLICT

To those vivid ironies describing his director's mode of action—"find-the-consensus, above-the-rabble, will-of-the-meeting, have-no-power-myself"—the dean added a sentence to make clear that in his opinion no institution could conceivably be run that way. The director left all internal management to the dean and the rest of the "barony" (the local term for deans, registrars, committee chairmen, and the like) and spent his time dealing with the outside world.

The two vice-chancellors, however, operate in both worlds, and part of the task they set themselves is to make their academics understand the outside world. In both cases the task turns out to be remedial. They concentrate on undoing or preventing a notion that the world outside is to blame for trouble in the university itself.

This attribution is easily made: one projects blame first onto the university's own administration and then onto the world outside, usually the government. At both levels "they" have a duty to provide the resources needed for "us" to function as scholars and teachers. "They" do not provide enough; therefore we fall to fighting over scarce resources; therefore "they" are to blame for conflicts within the university.

The dean would consider such an analysis, unless offered as manipulative rhetoric, to be puerile; nothing useful is achieved by blaming the world for being what it is. By all means make a fuss to get what you want, scheme, manipulate, and make outrageous accusations, but planning for reality starts with the fact of scarcity. Scarcity is always present. Besides, the one resource that is ever present in conflict is also, by definition, in short supply: power. The dean's search for the origins of conflict goes no further back than the fact of scarcity. To ask who is to blame is usually to procrastinate, to put off the unpleasant task of deciding who will go short. The dean never searches for witches; better spend time sorting out the mess. Witchcraft accusations logically require a moral collectivity, and for the dean there is no collectivity and no transcending morality. Backsliders and deviants and troublemakers are therefore not wicked: they are merely childish.

Vice-Chancellor High's institution was beginning to feel the pinch at the time he made one of his addresses. Indeed, the situation was serious enough to call for an explicit—if passing—distinction between the institution and its individual members: "certain individuals' careers have been very directly blighted." But this statement turns out to be a compassionate footnote to a main text asserting that this was not "the time to cry wolf" and that the university was being neither "damaged" nor "destroyed" by "financial constraints." There is a hint in this of trouble down at the departments, perhaps even agitation of the kind that so exercised Vice-Chancellor Low. But the agitators, if there were any, are not made into witches; they pass unmentioned. Nor is any blame attached to those in the outside world whose decisions caused the present "financial constraints." What matters—the institution itself—is unharmed and, although "various activities have been curbed, reduced, postponed," the twin virtues of serenity and excellence are still in command. In short, since the situation is defined as essentially without conflict, there is no talk about the origins of conflict.

Vice-Chancellor Low, alone of the three, is a witch-hunter. Trouble begins with malcontents inside the institution, those whose "radicalism is centered only on disruption and destruction." They are the ones who, shouting "the loudest about colonialism and imperialism," have so dismayed "our clients and our masters" (he also calls them "our benefactors") that the latter will take "no more buffeting." Vice-Chancellor Low cannot "in all honesty" disagree with that attitude.

In fact Vice-Chancellor Low's university was much the least affluent of the three and the one most immediately answerable to government and the politicians. But, he insists, government direction and government interference and government failure to be generous with resources (which were certainly not plentiful) are not the cause of conflict on the campus. Government and politicians are not to blame. The problem lies with those members of the faculty who, "guru-like," attempt to set up "their own constituencies." What is at stake, therefore, is less material resources than power. The problem lies with "bravado and personal popularity, which appears to be placed higher in the scale of values, than the institution's welfare." Such people "divide, but cannot rule." "True leadership," he adds, enigmatically, "also requires the ability to follow."

CONFLICT MANAGEMENT

Once its goal has been defined, any strategy should contain two parts. The first assesses the problem. What is given and unchangeable? What are the rocks around which a course must be steered? What room is left for maneuver? The second part specifies the maneuvers. In other words, first identify the relevant features of institutional conflict; second, decide what should be done about it.

There are few conceptual subtleties in the dean's definition of the situation. It is a compromise between the Platonic view of his colleagues (dingbats in need of a leader) and Aristotle's "political animal." The dean's intermediate view is a world populated mostly by rational-choice dingbats, but redeemed by leaders who are smart enough to manipulate the dingbats and at the same time to keep struggles among themselves within reasonable limits. Values and principles and ideologies can usually be discounted, because the dingbats, whatever they claim, are really concerned with interests, not with values, and because the elite are similarly agreed on the bottom line: "staying in business." That position is elitist (he is himself one of the supermen) but it is not hegemonic. His definition is not intended to reconcile subordinates to their own subordination. We have from him not an ideology ("bloody rhetoric") but a strategy.

Some finesse is required for the tactics that implement this strategy. The basic mechanism is the formula, protected by some degree of bureaucratic sacredness from frequent and incautious alteration. For example, distribute resources by student enrollment and be wary about making exceptions. Finesse is required first (and exceptionally) because exceptions to the rule are sometimes required, and second (more commonly) because the dingbats think of themselves as political animals and, if the institution is to run well, this self-definition has to be indulged, allowing them the appearance of decision making without much of its reality. Instructors, for example, should have the main say in designing their courses; deans are in error if they encourage minor dingbats (lecturers) to bypass major dingbats (departmental chairmen). The technique for control is like that which works with small children; tire them out with play and thus keep them from making chaos a steady state in the world of adults. But it is not a simple matter of parking them in a playpen and turning away from childish things. Inasmuch as the dean's world is a decentralized world ("lots of goals at different levels"), his manipulations have to be fine-tuned to both individuals and occasions: his politics are craftsman-politics, not mass-produced.

The dean's strategy for conflict management is based on the premise that conflict is ineradicable. Do not be foolish and suppose you can turn off the rain. Rather, stay indoors, buy an umbrella, or go live in an arid zone. The vice-chancellors, however, do not adapt themselves to the environment, but endeavor to control it. Each does so in a different way. Vice-Chancellor High asserts it is not raining at all, or at worst it is no more than a drizzle, and one can proceed on the assumption that really the sun is shining. Vice-Chancellor Low says, in effect, that if everyone pulls together, the rain can surely be turned off. Both these positions are what the dean would call "bloody rhetoric." Let us take them in turn.

It is not easy to find in Vice-Chancellor High's speeches any explicit statement about the genesis of institutional conflict. If one examines his rhetoric, however, it is very obvious that he is aware of its possibility. He underprivileges conflict and overprivileges consensus, but at the same time, in a somewhat contradictory fashion, he defines himself as being above the conflict.

He does so partly by donning a particular persona. First, he belongs to no particular part of the university but to all of it. Second, he is a special kind of individual, a leader not a manager. He makes frequent use of the phrase "I believe" and the resonances of the Book of Common Prayer suggest he is a man of principle, knowing what is right and steadfast in its pursuit. Who else, among these three, could speak without embarrassment of "the faith that is in us"? His task is more than a day-to-day solving of problems, mere pragmatics; he finds the direction, he sets the policy, he inspires others to follow his lead. Leadership is more than tactical skill, common sense, and a clear head: it is also a capacity for inspiring others. He endows institutional leadership with a mystique that is entirely lacking in the case of the dean.

Vice-Chancellor High is, so to speak, the Institutional High Priest, the *archon basileus*, proclaiming the True Institutional Faith. He also conveys a vision of a larger world that is, for the most part, as decent and considerate of the welfare of others as is the university itself. It is a world ruled by "better feelings." If times are hard, and cuts must be made, that is because times are hard: it is not the result of human wickedness. This is the philosophy of a secure elite, the members of which extend beyond the universities into the governing classes. They share a language and a morality.

In short, High proclaims there is no conflict and there is no necessity for conflict, either within or beyond the university. This has nothing to do with rationality: it is a matter of trust and of faith and of exercising the fundamental altruism that is within us all. Although he would be shocked to hear his colleagues described as "dingbats," it seems fair to say that Vice-Chancellor High is a Platonist. The world is populated mostly by worthy people, who nevertheless must be taught to have faith in the institution and its leaders. If they have faith, then all will go well. (Of course it will, because how well the world is going is not an objective matter, but is itself partly determined by faith. In other words, the world becomes the way Vice-Chancellor High says it is.)

Vice-Chancellor High does not admit to elitism (that is, to his own effortless superiority within the institution). His message is, however, distinctly hegemonic: privileging service to the institution is itself an obedience-inducing symbolic device.

But what is to be done to those whom the symbols fail to move? High's discourse does not contemplate an outage in his morale-conditioning system. But Low has just such a crisis on his hands: the system badly needs repair and he must do the job. "I cannot, because of the responsibility entrusted to me, permit an untidy system to gain roots." He stands with Hobbes: he believes in central regulatory action, and in the members "convenanting" to yield to Leviathan ultimate control over their own destinies, so that they will not be destroyed in a "war of all against all."

He is quite explicit about university life becoming nasty, brutish, and short, if his opponents do not cease their irresponsible addiction to "disruption and destruction."

Low's world is not the kindly world of High. It is a world of malevolence, in which a person is respected not for principles alone, but for strength. Inside the university are dissident and irresponsible elements; outside are "clients and masters" who, at best, look upon the university in a purely instrumental fashion, asking what they get rather than what they can give. It is a threatening world, and the threats are necessarily contagious, so that Low's discourses persuade by direct intimidation, a device entirely absent from High's addresses. Low's world is one of "witchcraft": find the evil ones, punish them, and when they are made harmless all will be well in the collectivity.

The strategies of the two vice-chancellors are similar in their main assumption, which is the need for Leviathan; but they result in different tactics. High's addresses are essentially maintenance routines, like an apple a day. In Low's case the disease has already struck and he is readying himself—threatening—to cut out the cancer. But, that surgery apart, both of them are into holistic medicine; the body politic as a whole is what matters. If the body is in good health, then so are its members. For the dean the metaphor comes out differently. Normality is a state of chronic but mild affliction. Medication, if any is used, is addressed not to the illness but to the symptoms, and not to the whole body but to whatever part hurts.

IDIOCOSM AND CARICATURE

It will have occurred to the reader that not only are the styles of conflict management different in the three cases, but so are the sets of material from which the descriptions are drawn. Two are taken from normative addresses on formal occasions; for the dean we have conversations interspaced with stories of how he conducted himself in battle. Obviously people vary the picture they present of themselves depending on the audience. If the contexts are different (a formal address against the less formal setting of a conversation), is such a comparison valid?

It is, because we are not looking, as a historian might, for an idiographic description of the three individuals and their motivations. We are dealing not with individuals in their psychophysical entirety but with the set of cultural constructs used by them. But how do we know that these are cultural constructs?

If the different styles are cultural constructs and not the unique attributes of individuals, they should be available, other things being equal, to other people, including any of the three contestants. To some extent they are; to some extent they are not. Culture is shared but not perfectly shared. What is shared and what is not depends partly on the office and partly on experience and personality. Some features they do not share. The dean does not pontificate. I knew Vice-Chancellor High when he was a dean, and, as a dean, he pontificated. Low sees witchcraft in every act of dissent; the dean thinks that silly, although he too has the task of manipulating troublemakers. But both the dean and Low use threats (the dean's threats being specific, while Low goes in for doomsday generalities). Both vice-chancellors pontificate (but in different ways); both also enter into the rough and tumble of internal politics. (Low, as one might suspect from the tone of his discourses, is in the thick of the fray and manages to inspire no little trepidation.) All three contestants, taken in the round (that is, from the point of view of their idiocosms), are well equipped with Machiavellian skills and command a similar, but not identical, repertoire of personae (masks) for use in conflict situations.

In short, the three discourses, albeit different in the context of their delivery, are comparable. Each yields a sufficiently clear definition of a distinct style of institutional conflict and conflict management, and of the masks that are appropriate to each style.

The word "style" goes along with "mask," "caricature," and "idiocosm." A mask is a presentation of self deployed to persuade other people to accept not only a particular role for the presenter but also a particular definition of the situation and of what is to be done about it. Caricature is the simplified definition of the situation. Vice-Chancellor Low offers himself as Horatio at the bridge, holding back the forces of institutional self-destruction. His caricatured version of the institution's situation is a hostile world, a siege, and traitors within the walls. Vice-Chancellor High is the Institutional High Priest, and the university is a congregation of true believers worshiping at Minerva's shrine. That is to say, a mask is a simplified and would-be persuasive presentation, selected out of a repertoire of cultural constructs of persons. Caricature is also a selection out of a larger set of constructs. The larger set, out of which both mask and caricature are drawn, is the idiocosm.

Idiocosm can be glossed as "a relatively individual view of the world." The dean's idiocosm, in its totality, is different from those of the vice-chancellors and each of them is different from the other. But they also share certain features. All have ideas about institutions and about conflict management in institutions (but the ideas are different in each case). Individuality lies in the particular selection and patterning of the ideas. A simple analogy is that of a construction set, which can be used to build a variety of distinct artifacts.

As soon as we compare different idiocosms, pointing out similarities, each idiocosm loses some of its individuality. The act of comparison generalizes and therefore abstracts away the particularity of an individual's view of the scene, and leaves a residue that is a cultural construct.

One could carry the process of abstraction further, talking, for example, about social science deans, about deans in general, about university officials, about bureaucrats in general, and so on until one reaches that somewhat vacuous level of "the person with power." At each level the component that makes "idiocosm" appropriate diminishes, and the cultural construct becomes more general.

Alternatively, one might construct a similar hierarchy using the concept of "mask," this time working downwards rather than upwards. A mask is taken readymade off a cultural peg, but modified in its design to suit the setting, the occasion, the personality of the wearer, and so forth. A mask that begins simply as "leader" acquires distinctive features at each step in the series: military leader—infantry general—infantry general in peace time—on a ceremonial occasion—with a peptic ulcer, and so on. At each succeeding lower level of generalization, the mask acquires more particular features, the lowest being equivalent to that of the idiocosm. (But it is not the same as an idiocosm; a mask is an item selected from someone's idiocosm.)

Or (a third way to find coherence in this incoherence) culture is made of constructs that range from the totally encompassing (and therefore very general) at the top, down through levels of particularity, to the most specific available. In this there are two kinds of hierarchy, which are logically separate from one another. One hierarchy has to do with the distribution of culture and answers the question: Who subscribes to this particular belief or value? The more people subscribe, the more general is the value. The other hierarchy is a matter not of distribution but of logic, as in the series: z is a type of y, y is a type of x, x is a type of w, and so on, w being the most general in that series and z the most specific.

The latter type of hierarchical ordering is significant in the process of conflict, since it is used by contestants as a weapon to define a situation. For example, what the dean describes as "bloody rhetoric" is (in his opinion) an attempt to divert attention away from the failure to provide a specific rational justification for one's own position. A common sign that such a tactic is in use is the declaration "This is a matter of principle!" Correspondingly, the phrase "bloody rhetoric" insists that a lower level of generality is appropriate in the situation: it is not a matter of principle, but a matter of interests. (But this also is, of course, "bloody rhetoric." The dean's own view of the world, although addressing itself to individuals and their particular interests, is itself exceedingly generalized: people act rationally in their own interest and one can assume that they are not much moved by ideologies.)

"Idiocosm" does not refer to the logical distinction between the particular and the general. Rather it is specific and particular *with reference to an individual*. It is, for example, the culture of Vice-Chancellor High, not the culture of vice-chancellors in general. Within itself, it contains a wide variety of logical domains, and within each there is a range from logically all-encompassing to the lowest level of particularity. When we assert that the study of conflict management will be deficient if it disregards cultural data at the most specific level available, we are referring to the specific individual. This is to say no more than that one must try to imagine all the different aspects of the situation that present themselves to a particular contestant, to comprehend all the different frames used to make sense of experience, to see the situation as Vice-Chancellor Low sees it, not as vice-chancellors in general are supposed to see it, still less chief executives in general, and even less leaders in general. As one moves up the hierarchy, there is a process of simplification and the frames available for interpretation diminish in number.

The reason for insisting on the idiocosm is simple. Conflict has within it an inherent push toward innovation, rule bending if not rule breaking, using any stratagem, in short, that will catch the opponent off balance. If you follow the rules precisely, while your every move cannot be known beforehand, the limitations on and consequently the range of possible moves can be anticipated (in theory) by anyone who knows the rules. But the matter is not so simple. "The rules" offer an array of choices. They form a hierarchy ranging from the general to the particular. For example, the dean has a general rule stating that control of information gives power; beneath that are more specific rules, advising that sometimes information should be leaked, and at other times kept out of the public domain. If it should be leaked, to whom should this be done? To allies, to rivals, to the general public? In what manner should it be done? Gossip, veiled speech, statement without attribution? Furthermore, in practice conduct in a conflict is guided not by a single set of rules, but by many different sets. If you are to anticipate the dean's next move, you must take into account not simply the rules he is likely to observe about information, but also his rules about how to differentiate among different kinds of colleagues (for example, dingbats as opposed to people like himself), rules that decide for him what is important and what is not, rules that tell him when to invoke formal rules and when to ignore them, and so forth.

Therefore, if you are to anticipate moves by a contestant, the more frames from his idiocosm available to you to cut down the area of darkness, the better your chances of success. If you know the moves specified by the rules of the dean's institution for a particular situation, that is one step; if you have a history of moves that have in fact been made in the past, that is a second step; if you know what the dean knows about these matters, that is a third step; if you know the dean's past history in organizational behavior, that is a fourth step; if you know his current and past extraorganizational concerns and commitments, that is a fifth step; if you know about his psychological hang-ups, that is a sixth step;

and so on. The thicker the description, to borrow a famous adjective, the better will be your chances of anticipating the competitor's moves (and therefore controlling him, if you are yourself a contestant). I could, for example, considerably thicken the idiocosms of my three sinners if I said more about their institutional frameworks and their personal histories. In the same way, it would pay each contestant to thicken his idiocosm of the situation (which includes, of course, his appraisal of other peoples' idiocosms) before deciding what move to make next.

That statement, however, must be qualified, because it does not take into account our limited capacity to gather and process information. In theory, the more that is known, the better one's chances of successful conflict management. In practice, however, the more detail gathered, the greater the cost because the move toward the specific and away from the general is made by discarding off-the-peg formulas, which make calculations cheaper because they are, so to speak, mass-produced. The statement "vice-chancellors always do X" is less costly in calculation time (supposing the research has been done) than a statement about what Vice-Chancellor Low will do, simply because in the latter case there is more specific information to be compiled, more frames to be used— historical, psychological, structural, and so on. Also, the greater the number of variables considered, the greater the difficulty of computation. Also, there is a distressing need for metaframes that will tell us how to balance off one frame against another. For example, if psychological tendencies are in conflict with conventional wisdom about how to conduct oneself, which will win? So in practice the contestants, including conflict managers, have no alternative but to play hunches. For that reason conflict management is always an art.

An art is any activity requiring skills not yet reduced to communicable procedures.[5] "Art" is an appropriate word, for it suggests the last of the problematic terms: "caricature." If any of my three sinners read this, they could justly complain that what I have presented of them is not an idiocosm, but a caricature, a grotesque overemphasis of certain features. To see a character truly, one must, to borrow a phrase from High, see it "in the broad." I have added that if one is to predict conduct, one must see the person, if not in the round, at least from as many aspects as is practicable. But in practice, we do not do that. We not only categorize, we caricature. We pick out in vivid emphasis that particular part of the idiocosm that, according to our hunch, is going to be the dominant factor in influencing decisions.

That is us, trying in a would-be detached and analytic mood, to understand what is going on. The antagonists themselves must be even more swift in their move toward caricature. They are quick to simplify for two reasons. First, they have to impose a definition of the situation on their competitors and sometimes on followers and spectators, and the more complicated and qualified that definition, other things being equal, the less likely is it to be persuasive. That was the Willy Horton stratagem in the 1988 election, caricature at its worst. The forms are rendered elemental, to caricature Durkheim, not for analytic but for rhetorical purposes. Second, antagonists are not like philosophers in search of the truth. They want not truth, but victory. They do not have the luxury of infinite doubt and infinite thought. Neither do they have much time to thicken descriptions. They have to take action—"even in academe," as Vice-Chancellor Low pointed out—and action is the foe of speculation.

What, then, is my proposal? Am I contradicting myself, advocating for the understanding of conflict management, both idiocosm and caricature, both a thickening of description and its simplification? I think not. Nor am I playing games with an oxymoron: detailed simplicity, ornamented plainness, and the like. I am talking about a procedure for the understanding of conflict management. The procedure is simple: reverse, so far as time and energy and computing capacity will allow, your own simplifying tendencies and use as many frameworks as possible to make an action profile of the antagonists and of the situation. The more you know, the better will be your hunches about which of their caricatures will be used for action. If you are yourself a conflict manager, then the better too will be your hunches about what caricatures will move the other antagonists in the way you want them to be moved.

In the end the best conflict managers will not be cultural outsiders. They will be those for whom the culture is second nature. The enlightened outsider, laboriously searching for the relevant cultural constructs, has too much to learn. The willful outsider, who disdains the search and thinks he has a formula good for all occasions and all cultures, has almost everything to learn.

NOTES

1. I thank Roy D'Andrade and Paula Levin for their comments and criticism.

2. The concept is derived from Theodore Schwartz, who uses the term "idioverse" (1978).

3. The universities concerned follow the British pattern, in which the vice-chancellor is the chief executive officer of the institution. The chancellor is a titular figure—a bishop, an elder statesman, or a member of the royal family.

4. In both cases the material comes from speeches made in the university and subsequently published. My argument does not require that I identify the institutions involved. "High" and "Low" are pseudonyms.

5. It follows that discovery (having a new idea) in the sciences is an art. Verification procedures, on the other hand, are routinized and therefore communicable.

REFERENCE

Schwartz, Theodore. 1978. Where Is the Culture? In *The Making of Psychological Anthropology*, ed. George D. Sprindler. Berkeley: University of California Press.

5

Interpersonal Conflict Management Styles of Jordanian Managers

Kamil Kozan

Writers on organizations have long stressed the need for an organizational science applicable to non-Western as well as Western cultures. In a review of the literature M. N. Kiggundu, J. J. Jorgensen, and T. Hafsi (1983:68) state that "there is a great deal of interest in the utilization of administrative theory and techniques in developing countries...[as] demonstrated by the sheer volume of published material on the subject." Despite this interest, however, conflict management practices in non-Western cultures have remained a much neglected topic of study. Indeed, Kiggundu, Jorgensen, and Hafsi report that although conflict management was one of the categories chosen for the analysis of the literature with respect to topics, it had to be dropped later because of lack of coverage.

Conflict management has received increasing attention in the organizational literature during the last two decades because of a shift in attitudes toward conflict in organizations. The traditional view of conflict as something harmful has changed to a view that sees conflict as a reality of organizational life. S. Robbins (1978) has actually argued that functional levels of conflict are conducive to innovation and higher quality decisions. K. W. Thomas (1976:889) notes that "social scientists are coming to realize—and to demonstrate—that conflict itself is no evil, but rather a phenomenon which can have constructive or destructive effects depending on its management." Hence, the emphasis has shifted toward an understanding of different styles of managing conflicts.

How conflicts are managed would seem to be of importance to organizations outside of Western countries as well. This is especially true in countries undertaking ambitious public development programs or encouraging private firms to open up to new technologies or markets. We need to understand how managers in different cultures deal with conflict as part of a larger concern for developing an organizational science having an international appeal. The present study aims at finding out about the interpersonal conflict management styles used by managers in one Middle Eastern country, Jordan.

Jordan is a country in transition from a traditional to a modern, industrialized society. Unlike petroleum-rich Arab countries on which most writing on Arab management styles has focused, Jordan strives for modernization with limited resources. Most economic activity centers around agriculture, mining, and manufacturing of chemicals, cement, paper, textiles, and food. Most finished goods are imported from abroad, but more and more are being locally produced, under the protection of import limitations against foreign competition. The state operates the public works and the utility companies, and has started agricultural development programs. The modernization this country is trying to achieve against a traditional background undoubtedly creates an interesting setting for the study of conflict in its organizations as well as other managerial practices.

Conflict occurs in several forms in an organization, including intrapersonal, interpersonal, and intergroup conflict. This study was confined to interpersonal conflicts. A model of interpersonal conflict management styles that has seen widespread use in the literature was used here too. This model, developed by R. R. Blake and J. S. Mouton (1965) and refined by Thomas (1976), identifies five different styles of managing conflicts: avoiding, accommodation, forcing, compromise, and collaboration or problem solving. These styles can be interpreted in terms of orientation toward conflict situations along two dimensions (Thomas 1976). The first dimension represents the degree (high or low) to which a person attempts to satisfy personal concerns. The second dimension represents the degree (high or low) to which that person attempts to satisfy others' concerns. Figure 5.1 illustrates how the different styles emerge as combinations of these two dimensions.

Forcing results from the production-oriented management styles that Blake and Mouton have identified in their managerial grid. It involves competitive behaviors and the use of power to have one's position accepted, even if it means ignoring the other's concerns. At the other extreme, accommodation represents overlooking or playing down the existing differences and trying to satisfy the other party's wishes. In between these two extremes lies compromising, or splitting the difference, with both parties giving up something in order to find a middle ground. Avoiding, a style reflecting low concern for self and others, takes the form of withdrawal, sidestepping the issue, or shying away from its open discussion. Collaboration, which is high in both dimen-

Figure 5.1
A Two-Dimensional Model of Five Interpersonal Conflict
Management Styles

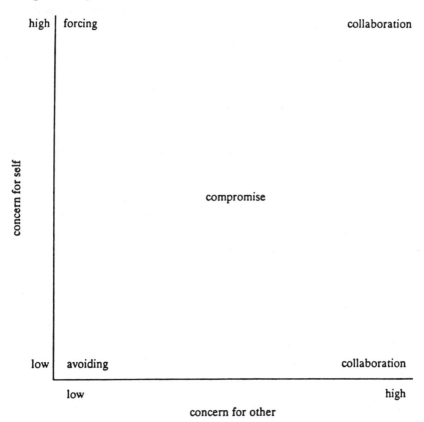

sions, involves facing the conflict, bringing all pertinent issues and concerns out into the open, and as a result, reaching a solution that integrates the different points of view.

Preference for these different styles has been shown to be influenced by a number of variables, including personality, the topic of conflict, and organizational factors such as the incentive structure and norms (Thomas 1976; Renwick 1975). The present study likewise is aimed at learning how the likelihood of using each style was affected when certain contextual variables were altered. Two variables were chosen for analysis: the authority relation between the parties and the topic of conflict.

The authority position of the other party to conflict, that is, whether that party is a superior, subordinate, or peer, seems to influence a manager's style. In a large-scale survey, M. A. Rahim (1986) found that managers were primarily obliging with superiors, collaborative with subordinates, and compromising with peers. Rahim explains these findings in terms of the constraining impact of hierarchical relations on the behavior of members in an organization. Organizations in Middle Eastern countries have often been characterized by centralized, authoritarian leadership (Badawy 1980; Wright 1981). One might therefore suspect the authority position of the other party could be an even more potent source of influence on the conflict behavior of managers in a Middle Eastern country such as Jordan.

Studies in the United States have also shown that conflict management styles are affected by the topic and the source of conflict. Renwick (1975) found a tendency to use problem solving when salaries, promotions, or performance appraisals were involved, and to rely on compromise in dealing with conflict concerning personal habits and mannerisms. She further reported that disagreements originating from substantive factors such as differences in knowledge or factual material were more likely to be openly acknowledged and confronted than affective conflicts that had their sources in personality or attitude differences. E. Phillips and R. Cheston (1979) also found problem solving to be used more in conflicts caused by communication failures and structural factors such as conflicting objectives, than in conflicts resulting from incompatible personal goals or values. The impact of culture needs to be examined here again. The organizational atmosphere in Latin America and the Middle East has been described as embodying a personal tone of administration and emotionally involved relationships (Bourgeois and Boltvinik 1981; Badaway 1980). Would this result in more assertive styles in dealing with conflicts involving personality issues than those concerning organizational policies or salaries?

The present study aims to understand responses to conflict situations within the culture studied. Studying the impact of topic and party jointly is expected to reveal more about how these managers adjust their styles in different contexts than when these variables are studied separately. Our understanding of conflict management styles in this specific culture will be enhanced, however, if we also make comparisons with the United States, where a wealth of studies exists.

THE STUDY AND ITS RESULTS

Subjects

Data were collected from managers in ten private and five public organizations in and around Amman, the capital city, which contains about 40 percent of the country's population. The organizations included natural resources administration units, development agencies, manufacturing and mining firms, and service organizations. In organizations with more than twelve managers, a random sample of twelve managers was chosen, while in small organizations all managers were included in the study. As a result, 150 managers were chosen from among 335, and usable data were obtained from 134 of those chosen. This group was 98 percent male, an average of 40 years of age, and with an average tenure of 10 years. About half of the managers had college degrees and a third were high school graduates. Among the college graduates 35 percent had degrees in engineering and 34 percent in business and economics, with the remaining graduates being equally distributed among humanities, sciences, and law. Finally, 14 percent of the sample came from top management (vice-president or higher), 49 percent from middle management, and 37 percent from among first-line supervisors.

Data Collection

Data were collected by means of a questionnaire. Conflict management styles were measured by statements derived from a conflict inventory developed by Rahim (1983a). These statements, representing avoiding, forcing, accommodation, compromise, and collaboration, respectively, are shown below.

1. I stay away from disagreement and avoid open discussion of differences (very likely, likely, depends, unlikely, very unlikely).
2. I am firm in my position and use my power to get my view accepted (very likely, likely, depends, unlikely, very unlikely).
3. I try to accommodate his/her wishes (very likely, likely, depends, unlikely, very unlikely).
4. I propose a solution halfway between my and his/her wishes to break any deadlock (very likely, likely, depends, unlikely, very unlikely).
5. I try to bring all of my and his/her concerns out in the open and work for a solution together (very likely, likely, depends, unlikely, very unlikely).

The respondents were asked how likely they were to use each style when conflicts involved a variety of topics. The same set of statements was repeated for each topic. Six conflict topics were identified by elaborating on a smaller set of categories used by Renwick (1975):

1. Salaries and other monetary benefits
2. Performance appraisal and promotion
3. Physical working conditions
4. Proper performance of responsibilities and compliance with rules and procedures

5. Work methods to be used and organizational policies
6. Personal habits, mannerisms, and values

Three different sets of questionnaires were prepared, each one for a different party to the conflict, for example, subordinates, peers, or superiors. A respondent randomly received only one of these sets, which identified both at the beginning and again when each topic was introduced, whom the party to the conflict was. Chief executive officers received only that set where the conflicting party was a subordinate.

The questionnaires were translated from English into Arabic jointly by two Arab colleagues of the author who were proficient in English. The Arabic version was then translated back into English by a third colleague to ensure reliability of translation.

Results

A split-plot factorial design (style x topic x party) with repeated measurement of style and topic over subjects was used for analysis (Kirk 1968). This design allows for testing whether the likelihood of styles differed in general from each other, as the party to the conflict differed, as the topic of conflict differed, or as both the party and the topic of conflict differed. Once a significant overall effect was found in any of these tests, pairwise comparisons between means were conducted using Tukey's (q) statistic at .01 level of confidence.

Figure 5.2 shows the mean likelihood of use of the different styles in general by managers. Mean likelihood of these styles differed from each other in general [$F(4,655) = 107.05$, $p < .01$]. Managers reported using collaboration significantly more often than compromise, compromise more often than avoiding or accommodation, and avoiding more often than forcing. The intercorrelations between the different styles are shown in Figure 5.3. As can be seen from this figure, the most likely style to be used, collaboration, is positively correlated with compromise, the second most likely style. Compromise is positively correlated with all other styles except forcing. Forcing is not only the least preferred style, but also unrelated to any of the other four styles.

Figure 5.4 shows the likelihood of using a style with different parties. A significant interaction effect was found between style and party [$F(8,655) = 5.60$, $p < .01$]. Pairwise comparisons between means showed that avoiding and accommodation were less likely to be used with superiors than with peers, and compromise was less likely to be used with subordinates than with peers. Collaboration is the first preference of managers with all conflicting parties. While compromise is the second most preferred style against superiors, however, avoiding as well as compromise turn out to be the second most preferred styles against peers.

Figure 5.2
Mean Likelihood of Use of Five Interpersonal Conflict Management Styles
(n = 134)

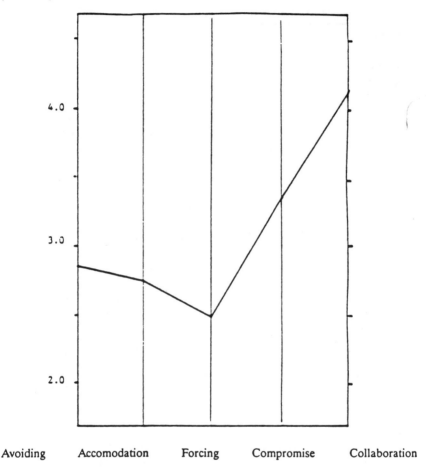

Avoiding   Accomodation   Forcing   Compromise   Collaboration

Finally, with subordinates all four remaining styles seem equally likely
to be used after collaboration.

Figure 5.5 shows the likelihood of using a style when different conflict
topics are involved. A significant interaction effect was found between
style and topic [$F(20,2620) = 8.76$, $p < .01$]. Pairwise comparisons
showed that whichever topic is involved, collaboration is the style most
likely to be used. Compromise is the second most likely, and it is preferred over the remaining styles in all but two of the topics. When
personal habits and mannerisms are involved, avoiding is used as often
as compromise. When conflicts involve responsibilities and compliance

Figure 5.3
Intercorrelations of Five Interpersonal Conflict Management Styles
(n = 134)

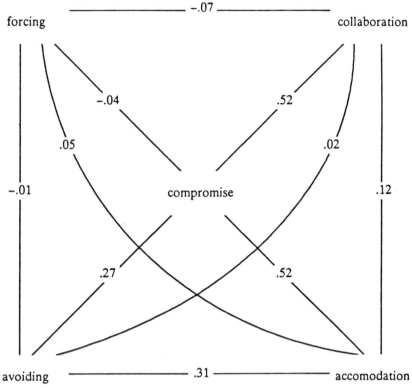

with rules, forcing is as likely to be used as compromise; otherwise forcing is the least preferred style.

The joint effect of party and topic on conflict management style turned out to be significant as well [$F(40,2620) = 3.00$, $p < .01$]. This interaction effect carries more information and should receive our attention more than the separate effects reported previously. Pairwise comparisons between means revealed some interesting contrasts. When conflicts involve salaries, performance appraisal and promotion, and physical working conditions, peers are avoided as compared to subordinates, and in the case of the latter two topics, as compared to superiors as well. Managers are also more accommodative toward peers than toward superiors when salaries and promotions are involved. When conflicts center around responsibilities and compliance with rules, managers use more forcing and less compromise toward subordinates as compared to superiors. A parallel tendency to use forcing toward subordinates could not be observed for work methods and organizational policies, however. When these

Figure 5.4
**Mean Likelihood of Use of Five Interpersonal Conflict Management Styles
with Respect to the Other Party to the Conflict**

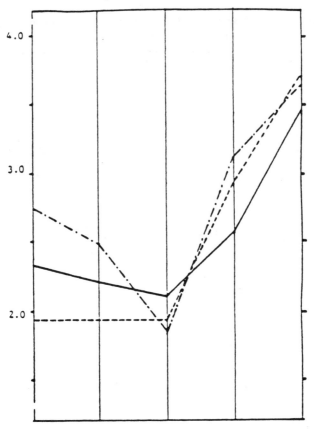

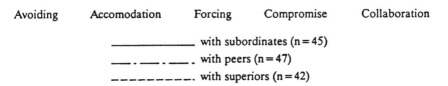

Avoiding   Accomodation   Forcing   Compromise   Collaboration

_____ with subordinates (n = 45)
_ . ___ . ___ . with peers (n = 47)
_ _ _ _ _ _ _ _. with superiors (n = 42)

topics are the issue, managers nevertheless use significantly less compromise toward subordinates than toward superiors or peers and less
collaboration with subordinates than with superiors. Finally, on conflicts
over personal habits, mannerisms, and values, managers tend to avoid
peers and accommodate subordinates' wishes as compared to those of

Figure 5.5
Mean Likelihood of Use of Five Interpersonal Conflict Management Styles with Respect to the Topic of Conflict (n = 134)

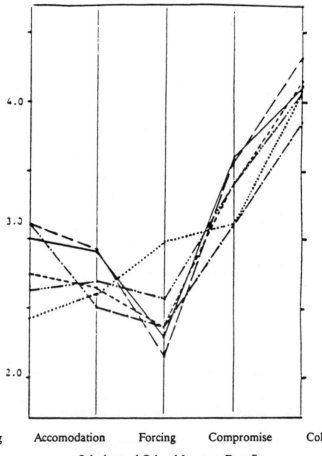

Avoiding   Accomodation   Forcing   Compromise   Collaboration

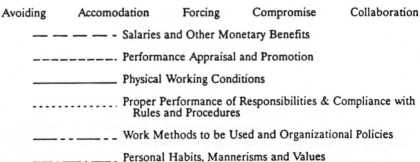

— — — — - Salaries and Other Monetary Benefits

— — — — — —. Performance Appraisal and Promotion

——————— Physical Working Conditions

· · · · · · · · · · · · · Proper Performance of Responsibilities & Compliance with Rules and Procedures

—— — — —— — — Work Methods to be Used and Organizational Policies

—— . —— . —— . Personal Habits, Mannerisms and Values

their superiors. Furthermore, they report using more forcing toward superiors than toward peers on personal habits and mannerisms.

THE EMERGING CONFLICT MANAGEMENT PROFILE FOR JORDANIAN MANAGERS

A consistent result obtained in the study across all parties and topics is the preference for collaboration. The prerequisite for this style is the acknowledgment of a conflict and open discussion of all the relevant issues. If there is such open discussion of differences, the parties are expected to eventually reach novel solutions satisfying both of their concerns. My observations during more than two years in Jordan actually confirm this initial tendency to discuss differences. Whether such discussion actually led to integrated solutions is another matter. Meanwhile, the following conflict episode, the most involved confrontation that I observed, may illustrate at least the tendency for open discussion of differences.

This conflict took place between a dean and some faculty members, including a chairman, in a teaching institution. These faculty members were unhappy with the managerial style employed by the dean, and in particular, his lack of consultation with the chairman and the faculty. The issue found a forum in a faculty meeting chaired by the dean, where some members freely stated their displeasure with the dean's style. Particular reference was made to a decision by the dean to recruit and place a couple of teaching assistants (actually prospective faculty members) on his own without consulting the department. In the meeting, where the two assistants were also present, the dean's style was openly criticized and the qualifications of the new recruits were questioned in detail. The dean's response was that it was within his formal powers to decide such issues. (He was actually serving as acting chairman for that department during the short span when the decision was made.)

This conflict found another forum with a meeting of the faculty and the dean with the president. The dean's style and all aspects of the conflict were discussed and once again, although this time in less candid terms. The president eventually agreed with the dissenting faculty that such decisions should be consultative, which seemed to calm the dissidents and close the issue. The recruits kept their jobs, however, and the dean got his term extended. The chairman later became the assistant dean. The centralized form of administration, being so pervasive in these institutions, did not undergo any change.

A tendency for open, heated, and prolonged discussion and debate is characteristic of this culture. In organizational life subordinates easily take issue with superiors on organizational policies or some personal concern, clients pressure public employees for some form of special treatment, who in turn get into lengthy arguments on the correct course of action, and so on. Judging from the responses shown by superiors, such conflict seems acceptable and within existing norms of conduct.

The high positive correlation between the collaborative and compromising styles suggests that these involved discussions are conducted somehow in conjunction with the compromising style. One interpretation of this finding is that the collaborative and compromising styles are used in sequence. According to Blake and Mouton (1964) and Renwick (1975), managers seem to use "response hierarchies" in dealing with conflicts; the dominant response is shown first, but if the desired result is not obtained, the next response in the hierarchy is adopted. Similarly, the initial response of these managers in a variety of conflictful situations may be interpreted as a tendency to "discuss" the matter. If this initial method does not seem to work, a manager may fall back on the next most preferred style, which was compromise in our case.

There is a problem with this interpretation, however: collaboration and compromise are not considered to be readily compatible styles in theory. Thomas (1976:902), for example, points out that "Bargaining may reduce the trust, candor, and flexibility required for problem-solving [i.e., collaboration] . . . [and] the disclosures made during problem-solving and the positive affect generated by it tend to discourage subsequent misrepresentation and bargaining." No consistent empirical evidence exists to suggest that the two styles are closely and positively related, either. Western researchers have come up with low to moderate correlations between the two styles, and with nearly as many negative correlations as positive ones (Van de Vliert and Prein 1987).

How, then, are we to interpret the moderately high positive correlation between collaboration and compromise? One explanation is that managers who report higher likelihood of using both styles may actually use them in different conflict episodes. This explanation then rules out the possibility of incompatible styles being used in sequence. A second explanation is plausible, however, and it accounts for their sequential use in the same conflict episode. For these managers, according to this second explanation, the "open discussion of concerns" inherent in the collaborative mode may possibly have stood for nothing more than an "opener" for what eventually constituted a compromising style. Such misrepresentation is frequent in measures using self-reports of actors. Self-reports of conflict behavior, likewise, have been found to be vulnerable to social desirability bias, usually in favor of projecting a collaborative profile (Thomas and Kilmann 1971; Rahim 1983b). In fact, Blake and Mouton (1964) have suggested that, because of the social desirability bias, the second most preferred style may better reflect a manager's "true" style.

My observations also support this last interpretation, that is, these discussions often constitute the initial phase of a bargaining process.

Most of these discussions eventually end up with no change in the status quo, as in the case of conflict among faculty described above, or in some form of give and take, but nevertheless in solutions that were apparent from the start. Rarely have I observed a new systemic solution arising from these discussions, although the problem-solving or collaborative style is expected, in theory, to help in achieving innovative solutions to problems that conflicts help to surface. The lengthy discussions that are commonplace seem rather to serve to "wear out" the other party without directly forcing the decision, a mark of the bargaining approach.

A major finding of the present survey was indeed the relative absence of forcing in the conflict styles of these managers. It will be recalled from Figure 5.3 that forcing was also perceived in isolation from the other styles. These results seem to parallel those in the West, where self-reports of managers show low preference for forcing (Rahim 1983b) and where forcing is uncorrelated with the other styles (Van de Vliert and Prein 1987).

The Jordanian aversion for forcing still seems unique. For one thing, a very low level of forcing would not be ordinarily expected in organizations where centralized decision making is the norm. We will momentarily see that Jordanian organizations upheld such norms. For another, some U.S. studies have found preference for forcing in specific situations. Lawrence and Lorsch (1967) have noted that effective organizational performance may require some forcing as a back-up mode for collaboration. Phillips and Cheston (1979) have found forcing to be the more successful method when a fair, clear solution for the benefit of the organization is available. In contrast to these U.S. findings, the managers in the present sample reported using forcing toward subordinates and peers only when conflicts involved responsibilities and compliance with rules. Forcing was absent from the other topics, including work methods and organizational policies.

This tendency to avoid forcing seems to blend well with the extraordinarily slow way in which work gets done in these organizations. In addition to a general "laid-back" atmosphere, an employee may find it easy to question decisions made or methods used, resulting in detailed discussions with coworkers or superiors. Even when violations of rules are involved, such as being absent from work during work hours, tardiness, or delaying work, purposefully or not, a manager will be reluctant to use coercive means such as disciplinary action. The ideal manager is one who is soft and tolerant, and who tries to persuade subordinates when differences arise.

Lack of forcing did not necessarily imply participative decision making, however. Centralized decision making is an acknowledged characteristic of management in Jordan (Adwan 1983; Al-Faleh 1987) as well as other Arab countries (Badawy 1980). For example, nearly three out of four high level Jordanian public administrators surveyed by Adwan reported that they make decisions without involving their employees. The present data, too, showed that managers are jealous in protecting their prerogatives on the issues of work methods and organizational policies, as evidenced by significantly less use of collaboration or compromise toward subordinates on these topics. A curious situation therefore emerges: power is sought and well guarded but not forcefully used in achieving organizational objectives. This finding lends some support to the argument that administration in developing countries is characterized by ritualistic formalism and lack of delegation, but "the absence of delegation does not imply that there is effective centralization, only that there is the appearance of centralization" (Milne 1970:58).

Another conflict episode that I observed may help to illustrate this last point. The administration of a higher education institution had been troubled for some time with the return of faculty members from their yearly summer vacation several days later than the officially announced date. The problem mostly involved non-Jordanians (Arabs and non-Arabs) who were going abroad during this time. Finally, this behavior was penalized by direct cuts in salaries in proportion to the number of days past the announced date. Each department was asked to report the return date of its members. One department, however, reported that *all* its members returned exactly on the announced date. A few members of the other departments were furious about the practice in general and the way it was executed. Their chairmen agreed with them, and a joint meeting involving a couple of faculty members, their chairman, and the academic vice-president was held. The vice-president listened to the complaints and discussed the matter in detail, but would not back away from the decision. When reminded that one department had given false reports, and that not only everybody knew it but it could also be easily proved, he closed the issue by saying that he could not do anything about it since he could not possibly accuse this chairman of giving false information.

While this case supports the argument for ritualistic formalism and the appearance of control hypothesis of R. S. Milne (1970), the notion of ineffective centralization may nevertheless be confined only to the formal business of the organization. When it comes to resources seen as critical or the assertion of personal power, control is not in appearance but in reality as well. A university president, for example, may not always ensure that policy decisions are being implemented throughout the university, but will have total control over who gets into the university housing. The control of critical resources may be the actual reason for acquiring power in the first place. But the reasons for not using this power in forcing the accomplishment of organizational goals require further exploring.

A plausible explanation for lack of forcing may be a general aversion to confrontation and use of force prevalent in the culture. Islam preaches patience and getting things done through consent, without breaking hearts. These values find their way into managerial practice, giving it a benevolent-autocratic character. For example, even under the open conflict of interest that exists in the process of collective bargaining, it is management, be it in the private or the public sector, more than the workers or their associations, who bears the responsibility of solving the dispute without escalation into strikes and lock-outs (Copur 1984).

Values alone may not be sufficient, however, to explain fully the very low level of forcing found. As an Arab colleague who had served in high government posts remarked when discussing the present results: "They will use forcing if they can." The difficulty of using forcing in many cases may well be due to the artificiality of the modern organization and its policies in a traditional society. A complex organization calls for universalistic practices, to use Parsons's (1951) terminology, from employees who are accustomed to specific ways of relating to each other in traditional cultures. It becomes very difficult for individuals to strip organizational role relations from the role relations that exist in the larger society. Family relations, for example, interfere with formal relations in the organization, as Nusair (1982) demonstrated in his study of Jordan Valley Authority. Status differences between families may also create incongruence with the organizationally defined status differences. The artificiality of formal organizational practices is further reinforced by the fact that performance may not always be perceived as directly related to strict adherence to modern management practice. A minimally competitive environment existed for most private firms in Jordan, for example, largely due to import regulations. Government agencies, likewise, are mostly beyond public scrutiny. All of this amounts to a reduction in the relative importance of modern organizational practices and policies. As models of conflict behavior would suggest (Thomas 1976), when stakes are low under low conflict of interest, so is the tendency to use forcing. A manager working within such a societal and organizational context may be well advised not to force abstract managerial principles upon peers and subordinates and, as a result, make a lot of enemies in what Almaney (1981) has described as a "revengeful" society.

The present sample of managers also seems to avoid peers more than they do superiors or subordinates on the issues of salaries, performance appraisal and promotion, and physical working conditions. Renwick (1975) had found a problem-solving approach to salaries and performance appraisal in a U.S. study. But no further study has been done on the differential treatment of these topics when dealing with superiors versus peers. An attempt will be made here to explain the present findings on the basis of Thomas' (1976) theoretical model. According to this model, avoiding behavior will emerge under conditions where parties have mostly conflicting interests but the stakes involved are low. Stakes are low when a party is not dependent on the other for the satisfaction of important concerns, as well as when an issue is unimportant. The higher likelihood of avoiding found against peers when salaries, promotions, or working conditions are involved would make sense because of the low stakes involved in this relationship. For the resolution of these issues, a manager is usually dependent on superiors not on peers, and manifest conflict is hierarchical, although the conflict of interest is basically among peers.

A similar tendency to avoid peers more than superiors is observed when personal habits, mannerisms, and values are involved. If we interpret this finding according to Thomas' model it would mean that personal style is more important when the other party is a superior. Thomas' model also predicts that assertive behavior would emerge when higher stakes are involved. This indeed seems to be the case with these managers, who use more forcing and minimal accommodation toward superiors when personality issues are at stake. The impact of culture is evident here, as these findings seem contradictory to the situation that exists in the West. In her U.S. studies Renwick found that issues of personal habits and mannerisms are likely to get compromised. Phillips and Cheston (1979), on the other hand, have reported more use of forcing, mostly toward subordinates, on personal conflict involving value differences.

The present findings seem to be consistent, however, with the overall personal tone of administrative relationships in and around organizations in Jordanian culture. As explained earlier, personal relations play a more important role in shaping behavior than formal, organizationally prescribed relationships. Furthermore, the culture places extraordinary emphasis on pride and face saving (Almaney 1981; Patai 1983). Any degrading form of treatment, particularly from somebody whose superiority rests in formally conferred rights, would therefore be quite unacceptable.

A conflict episode between a cabinet minister and a visitor provides an example of this sensitivity. This visitor, a member of one of the large families in the country, got quite nervous for having been kept waiting for nearly an hour by the minister. He responded to this degrading behavior on the part of the minister by walking into his office, as the minister was being interviewed by a team of researchers, and telling him of his frustration. The minister responded by telling the intruder that he should wait as long as necessary for him to finish his business, and asked him to get out of the office. The visitor left, hinting, however, that they were not finished with each other yet!

The emerging profile for this sample of managers from Jordan may be summarized as follows. These managers exhibited a tendency to discuss freely any disagreements they had with coworkers, superiors, and subordinates, and seemed to seek settlement of these differences through discussion and compromise. Persuasion was preferred over forcing, which seemed to contradict the prevalent organizational norms for centralized action. Hierarchical conflict seemed to occupy the energies of these managers more than conflict with peers. Direct conflict with peers was typically avoided, as exemplified in conflicts over salaries, promotion, or working conditions. Discontent on these issues was taken up the hierarchy. Hierarchical relations were also a sensitive spot for conflict over personal habits and mannerisms. Personal conflict with a formal authority figure was often taken as a matter of pride and received due reaction.

THEORETICAL AND PRACTICAL IMPLICATIONS

The theoretical implications of the present study lie mainly in the field of comparative management. It has long been recognized by writers in this field that cultural forces in the environment play an important role in shaping behavior in the organization (Ronen 1986; Kiggundu et al. 1983). Kiggundu et al., for example, state that "In general, each time the environment is involved, the theory developed for western settings does not apply, because it assumes contingencies that may not be valid for developing countries.... To the extent that contingencies for the utilization of administrative science in developing countries differ from those of industrialized countries, the transfer of management knowledge and technology (...) should emphasize *process* rather than *content* theories (...) and methods" (p. 81).

The present study supported the notion of external cultural forces shaping the behavior of managers in the area of conflict management. But more important, the study provided a specific application in support of Kiggundu et al.'s last suggestion that process rather than content theories should be emphasized. While the findings differed in several respects from Western ones, they still found their interpretation in theory relating conflict behavior to variables such as degree of conflict of interest and the stakes involved. In a different culture, these theoretical relations still seem to hold explanatory power; only the specific content of these variables, that is, the meaning they assume changes. For example, the stakes involved in conflicts over personal habits and mannerisms seemed to be quite high in a traditional society like Jordan. Hence, the impact of culture may have to be dealt with at the stage of deriving specific hypotheses from theories that may have a more universal applicability.

On the practical side, the study may have implications for managerial practices of foreigners doing business in the Middle East or in their relations with managerial counterparts in subsidiaries. A comparison of the stylistic differences between Jordanian and U.S. managers may be helpful in this regard. Based on the present study and U.S. findings (Renwick 1975; Phillips and Cheston 1979; Rahim 1986), the following two main differences seem to emerge between the two countries.

First, a high level of sensitivity exists in Jordan over issues involving personal habits, mannerisms, and values, especially toward those in power positions. Managers seem to be well aware of these tendencies, and show signs of accommodation toward subordinates on personality issues. These tendencies contrast with Phillips and Cheston's findings on U.S. managers, who seemed most assertive toward subordinates when value differences emerged. Contrary to what Renwick concluded from her data from the United States, the Arab managers studied also seemed to be more assertive on affective issues, such as personal habits and mannerisms, than on substantive issues, such as work methods, organizational policies, rules, and procedures, when authority figures were involved.

Second, relatively low levels of forcing exist down the hierarchy over substantive issues, despite centralized decision making. In the United States, low levels of forcing seem to accompany participative decision making. Furthermore, Rahim's discriminant analysis results indicate that conflict behavior of subordinates toward superiors is characterized by higher levels of accommodation in the United States. Hence, managers in the United States seem to elicit accommodative responses from subordinates while exercising participative styles of management. The same combination does not seem to hold for managers in Jordan. Infrequent use of forcing down the hierarchy is coupled here with low levels of accommodation on the part of the subordinates. Consequently, Jordanian managers seem to rely more on persuasion and "selling" than on participation or authoritative command in managing differences with subordinates.

These stylistic characteristics of Jordanian managers may contrast with popularly held views of Arabs in the West, formed largely through media coverage of political conflicts in the region. This is not to imply that conflictful behavior was uncommon among the managers studied. To the contrary, discussion, disagreement, and bargaining seemed to be quite natural parts of organizational life, and are likely to take place in business or interorganizational role relationships of foreigners with Arab managers. But even when intense bargaining is involved, this is best done in style: in a soft manner without giving an impression of hostile and deliberate use of power.

The importance of resisting temptations to force for fast results cannot be overemphasized here. As A. Ali (1987) has observed, "familiarity with sociocentric and family-tribal orientations is indispensible for under-standing the decision making process in Arab society. Those who are not informed about Arab values tend to get frustrated in slowdowns in decision making" (p. 100). A Western manager, who feels under pressure to get things going may still be wiser to avoid forcing issues. This is a society that lives in a long-term time frame, and here long-term relations may need to be preferred to short-term results. Understanding Arab conflict management processes should also help foreigners be more em-pathetic with their Arab counterparts. These Arab managers cannot be very results-oriented even if they wanted to; they have to work through their differences by a process of extended discussion, persuasion, and compromise.

A foreigner may also have to be careful not to turn a difference into a personal matter with the other party. Forcing the issue will invariably turn into a personality conflict in this culture. So will insensitivity to the rituals, behavioral norms, and values of Arabs. A thorough knowledge of these cultural specifics seems necessary, and various books, articles, and films on doing business with Arabs can be useful training material. Just as personal frictions may render conflicts unmanageable, friendship, even when not so deep, may make likely conflicts disappear in this cul-ture. It is no wonder that most training material on the Middle Eastern culture emphasizes establishing good personal relations before getting down to business.

As critical as interpersonal relations in this culture may be, competence in relating to members of a foreign culture is not easily acquired. Foreign managers who do not feel confident in this area may do well by not trying to solve their own differences. It may be best for them to let Arab managers deal with their subordinates or peers, as they are far better equipped in the art of persuasion and compromise required for handling differences in this culture. The centralized nature of managerial practice prevalent in Arab organizations comes in handy here, as it may be suf-ficient for foreign managers to deal only with their high level Arab counterparts.

In addition to practical implications for foreigners, the study points to an important problem facing the attainment of organizational effec-tiveness in Arab countries. A tendency to openly acknowledge and dis-cuss disagreements is an admirable property for managers in any society. If also coupled with more information sharing and participative decision making, which are lacking today (Badaway 1980), these conflict man-agement styles may well be strengths for the future. But effective or-ganizational performance would also require enforcement after such discussion results in a thorough analysis *and* a solution. Observers of Arab culture have argued that Arab society is basically an expressive, verbal society (Ajami 1981; Almaney 1981; Patai 1983), reluctant when it comes to action. A related potential problem in the area of conflict resolution was discovered here, and it deserves further study. The present survey was essentially a descriptive study, and its data collection methods emphasized breadth rather than depth. Future in-depth studies on the effectiveness of the different styles, not only from the point of view of the individual employees but also the larger organization, would be welcome additions to our present knowledge of this problem. Also worth investigating are mediation and third party roles in handling conflicts within organizations, methods which, according to Patai (1983), have a long tradition in Arab society.

REFERENCES

Adwan, Y. M. 1983. Patterns of Administration—Citizen Relationship: Administrators' View. *METU Studies in Development* 13:325–38.

Ajami, F. 1981. *The Arab Predicament: Arab Political Thought and Practice since 1967.* Cambridge: Cambridge University Press.

Ali, A. 1986–1987. The Arab Executive: A Study in Values and Work Orientation. *American-Arab Affairs* (Winter): 94–100.

Al-Faleh, M. 1987. Cultural Influences on Arab Management Development: A Case Study of Jordan. *Journal of Management Development.* 6: 19–33.

Almaney, A. J. 1981. Cultural Traits of the Arabs: Growing Interest for International Management. *Management International Review:* 10–18.

Badaway, M. K. 1980. Styles of Mideastern Managers. *California Management Review* (Spring): 51–58.

Blake, R. R., and J. S. Mouton. 1964. *The Managerial Grid.* Houston, Tex.: Gulf.

Bourgeois, L. J., III, and M. Boltvinik. 1981. OD in Cross-Cultural Settings: Latin America. *California Management Review* (Spring): 75–81.

Copur, H. 1984. Collective Bargaining in Jordan: An Industrial Relations Systems View. Paper presented at the 10th Annual Convention of the Eastern Economic Association, New York.

Kiggundu, M. N., J. J. Jorgensen, and T. Hafsi. 1983. Administrative Theory and Practice in Developing Countries: A Synthesis. *Administrative Science Quarterly:* 66–84.

Kirk, R. E. 1968. *Experimental Design: Procedures for the Behavioral Sciences.* Belmont, Calif.: Brooks/Cole.

Lawrence, P. R., and J. W. Lorsch. 1967. *Organization and Environment.* Homewood, Ill.: Irwin.

Milne, R. S. 1970. Mechanistic and Organic Models of Public Administration in Developing Countries. *Administrative Science Quarterly:* 57–67.

Nusair, N. 1982. Regional Development and Planning in Jordan: Jordan Valley Authority, 1973–1980. Unpublished Doctoral Dissertation, State University of New York at Albany.

Parsons, T. 1951. *The Social System.* London: Tavistock.

Patai, R. 1983. *The Arab Mind.* Rev. ed. New York: Scribner's.

Phillips, E., and R. Cheston. 1979. Conflict Resolution: What Works? *California Management Review* (Summer): 76–83.

Rahim, M. A. 1983a. A Measure of Styles of Handling Interpersonal Conflict. *Academy of Management Journal*: 368–76.
———. 1983b. *Rahim Organizational Conflict Inventories: Professional Manual*. Palo Alto, Calif.: Consulting Psychologists.
———. 1986. Referent Role and Styles of Handling Interpersonal Conflict. *Journal of Social Psychology* 125(1): 79–86.
Renwick, P. A. 1975. Impact of Topic and Source of Disagreement on Conflict Management. *Organizational Behavior and Human Performance*: 416–25.
Robbins, S. 1978. Conflict Management and Conflict Resolution. *California Management Review*.
Ronen, S. 1986. *Comparative and Multinational Management*. New York: Wiley.
Thomas, K. W. 1976. Conflict and Conflict Management. In *Handbook of Industrial and Organizational Psychology*, ed. M. D. Dunette. Chicago: Rand-McNally.
Thomas, K. W., and R. H. Kilmann. 1971. Some Properties of Existing Conflict Behavior Instruments. Research Paper No. 38, Division of Research, Graduate School of Management, UCLA.
Van de Vliert, E., and H.C.M. Prein. 1987. The Difference in the Meaning of Forcing in the Conflict Management of Actors and Observers. Paper presented at the First International Conference of the Conflict Management Group, Fairfax, Va., June.
Wright, P. 1981. Organizational Behavior in Islamic Firms. *Management International Review*: 86–94.

6

Conflict Resolution and Moral Community among the Dou Donggo

Peter Just

Although it is something of a commonplace, in an anthology like this one it is well worth recalling that in a great many societies there may be a wide variety of culturally legitimated paths of behavior dedicated to the resolution of conflicts, the settlement of disputes, and the allocation of responsibility for trespass against personal rights, communal interests, and public morality. To the casual Western observer many of these paths may seem to be "informal," "extralegal," "nonbinding," and somehow preliminary or ancillary to formal legal and penal institutions. But students of conflict resolution and comparative law neglect or underestimate the importance of such local institutions for the mediation, arbitration, and adjudication of conflicts and disputes at their peril. For although they lack the formality of written legal codes administered by specialists and enforced by means of coercive powers to exact restitution or retribution, they are often the principal means by which disputes are settled, conflicts resolved, and the moral fabric of the community maintained and enforced. To be sure, in many societies where "informal" or "customary" law prevails there may also be more recognizably conventional legal and penal institutions to which members of the community have alternative or simultaneous recourse. Indeed, an important aspect of the dynamics of conflict resolution in such societies lies precisely at the junction and interrelationship between such dual (or multiple) legal systems, and in the ways individuals choose to manipulate differences between the systems.[1]

But in many societies composed of small-scale, morally cohesive communities, there is often an incomplete understanding and a fundamental mistrust of formal state-run legal institutions, which are perceived as exogenous, intrusive, uncontrollable, and ill-suited for representing indigenous concepts of justice. For this reason, there is often a distinct—almost exclusive—preference for resolving conflicts within the community and according to endogenously defined concepts and procedures. While national or regional formal systems of law may provide a context within which local law operates, "a sharp distinction is drawn between the two types of dispute management at the ideal as well as at the practical level" (von Benda-Beckmann 1984:72–73; see also Just 1986a:47). It should be noted, too, that these endogenous systems of "customary" law run a formidable gamut from highly formalized and richly articulated systems of courts and judges, to situations in which a vague mediation by respected members of the community seems to be the only alternative to the violent, "self-help" resolution of conflicts.

The system described in this chapter, that of an Indonesian people called the Dou Donggo, falls somewhere in the middle of this spectrum. Among the Dou Donggo, conflicts are resolved, disputes are settled, and the sociomoral order is enforced almost exclusively within the village community. Within the village, some mediation, arbitration, and adjudication are undertaken by the village headman or by members of his appointed staff in the name of the formal village government.[2] The majority of cases is resolved, however, not by village government officials, but by community elders who have exceptionally broad and flexible powers to interpret evidence and impose judgments. Yet they can neither exert nor threaten to exert coercive sanctions. If one stops to think about it, this in itself is a bit problematical. Who are these elders, anyway, and if they are not appointed or elected, how are they chosen? If these elders have no power to enforce their judgments, how can they operate effectively? Why should anyone listen to them in the first place, especially those they have decided against?

THE DOU DONGGO

Subsisting mostly on the cultivation of swidden (slash-and-burn) and irrigated rice, the Dou Donggo number about twenty thousand and inhabit Donggo District, a highland massif to the west of Bima Bay at the eastern end of Sumbawa, one of the long chain of islands stretching east from Java and Bali. For some three hundred years after the lowland (Dou Mbojo) population accepted Islam, a special political status allowed the Dou Donggo to preserve their traditional religion. Since the postwar absorption of Donggo by the independent Indonesian nation, most Dou Donggo have become at least nominally Muslim, although about one thousand have been converted to Christianity.

Most Dou Donggo villages are built atop high ridges between the gorges that cut across the massif at frequent intervals. Villages tend to be compact; social life is dense and intense. In Doro Ntika, the most populous Dou Donggo village, a population of about three thousand is divided among eight hamlets. The oldest part of the village, where my wife and I lived for two years, holds about half of the population, tightly clustered in four hamlets.[3]

Gender and age are the principal dimensions of social differentiation in what is generally a highly egalitarian society.[4] Personal charisma, as embodied in the command of esoteric healing lore, oratorical ability, and persuasiveness and diplomatic skill in the mediation of disputes, counts far more than any other dimension of social differentiation in the composition of what little community hierarchy there is. Formal government is in the hands of an elected village headman (*kepala desa*, locally termed a *gelara*), who appoints a staff of six or eight assistants (*pamong*), augmented by elected hamlet captains (*kepala dusun*). The headman is responsible for enforcing codified national law and has as a major duty the adjudication of disputes within the village community. He may assess fines or order restitution, although he is supposed to arrive at such judgments through a process of discussion and consensus building (*musawara* and *mufakat*).

There is a strong feeling that disputes, conflicts, and misbehavior are matters for the community to deal with internally. There is a strong disposition to avoid washing dirty linen in public, and a general reluctance to involve authorities from outside the community. As far as I know, virtually never in recent years have the police been called in to respond to a complaint lodged by one villager against another, nor has one member of the community taken another to court over a dispute. In part this is a matter of community solidarity, but it is also the result of pragmatic considerations, for to involve outsiders is to relinquish a share of control over the outcome of a dispute: bribes could become a factor and there is far less assurance that the outcome of a legal proceeding left to strangers to resolve will be as sensitive to local needs as one resolved by people who have to continue living together as neighbors.

While the headman and his staff are recognized by the government as the lowest level of government and law, most disputes and conflicts within the village are resolved through the mediation of one or more of the village elders (*doumatuatua*), who constitute a parallel and independent source of politicojural power in the community. When a dispute arises, or a long-standing conflict comes to a head, one of the parties involved will usually solicit the help of a respected elder in negotiating a resolution. If initial efforts fail, other elders, perhaps more skillful or acceptable to the opposite party, may become involved as well. It is their task to carry back and forth representations of each side's position, using their own judgment and position of moral ascendancy to find a solution acceptable to all.

In complicated cases, particularly where there has been violence or a serious threat of violence, an ad hoc panel of elders, representing not only the parties involved but the interests of the community at large, may be set up to investigate and adjudicate the conflict. In such instances there is a trial-like proceeding (*paresa*) in which evidence is publicly presented and weighed, a ruling is made, and sanctions may be applied (see Just 1986a:49–54 for an example). It is also possible for a panel of elders to investigate rumored allegations of wrongdoing, even though there is no two-party dispute or conflict and no one has made a formal complaint. (By example, such was the case when there were rumors that the parents of an unwed mother had smothered their grandchild at birth because the child was unwanted. Although no formal suit was filed, an investigatory panel of *doumatuatua* questioned those involved and assessed a fine.)

To be successful, the mediations and adjudications of the elders must be reasonably acceptable to all the parties involved. A disputant dissatisfied with the outcome of a *paresa* conducted by the elders has the option of formally taking the issue to the village headman or one of his subordinates. The headman's ruling is almost always definitive, since the only remaining recourse is to move into the realm of formal courts and judges, which, as I have said, Dou Donggo are extremely reluctant to do. In some instances, the parties to a dispute may take their case to the village headman from the outset.

One additional thing may be said before proceeding to a more elaborate description of the *doumatuatua*. Although resolutely egalitarian with respect to most ascribed statuses, Dou Donggo society recognizes and strongly defends social differentiation based on age and gender (see Just 1986b:135–51). Violations of canons of behavior impelling deference and respect by juniors for seniors or protecting women against male violence tend to be enforced with great vigor and little room for mitigation. Sanctions applied in cases involving such violations may be seen as instances of the society defending itself against breaches of its most fundamental values.

In part it is this deference for age that grants moral authority to the *doumatuatua*. While a degree of deference and respect attaches to anyone who has attained the grandparental generation of the community, among the *doumatuatua* deference and respect are augmented by an authority based not necessarily on wealth or coercive temporal power, but on a general and consensual recognition of moral standing. *Kandede nggahi doumatuatua*, ("This is what the elders say") is the prefatory formula to almost any formal authoritative statement of ideology, particularly when addressed by an older person to a junior. It is a way of saying, "this is the consensus of what it is right and proper for a member of this community to do; this is what your elders, who are wiser than you, know to be best."

The *doumatuatua* do not constitute a formal government body. Indeed, inasmuch as their authority is consensually acquired, consensually maintained, and consensually enforced, there is no unanimous agreement within the community as to precisely who is or is not to be considered a *doumatuatua*. (Indeed, it is somewhat misleading to suppose that Dou Donggo villagers even think in terms of a specific individual as "being a *doumatuatua*," as against others who are not). Nonetheless, at any given time in a community the size of Doro Ntika, there will be four or five individuals universally recognized as representing the moral ascendancy of the community. There will be perhaps a dozen or a score of other persons who take on such a position periodically or in some quarters of the village, who are gradually coming to occupy such a position, or who merely have pretensions to doing so. The proof of an individual having achieved a social identity as a *doumatuatua* is found in the extent to which that person is called upon to act in the ways expected of a *doumatuatua*.[5]

What, exactly, is expected in and of a *doumatuatua*? To begin with, a *doumatuatua* is a mature member of the community. Relative age is a principal dimension of social differentiation among the Dou Donggo, and a show of respect for one's elders is a fundamental tenet of Dou Donggo social values and behavior. Moreover, as with all older members of the community, it is generally expected that a *doumatuatua* will have married and reared a family. Therefore, although there are exceptions, most *doumatuatua* are assumed to be of the grandparental generation of the community (see Just 1987a for a discussion of Dou Donggo procreative generations and "teknocentrism").

Second, a *doumatuatua* retains a reputation for moral rectitude. This, obviously, is a far more difficult characteristic to specify. The position of a *doumatuatua* is attained over time and retained in a context of a person's total moral character. A *doumatuatua* becomes one gradually, through community consensus and usage, and earns the position by dint of practice. There is more to this than simple good behavior over time. As will be seen in greater detail, disputes in Donggo are usually settled in large part through sometimes lengthy consensus-building meetings (*mbolo*). A young person of obvious intelligence and social grace attending such meetings will more and more frequently be asked to venture an opinion or proffer a solution in the resolution of a case, at first, perhaps, in only those cases in which he is directly involved as an interested party.[6] In general, however, it may be said that a person has a right, sometimes construed as an obligation, to participate in decisions regarding a member of his asymmetric kindred (see Just 1986b:417–26), but that the extent to which he is sought out or is welcomed to participate, turns on matters of maturity and personality. If his opinions are useful and wise, if—more to the point—he is persuasive in making a case for them, then he will continue to be consulted. As his reputation for wise and persuasive counsel spreads, he may come to be brought in as a mediator or adjudicator more and more frequently and increasingly beyond the narrow confines of his own hamlet.

Nevertheless, most of the work of a *doumatuatua*, and much of the authority that attaches to him, does not derive from performances in formal gatherings. As will be discussed more fully below, the great part of conflict resolution in a village like Doro Ntika takes place in the consensus-building processes of gossip among friends and neighbors and in whispered intrigues among a disputant's kinsmen and allies. It is here, in the interstices of formal process, that a *doumatuatua* operates most effectively, and it is in these matters that he is most likely to be called upon for help. In many ways, then, a person becomes a *doumatuatua* not so much by the delivery of opinions in formal legal settings, but by being asked to negotiate a brideprice, or muster arguments in a land dispute, or to lend his good offices to the termination of a betrothal, or to intercede more immediately in preventing a dispute from erupting into violence.

In this context, then, it is not surprising to find that virtually all *doumatuatua* are also *sando*, that is, healers and diviners in the autochthonous religion. Although one need not be a *sando* in order to be a *doumatuatua*, the same characteristics of personality that make for a good *doumatuatua* also are found in the most respected *sando*, and it is certain that the most called-upon and respected *doumatuatua* are also the most powerful *sando*. In a metaphoric sense as well, there is a considerable consonance between the good works of a *doumatuatua* and the good works of a *sando*: both are engaged in divining ills and healing them, whether they be bodily ills or the ills of the body politic. The greatest of the community's *sando* are also those who serve as officiands for the rituals (mostly agricultural) performed on behalf of major groups of farmers and on behalf of the community at large (see Just 1986b:196–201). To their quality as healers, then, is added a sense of protector. Also implicit in this liturgical service, and more important for their function as adjudicating elders, is the position of the great *sando-doumatuatua* as the embodiment of community identity and solidarity.

At the same time, those with the necessary charisma, esoteric knowledge, and spiritual courage to become healing *sando* must at least potentially be regarded as sorcerers as well, for the same sort of knowledge that allows a person to banish vexing spirits may also be employed to summon and direct them.[7] All *sando*, and by extension all *doumatuatua*, must be regarded as double-edged swords: openly healers of the physical and social body, repositories of communal solidarity, but perhaps secretly destroyers as well. Needless to say, this adds greatly to the practical authority of a *doumatuatua*, for not only is almost everyone in the community likely obligated to him for the services he has performed in healing the sick and protecting the health and well-being of the group, but a powerful *sando-doumatuatua* is manifestly not someone lightly crossed. One can never be certain that a *sando-doumatuatua* whose authority has been too abruptly challenged might not turn and secretly visit sickness or calamity on the challenger. I do not wish to imply that the *doumatuatua* of a village like Doro Ntika are somehow a claven of warlocks, ruling by terror; nothing could be further from the truth. But if the association between *sando* and *doumatuatua* helps us to understand the authority vested in the *doumatuatua* of the village, we ought to consider everything that being a *sando* implies.

In addition to maturity, moral rectitude, and spiritual accomplishment, a *doumatuatua* is also always possessed of a powerful personal charisma that is at the heart of being a *sando* or a *doumatuatua*, and is most palpable in those who are among the most illustrious of both.[8] It is a charisma far easier to perceive than describe. While no characteristics of dress or deference distinguish an eminent *sando* or *doumatuatua*, one cannot enter a room occupied by such a person and long be unaware that he is the moral center of gravity for all who sit with him.

THE NATURE OF DISPUTE AMONG THE DOU DONGGO

A society's system of conflict resolution and dispute settlement is best comprehended when we understand the moral economy of which it is part. By this I mean that a legal system will to a large extent reflect and support underlying cultural assumptions concerning the nature of human nature, of the individual, of social behavior, and of the social order itself, all of which have a moral valence. It is only to the extent that a community can assess the outcomes of its legal proceedings as consistent with and constitutive of a basic set of norms that an enduring sense of justice can be achieved. These norms themselves rely on assumptions about what people are like, how they can be expected to act, and what is possible, necessary, or desirable in modifying or controlling their behavior. It is for this reason that we begin a consideration of the nature of dispute among the Dou Donggo with a brief discussion of the way in which they perceive themselves and human nature.

In many parts of Indonesia—most particularly Java and Bali—proper social conduct entails restraint, indirection, discretion, and soft-spoken courtesy in the conduct of everyday social relations. As Hildred Geertz (1974:251) observes of the Javanese, they "rarely quarrel openly, rarely raise their voices in anger or their hands against one another. There are just as many quarrels in a Javanese village as elsewhere ... but the arguments are kept in a low key, carried on by hints, slights, and allusions rather than by direct accusation and attack; and if a quarrel threatens to erupt into an uncontrollable fight, the opponents forestall it by cutting off relationships with one another."

Clifford Geertz (1983:211) describes a similar situation for Bali, where conflict resolution "is a matter of what one can only call high etiquette, of patient, precise, and unexcited going through the elaborate forms of local consensus making." This is certainly what most Westerners expect of Indonesian—even pan-Southeast Asian—demeanor and dispute settlement: an at least superficial gentleness and elaborate courtesy in interpersonal relations, even if it masks resentments that may later erupt on an occasion of massive general violence.

Elsewhere in Indonesia, however, a more open style of social interaction, featuring greater bravado and more aggressive posturing is a cultural norm (see Bruner 1974).[9] The Dou Donggo, like their lowland neighbors, are counted among the more open and less restrained of Indonesian peoples, falling into the category of the fiery-tempered— quick to anger, but quick to make amends as well. Speaking of themselves, Dou Donggo say, "If you are good to us, we are better than good in return; if you treat us badly, we will be worse than bad to you in reply." Another informant once told me that a Dou Donggo would take an insult twice and beg forgiveness, but insulted the third time, would *"veha buja, ramba cila"* ("take down the spears and sharpen the bush knives"). Informants enjoyed regaling me with stories in which Dou Donggo fierceness intimidates cowardly Dou Mbojo. One friend, whom I had never imagined to be other than the gentlest of souls, told me of the time in a nearby lowland marketplace he had heard one lowlander tell another "You act like a Dou Donggo." On hearing the name of his people used as a slur, he grabbed the speaker by the scruff of the neck and threatened him with a knife, while the onlooking crowd scattered.[10] "Imagine," he laughed, "a hundred Dou Mbojo running away from one Dou Donggo! They're just like dogs: they yap and they snarl, but shy a rock at them and they run away whimpering."

The Dou Donggo self-image, then, is one in which they portray themselves as tough but fair, initially conciliatory but with a quick fuse if insulted or treated unfairly. There is, in other words, a general feeling that a person should not go looking for trouble, but must be willing to defend his interests when threatened, violently if necessary.

In this context, then, it should not be too surprising to find that Dou Donggo regard human nature as more or less unpredictable and expect everyday social relations to be marked by the occasional flare-up of violence. Nor are Dou Donggo generally inclined to look upon people as essentially good at heart; a traditional formula holds that by nature people are inclined to be selfish and do evil three-fourths of the time.[11] In consequence, human behavior—one's own as well as others—is seen as requiring fairly continuous monitoring and subject to the exercise of fairly constant control.[12]

Another person's misbehavior is regarded as more than just a threat to one's own well-being; Dou Donggo notions of human nature and social behavior go well beyond self-defense and self-help. There is a definite sense of a communal moral order, which may and must be maintained in the name of the community itself. Sexual misconduct in particular, even if it is covert and by mutual consent, is regarded as dangerous to everyone, since it angers the village's tutelary spirits whose response may include the visitation of agrarian natural disaster on the entire region.

More can be learned about the assumptions underlying Dou Donggo concepts of human behavior by considering the way in which praise and criticism are made in social contexts. Public praise and criticism are by far the most frequently used means of applying social sanctions, both positive and negative, not only to children, but to adults as well. Dou Donggo are not given to lavish expressions of gratitude immediately on receiving the benefits of another's actions; indeed, the term for "thank you," *tarima kasi*, is almost certainly a recent loan from Bahasa Indonesia's *terima kasih*. Nor is it common to praise someone's laudable actions at the time they are performed. Instead, it is far more common to reserve expressions of gratitude and praise for a public context and to praise another's behavior in his or her presence and before as many other people as possible. For one person to praise another's generosity or virtue in his or her presence alone is, in a sense, a waste; that person knows, or should know, that what he or she has done was praiseworthy. Praise is far more meaningful and useful when it contributes to a person's public moral standing, and that is the appropriate arena for its expression.[13]

Similarly, expressions of disapproval for a person's behavior are most effective when public. Preadolescent children are regarded as morally unformed, not fully responsible for their actions. But as they grow older, children are increasingly expected to behave in a socially acceptable fashion. A youngster who consistently misbehaves may be publicly taken to task for bad behavior at an occasion that calls for a large gathering of people, as one or more *doumatuatua* gives "advice" (*naseha*) as to how behavior can be improved. Thus, for example, I can recall one instance in which the *sando* who had been called as ritual specialists in the consecration of a new house for a young couple, used the occasion to give a lengthy and embarrassing critique of the young husband's tendency toward financial profligacy. The young man was appropriately embarrassed, especially because it was on what for him was a particularly important and auspicious occasion.

All of this implies that the moral economy of Dou Donggo society emphasizes "shame" rather than "guilt" as the principal locus of social control (in Benedict's [1946:222–27] sense of this distinction). Action is evaluated not on the basis of its phenomenal consequences and in reference to abstract notions of good and evil, but in the context of the status relationships that constitute its social environment and the effects of action on that environment. Hence, the most appropriate use of both praise and criticism is in the public, social arena, where a person's behavior is given public evaluation and has consequences for that person's moral reputation. Good behavior is good not for its own sake, but for its social benefits; bad behavior is not inherently wrong, it is wrong because it damages society. One of the consequences for dispute settlement that flows from this attitude toward human nature and human behavior is that society is more concerned with the effects of a person's behavior than with its motivations. As will be discussed more fully below, there is an important sense in which an individual is held liable for even the potential consequences of his or her actions, regardless of intent (cf. Just 1990).

Dou Donggo do not make a sharp distinction between strictly public, legal affairs and private or personal matters. The heart of Dou Donggo jurisprudence is not the protection of individual rights and liberties so much as it is the recreation and reaffirmation of proper relationships within society. The object of conflict resolution, therefore, is not so much to punish or deter bad behavior, or even to regulate behavior into correct channels, as it is to restore the proper social relationship between individuals who for one reason or another have ceased to relate with each other in a proper way. This means that the resolution of a conflict ought to be made in such a way that the disputants can be restored to appropriate relations. The acceptability of a solution may take precedence over assessing actual responsibility for the initial breach in the relationship, and the solution itself must reaffirm those appropriate status relations. Thus, for example, the settlement of an argument between siblings is almost always contingent on the younger first making apology to the elder, even if both recognize the elder was in the wrong. The moral imperative dictating respect for age is a more general and perdurable principle than a transient dispute and is the most cogent aspect of the relationship between siblings. Therefore, before the dispute can be resolved, the relationship must be restored to its proper value. Only then can accommodation be made for who may have been right or wrong in the present issue.

Dou Donggo do not make a sharp distinction between problems that are amicably solved through the mediatory good offices of a *doumatuatua* and formal cases brought before the village headman or a committee of *doumatuatua* for adjudication. In the vocabulary of dispute, there is little, if anything, to distinguish a *masala*, a problem, from a *parakara*, a legal case or suit.[14] Similarly, to resolve a case is to *kanggori parakara*, to end it or, more literally, to "set a case free." At the same time, one can speak of the resolution of a dispute in terms of *kataho eli ro nggahi*, repairing [bad] sounds and speech.[15] This turn of phrase, I think, reflects the sense in Dou Donggo jurisprudence according to which conflict resolution may be seen as the restoration of damaged status relationships rather than the pursuit of equity or the imposition of retributive punishment.

THE DISPUTING PROCESS AMONG THE DOU DONGGO

As the core of my contribution to this anthology, I would like to give the reader a relatively intimate account of a Doro Ntika dispute settled not by means of a formal *paresa* but through the mediatory agency of several *doumatuatua*. The case in point, one of the breaking off of a betrothal, will be used as a means for describing processes of mediation and for discussing the ways in which accommodations can be made between articulated rules and more deeply held but less determinate norms. I shall also use this case as an example of Dou Donggo responses to the moral and jural challenges posed by the structural changes brought on by their incorporation in a wider world over which the village and its elders have little control.

The annulment of a betrothal, is a civil case in the law of contracts rather than torts or a criminal proceeding. As in many societies, a marriage among the Dou Donggo is not a matter to be decided by two individuals; it is an alliance between two groups of kin, all of whom to varying degrees have a vested interest in establishing the relationship. Marriages are often contracted by parents while children are very young; indeed, pregnant women sometimes even agree to prenatal betrothals (providing, of course, their newborns are of opposite sex. While such "*cepe kanefe*" infant betrothals are more an expression of mutual esteem between the parents than a realistic expectation of marriage, they do represent a loose commitment.

A firmer and more formally recognized commitment is constituted through a process call *sodi angi*. *Sodi angi* may be glossed as "betrothal," but literally means "ask [a] friend," ambiguously suggesting both asking a friend for a spouse for one's child and asking for someone to be a friend and spouse to one's child. In any event, there is a strong ideological connection between betrothal and friendship, and an implication that the relationship of prospective co-parent-in-law (*vai kata'ari*) is one of amity, goodwill, and voluntary mutual support. The formal establish-

ment of a betrothal and subsequent negotiations over bridewealth payments are undertaken through the agency of intermediaries on both
sides (*panati*). But from the time a betrothal is first contracted until well
after the final installment of bridewealth is paid off, years after the
wedding, the relationship between the extended bilaterial kindreds of
the betrothed couple is characterized by frequent reciprocal exchanges
of gifts and services, all of which are seen to *katenggo sodi* ("strengthen
the asking"). Among the most important of these transactions are exchanges of labor, which Dou Donggo ironically call *cepe maki* or *cepe hovi*
("swapping fatigue" or "swapping sweat"). When the parents (or, more
frequently, an elder sibling, uncle, or aunt) of a prospective bride or
groom are about to undertake an agricultural project of some magnitude—planting, threshing soybeans, harvesting swidden rice—they will
inform their *vai kata'ari*. Someone in the corresponding kindred will
then be responsible for organizing a labor party to assist in the project.
These labor parties may include more than a score of the organizer's
friends and relatives, and may even be filled out with unrelated workers
hired for the occasion. Reciprocity is observed on two levels: first, the
kindred of the prospective bride always contributes female labor (planting, harvesting, weeding, etc.) while the kindred of the prospective
groom always respond with male labor (swidden clearing, soybean
threshing, transport of the harvest, etc.); second, there is a general attempt to achieve parity in the amount of labor exchanged. Determining
this latter parity is a bit complex, since labor is not necessarily calculated
on a person/hour basis, but tends rather to be seen in terms of the labor
contributed as a proportion of the project's total labor requirements.
This, at least, is the position taken by the winning side in the dispute we
are about to consider; the principle itself is not unambiguously
established.

Dou Donggo marriage patterns have undergone considerable change
in the past three decades, as have many of the rules governing bridewealth, postmarital residence, and inheritance (Just 1987b). About a
third of the marriages solemnized in Doro Ntika before 1960 were the
result of infant betrothals; while most marriages in the early 1980s were
also the outcome of parental arrangement and negotiation, all but a few
of the couples had become betrothed when they were already teenagers.
The reasons for it are complex, but overall there has been an increasing
trend toward shorter betrothals (three or four years) and younger ages
of marriage (late teens rather than mid-twenties). Moreover, it had become not uncommon for teenagers to reject their parents' initial selec-
tions, pushing for a betrothal with someone of their own choosing. By
1983 there were even some younger adult members of the community
who had begun to feel that betrothals need not precede weddings by
more than a year or two, and that some youngsters at least ought to be

allowed to arrange their own marriages. In many ways this new attitude can be seen as a response to just the sort of trouble la Di's parents had with his betrothal. Here is their story, largely as recorded in my field-notes, with periodic interruptions for discussion and analysis:

Early one morning toward the end of June, when the harvest was in and the villagers had returned to the village from their swiddens, I was standing near my house, chatting with a neighbor and her husband. A passer-by informed us that ama Di[16] was holding a meeting (mbolo) at his house in the adjacent hamlet, to discuss the dula sodi (literally, "sending home of the asking") of his son's betrothal to la Fia. I went to ami Di's house and found him and eight or ten men related to him. They brought me up to date on the events that had led up to this mbolo: la Di, ama Di's eldest son, had at great expense been sent away to attend police academy. He had been quite successful and had just been promoted to sergeant second-class, after which he had been posted to Larantuka, Flores, a great distance from Bima. La Di and la Fia had been engaged since infancy, a cepe kanefe betrothal of some twenty-odd year's standing. A few days before the mbolo, ama Di had received a letter from his son informing him that he was hoping to be admitted to officer candidate's school in the near future. If accepted, he would be unable to marry while attending, and he felt that given the requirements of his career as a policeman, it was most likely he would be unable to marry for the next ten years. It would be terribly unfair, he wrote, to expect la Fia to wait that long, so in consideration to her he thought it best the betrothal be called off. As I was to learn in subsequent conversations, it was most likely that since la Di had his sights set on becoming an officer in the national police, an illiterate and unsophisticated village wife who could not even speak the national language would be a considerable hindrance to his career.

There are no secrets in Doro Ntika, especially not within a single hamlet, and word of la Di's letter had reached la Fia's parents the same day. They were more than a little upset, for not only had they and their daughter punctiliously observed the obligations of betrothal—only recently having provided a twelve-person harvest labor party for ama Di—they had also eagerly anticipated access to la Di's policeman's salary. Their initial reaction had been one of great anger, and they had been heard threatening to veha buja, ramba cila ("take down the spears and sharpen the bush knives") portending a violent encounter with ina and ami Di. Ina and ama Di were now afraid to approach their vai kata'ari directly, and had called this meeting of kin to decide how to proceed. They were aware that ama and ina Fia had likewise called a meeting of kin and that some representation on their part was called for. They discussed general principles and several of the older men made brief but fairly tendentious orations summing up the situation in a way that made their side look as good as possible. In particular, ama Di spoke at some length about the heavy responsibilities of a police officer: how he must sacrifice himself for the good of the nation, how he must be willing to forsake his home village and go wherever assigned, brave great dangers, jump off of trucks,[17] be a wise leader of the community to which he is posted, and so on, but especially how these responsibilities also fall on a policeman's wife. La Fia should be relieved to be let off the hook, said ama Di.

This line of argument met with general approval and others spoke, elaborating on its theme. Most of the men remained silent, but when the eldest among them had all had an opportunity to speak, it was decided that ama Hamu would be delegated to go up the hill to ama and ina Fia's house and formally ask for an annulment of the betrothal. Ama Hamu was the *pamong* (headman's subadministrator) of a nearby hamlet, ama Di's mother's sister's son and also the younger brother of the village headman. He would be accompanied by ama Kari, ina Di's father's sister's daughter's husband, *doumatuatua*, and a respected leader of the Catholic community. I, too, went along.

Let us break the narrative here to note several points. First, we may consider the meeting at ama Di's house as an example of the *mbolo* as a forum for kin group solidarity and as an arena for rhetoric. Ama Di's kinsmen gathered about him to show their solidarity in the face of a socially difficult and potentially dangerous situation. But this solidarity would take its most effective form in the way ama Di's kinsmen would subsequently go about making his case among the more or less neutral members of the community. As will become apparent, Dou Donggo disputes tend to be settled as much in the court of public opinion as they are in formal mediatory or adjudicatory proceedings. Such proceedings often act more to articulate verdicts already formed by a consensus of opinion than they do to actually determine guilt or innocence. No one, therefore, enters into a dispute alone. Ami Di's kin were obligated to support him in his dispute with his *vai kata'ari*, but as with any obligation of kinship, participation can range from the enthusiastic to the lukewarm to the nonexistent. Calling the *mbolo*, therefore, was an important means of calling his kin to his side, alerting them to his need for their support, and convincing them to support him enthusiastically. But—and this is crucial—it was also the appropriate means for formulating the position they would take in the dispute. In this instance ama Di was the one to formulate the position, mostly, I think, because he was the eldest of his sibling set and held a certain authority over them. In other instances, the disputant may say nothing at all, but defer to elders in the formulation of a rhetorical position. In either case, *mbolo* are pivotal arenas in which legal arguments are tried out and a consensus position reached in advance of public dissemination. There is a tendency to preserve an air of righteous indignation in formulating a complaint or of injured innocence in proposing a line of defense. There is no open calculation of strategies per se; even when those present are aware that what they are saying is not strictly true, they all speak as if it were. (In this case, for example, it seemed clear that la Di's desire to be free of his betrothal to la Fia was not entirely—or even principally—a matter of his unselfish concern for her fading youth, but rather his own growing realization of her inappropriateness as a civil servant's spouse; she was just too hick for what he had become.) There is an attempt to create a representation of the facts that corresponds to the deeper issues as the disputants see them—or at least as they would like their neighbors and *doumatuatua* to see them. Having done so in conjunction with his kin, ama Di was now prepared to dispatch an agent to represent this version of the truth. Needless to say, la Fia's kin had been doing precisely the same thing.

I am not prepared to speculate on the degree to which a given speaker at a particular *mbolo* believes his own rhetoric. But I think it is fair to say here, that Dou Donggo jurisprudence admits of a kind of "dualistic epistemology" in which representations of events known to be at variance with phenomenal facts are treated as "more true than what really happened," so long as such representations clarify rather than obscure the moral issues at hand. To some extent, at least, the participants in *mbolo* work up such representations of the "sociological truth" of their circumstances. The public at large, mediators, and, if necessary, *doumatuatua* or the headman acting as adjudicators in a formal *paresa*, would decide which of these alternative representations was most "true of what really happened," regardless of phenomenal events.

Next, we should stipulate that whatever ama Di might claim, la Fia's parents—indeed, her entire kindred—were quite justified in their disappointment and chagrin over losing la Di as a son-in-law. The case highlights two related structural problems posed with increasing frequency by the intensifying incorporation of Donggo in a wider world: the strain on the behavioral expectations surrounding betrothal created by the departure of affianced young men who leave the village for lengthy periods to attend high school and teachers' training college; and a growing general concern with access to cash money, needed in part to finance the educational expenses of one's own children. Infidelity on the part of the prospective wives of absentee fiances had become a persistent problem in recent years as more and more sons of the village had gone off to Lombok, Sulawesi, and even Java in pursuit of education and fortune. (Similarly, la Di was not the first of these absentee fiances who, having seen the bright lights of the big city, had lost interest in the girl back home.) Yet la Fia had steadfastly held herself aloof from local romantic entanglements in anticipation of her marriage to la Di, a steadfastness more than a little encouraged by her parents. Much was riding on this fidelity: the alliance established by a marriage entitles affines to call upon one another's financial resources and cash is an extremely scarce commodity in the economy of Doro Ntika. As long as the community had been homogeneously composed of farmers, swidden land was in plentiful general supply, and the Dou Donggo economy was almost exclusively one of subsistence, the mutual obligations of affines were relatively inconsequential economically. But in the past decade or so the education of Doro Ntika's children both required the expenditure of cash money and provided a means toward its acquisition. Indeed, the village economy in general has become more entwined in the monetized markets of the region, and so the importance of access to cash—and hence the economic significance of marriages—has increased substantially. In this context, then, the lost access to la Di's policeman's salary, money that la Fia's parents and kin had probably already spent in their imaginations, was keenly felt and bitterly regretted. And their disappointment was all the more bitter because la Fia's parents had recently gone out of pocket to hire nine workers to harvest for la Di's parents. In any event, the annulment of the betrothal had a relevance to issues of current change in Dou Donggo society that went far beyond the concerns of la Fia, her kin, and their access to la Di's salary.

Finally, we may pause to consider in greater detail la Fia's parents' threat to "take down the spears and sharpen the bush knives." In part we may see this as another example of the "bad sounds and speech" that seem to signal the opening of any public dispute. The aesthetics of Dou Donggo social life admit of considerable drama. Without too much indulging in dime-store psychological anthropology, one might suggest that the success Dou Donggo children experience in having their prolonged whining and fretting demands (*ongu ro weta*) rewarded with parental indulgences, resurfaces in their litigatory lives as adults. There is little in the childhood experience of Dou Donggo to suggest that a calm and reasoned request will produce a satisfactory response, and so it is hardly surprising that a hurt and offended adult Dou Donggo will do any less than throw an adult temper tantrum in seeking a redress of grievances.

Regardless of their origins, extravagant displays of passion and threats of violence are certainly a prominent feature of the disputing process and can equally be regarded as characteristic of social discourse. Such displays and threats are also a potent reminder to everyone in the community, but especially to one's antagonists in a dispute, that village justice depends on achieving a settlement acceptable to *all* parties, for self-help remains a plausible, if extreme, option, and that way lies vendetta and anarchy, or at least the arrival of the police, and the consequent loss of communal autonomy. It is a way of announcing the seriousness of one's feelings and of voicing a demand for redressive attention.

The threats of la Fia's parents also illustrate another sense in which Dou Donggo jurisprudence may be seen as "the repair of bad sounds and speech" alluded to above, and it may be worth a general comment at this point. The presence of a dispute or conflict within the community is almost always announced by some public display of sound or speech: a prolonged session of screaming and weeping directed at no one in particular but detailing the injuries inflicted on the weeper; an unexpected visit from an offended neighbor or kinsman, who stands before one's house shouting his complaints at one's behavior; an argument shouted before onlooking neighbors; threats of imminent violence. These are the most common ways in which disputes begin their social lives. It is not unknown for a dispute to become public knowledge because an accuser has lodged a complaint against someone with the headman, one of his staff, or a leading elder. But it may be said that in order for a dispute to become eligible for settlement there must first be expressed some variety of "bad sounds and speech." It might be added that there is an almost constant public monitoring of what might be called the "state of sounds and speech" among citizens of the community. As anyone proceeds through the village he or she is greeted at almost every turn. Greetings are conventional, even superficially idiotic. To a woman sitting at a loom, one might say *"Muna ro?"* ("Are you weaving?")—as if she would be doing anything else—but no response other than *"Iyo, muna-e!"* ("Yes, I'm weaving, all right!") is expected. The purpose of these greetings, of course, is not to find out that someone is indeed doing what he or she is manifestly doing, but as a way of saying, "You and I are on friendly terms, and I may greet you and be greeted in return." This is because among Dou Donggo a person who feels angry with or injured by or guilty about someone else feels "too shy" (*maja ade lalo*) to speak with or look directly at that person. The root cause of this bad feeling may not be apparent, and it may be the result of past behavior on the part of either party, but a persistent failure to give or return a greeting is a clear warning that all is not well between them. Certainly this was the state of affairs between la Di's parents and la Fia's parents, who had formerly been such good friends. But let us return to our story:

I accompanied ama Hamu and ama Kari to the house of la Fia's parents, where a group of their kinsmen was gathered. Since the matter had already reached a point of threats and gatherings of kin, the *dula sodi* had now become a matter of formal negotiation and representation, subject to mediation; it had, in other words, become a *masala*, a problem, a *parakara*, a case (see Just 1986a:47). Ama Hamu and ama Kari sat together, adopting the posture and demeanor reserved for meetings at which serious and weighty business is to be conducted. They accepted hospitable offers of betel and tobacco, after which ama Hamu conveyed what everyone already knew: that la Di was hoping to continue his education, would probably not marry for another ten years, and therefore was willing to "release" la Fia from the betrothal. His tone was conciliatory and he spoke softly, apologetically.

La Fia's parents were represented by ama Tali, the husband of a distant cousin, who was also a leader of the Catholic community, but the principal negotiator was ompu Siwe, one of the most respected *doumatuatua* in the village and the *panati siwe* (woman's marriage broker) for la Fia. Their response was not at all conciliatory. After considerable discussion it became apparent that la Fia's parents were demanding compensation as a condition for breaking off the betrothal. They wanted the return of two very fine black sarongs that had been given to la Di's parents in earnest of the betrothal, and were asking to be paid Rp40,000 in repayment of *sodi angi* labor la Di's parents had received over the past several years apparently calculated on the basis of numbers of workers provided.[18] Ama Hamu and ompu Siwe conferred privately in a whispered conversation to which, alas, I was not privy. Afterwards, ama Hamu was noncommittal, and politely took his leave in order to confer with the group assembled at the house of la Di's parents. After he had left, the group at la Fia's house began discussing matters more openly. Like the session at ama Di's house, the senior men present made speeches presenting their arguments. One position that developed and later became a prominent argument heard around the hamlet was that la Di's parents had spoiled things from the outset by calling on a formal intermediary rather than broaching the matter in person, as friends would. They found ama Hamu an offensive representative (for reasons I will adumbrate shortly). The mood was one of defiance and anger, and it was in this context that one of those present "remembered" that ama Di had promised to give them a buffalo "to strengthen the asking." This, too, would be added to the demands, and ompu Siwe was dispatched to convey their demands to la Di's parents. I left before he did, however, anxious to return to the group at the house of la Di's parents.

Let us pause a moment to consider the arguments of la Fia's kin. La Di's parents knew that breaking off the betrothal would be bound to provoke hard feelings and possibly real violence, and for these reasons they preferred to approach ama and ina Fia through mediatory agents. Yet la Fia's parents, and a good deal of public opinion, held that the *dula sodi* could have been handled discreetly and amicably if la Di's parents had approached them directly. Initially I found their position surprising, since many delicate negotiations between *vai kata'ari* are properly handled through marriage brokers. But since the idiom of betrothal is one of a formalized relationship between friends, it could be argued that if the termination of that relationship is to take place, it is best done without intermediaries, so as to restore the relationship to one of ordinary and informal friendliness and neighborliness. Such, at least, was the rhetoric expressed; I myself am doubtful that a direct approach would have yielded a welcoming response and I also strongly suspect that their position allowed them to most fully represent themselves as a wrongfully injured party.

This brings us also to the suitability of ama Hamu as intermediary. If the use of an intermediary at all was offensive, then the use of ama Hamu as that mediator exacerbated hurt feelings. As ama Di's matrilateral cousin he could not authoritatively represent la Di in negotiating issues of marriage; this is a right reserved to a child's father's male agnates. Moreover, as a member of the formal village government and the headman's brother, ama Hamu was perceived as offensive to la Fia's parents—an implicit threat that ama Di could bring his influence with the village government to bear on the matter if it should become a matter for adjudication. The annulment now began to look more and more litigious, and ama Hamu may have seemed more than a little threatening. For all these reasons, then, the situation was one in which hackles were raised.

Back at ama Di's house tempers were also inflamed. Ama Kari had arrived earlier and informed them of the demand for Rp40,000 in compensation of the labor provided during the preceding years of the betrothal. He argued that this demand ignoring the reciprocity of the relationship was unfair; it was not as though la Fia's kin had received no labor from la Di's kin in return. Ompu Siwe then came in and announced the additional demand of the buffalo that "had been promised to strengthen the asking." It was agreed that the intermediaries would meet again at la Fia's parents' house at dusk (magrib). That much time would be needed for ama Di to marshal his resources: of cash if compensation was to be paid, of personnel if the case was to be taken further in litigation.

Conversation continued peevishly until ama Panci arrived. As the panati representing la Di's kin in their earlier betrothal negotiations with la Fia's parents and kin, ama Panci was a crucial player in the unfolding social drama. Not only was he in a position to authoritatively testify as to what had or had not been promised "to strengthen the asking," ama Panci was also an important figure in the affairs of Waduna'e hamlet, of which both la Di's and la Fia's parents were citizens. Waduna'e is the smallest and most predominantly Catholic of Doro Ntika's several hamlets and although only in his mid-thirties, ama Panci is widely recognized as the most charismatic of its residents, and that he will almost certainly be its most influential elder as his generation replaces the current one. He is, moreover, well known for defending the responsibilities of betrothal, and had done so in the past (see Just 1986a). Without hesitation ama Panci averred that no buffalo had been promised. "A buffalo? That's bridewealth talk," he snorted, "and no one had started to talk bridewealth yet."

As things stood ompu Siwe, the panati for la Fia and a doumatuatua of irreproachable dignity and moral stature, had claimed the promise of a buffalo. Ama Panci, panati for la Di and a younger man but of no inconsiderable moral stature and charisma himself, said no such promise existed. Had a buffalo been promised? I have no idea, but I will say that I have never heard of anyone giving away a buffalo to "strengthen the asking." Most bridewealth payments include a buffalo, but this is usually one of the last items of the bridewealth conveyed, often after the marriage itself has taken place. I suspect that at some point in previous discussions about the marriage someone on la Fia's side—perhaps ompu Siwe—had suggested the gift of a buffalo would "strengthen the asking" and that someone on la Di's side—perhaps ama Panci—had affably but noncommittally said yes. Dou Donggo hate to say "no" to any request, and laugh at themselves by saying that the only way anyone can bring himself to answer in the negative is to say "Iyo, vati" (yes-no).[19] Answering "yes" to any request is most often ambiguous and usually means "I'd love to *if* I can." Dou Donggo themselves love to play ironically with this ambiguity. Asking for things is a feature of daily discourse so ubiquitous as to be a kind of background noise. Trivial requests or requests so outrageous as to become trivial are a kind of social grace among Dou Donggo, a friendly sort of thing done with friends and kin so that they "do not become distant" (see also Just 1986b:189–90). This kind of behavior is called *raho hakokai*, begging to tease, but sometimes the boundary between playful begging and a request is fuzzy and open to misinterpretation and reinterpretation. In this particular case it appears that an ambiguously meaningful promise was being revived and reinterpreted as a bargaining point and as a way of further placing ama Di's people in a position of moral inferiority. They were being publicly portrayed (for all of the claims made by both sides were instantly known to everyone in the hamlet who cared to know) as people who break their promises. Ama Panci's point that "buffaloes are bridewealth talk" was a valid one, however. In claiming that a buffalo had been promised to "strengthen the asking" la Fia's people were making a statement more symbolic than realistic.

Much of the tension generated by ompu Siwe's additional demand now dissipated; it was clear that the demand for a buffalo was most likely a bargaining position rather than a real or enforceable expectation on the part of la Fia's kin. The conversation turned to a more relaxed and abstract discussion of the virtues of love matches versus arranged marriages. I was asked how my own marriage had been arranged and ama Panci seemed almost wistful when I described betrothals determined by the two young people alone and involving no negotiations, prestations, or labor exchanges. "So simple!" he said. Some of the men complained at length about how vexing the business of marriage had become now that young people seemed to feel they knew so much better than their elders. "Go to all that trouble to fix a marriage, and then the kid doesn't want any part of it," grumbled one man. "Maybe we'd be better off letting them arrange it for themselves." After a time ina Di served those present a lunch of rice and vegetables followed by sweet coffee, and the meeting adjourned until the afternoon.

With the showdown meeting set for *magrib* (sunset), I headed back to ama Di's house around 5:00 o'clock, stopping by ama and ina Fia's house en route to confirm the time of the meeting. Ama Di had just dispatched someone to fetch me and his kinsmen had only begun to arrive. He asked me for some antimalarial medicine, which I returned home to get, so that by the time I arrived at his house it was starting to get dark and the meeting was ready to begin. Eight men were present, most of them ina Di's kinsmen. The group decided that la Fia's parents' demands for Rp40,000—which in the meantime had been reduced to Rp25,000—was out of the question. They would return the two black sarongs and add a sarong as a token of generosity (and a tacit, symbolic, admission of guilt). They would also offer to pay a cash settlement of Rp10,000. The money and sarongs were put together and I accompanied the same deputation that had been to la Fia's parents' house earlier back to their house to present this counter-offer. By then it was almost 7:30, an hour and a half after sunset and so an hour after dark. Technically we were late, but punctuality is not a general virtue among Dou Donggo, and in any case it was Ramadan and one might have expected that the more pious Muslims would have been given the chance to break fast before attending a meeting. So it was with some surprise that we found la Fia's parents' house empty. Ina Fia arrived after a while and said that they had waited for an hour and then given up. "You promised to be here at sunset," she said, "and you didn't keep your promise. That's the kind of people you are. You don't keep your promises." The delegation returned to ama Di's house.

Everyone was now thoroughly offended. La Fia's parents were offended that the engagement was being broken, that la Di's parents had not come to them directly, and that they had been late to the meeting. La Di's kin were offended that la Fia's parents were being so intractable, were making unreasonable de-mands, and had not waited for them—or at least sent a child to inquire when they were late. One of ina Di's kinsmen, a haji and member of the village headman's staff with a reputation for contentiousness and a quick temper, urged that they refuse to pay any compensation, saying, "If they want to sue [*tuntu*], just let them try!" Ama Hamu was also irked. "If they want to play games," he said, "I can play games, too. I'll go directly to ompu Siwe and tell him we'll return the sarongs and the Rp2000 they contributed to la Di's schooling. That's all. They can take it or leave it." And with that, he and another man went to the neighboring hamlet to see if ompu Siwe was at home there. I followed.

Ompu Siwe was not at home, but in a nearby house belonging to a woman who had recently made it through a difficult childbirth. She had promised to conduct a thanksgiving ritual if the birth was successful and was now having ompu Siwe perform one in fulfillment of the promise. That, explained ompu Siwe, was why he had not waited long earlier; he had this obligation to perform. "But you were late. You were wrong and you should act to repair the situation as quickly as possible." Ama Hamu replied in conciliatory tones. "We were all set to give back the sarongs with an additional one, and pay Rp10,000 to boot," he said. "But there was no one there to receive it, and now abu la Rudi [the contentious haji] and the others don't want to give anything, but are content to see this go before the headman for adjudication."

Ompu Siwe and ama Hamu then began serious negotiations, starting by agree-ing that abu la Rudi was a contentious and divisive influence who should not be listened to. After about an hour of discussion it was agreed that la Fia's parents would accept the three sarongs and Rp10,000 now, along with a promissory letter stipulating a payment of an additional Rp15,000 when la Di began to send home money from his salary. There was no further mention of buffaloes (much to everyone's relief, I suspect) but ina Fia's people had remembered some wood that they had stored with ama Di, but which ama Di had contributed to the rebuilding of the village school hut. "This wasn't right," said ompu Siwe. "Even if it wasn't for his own gain, ama Di had no business giving away wood that wasn't his." Ama Hamu agreed in principle that the wood should be replaced. A youngster was dispatched to ama Di's house to inform those waiting there of the proposed settlement, which they would have to ratify. The negotiators and I hung around chatting a bit longer, basking in the glow of concord, and enjoying the sweet coffee and betel offered by the new mother. We all took great pleasure in slandering abu la Rudi, whose position in the village as a haji and member of the headman's staff insured him a polite audience at every gathering, but whose contentious and vituperative spirit made him an unlovely companion. His nastiness was one thing we all could agree upon. Feeling the issue satisfactorily concluded, ama Hamu left for his home in the hamlet across the river to the north, and I set off for ama Di's house to see if there was any mopping up to do.

The negotiations between ama Hamu, ama Kari, and ompu Siwe had proceeded with reasonable dispatch and equanimity. Ompu Siwe had left ina Fia's house because he had had another obligation, not because he was angry at their late arrival. That everyone else at ina Fia's house had vacated rather than waiting was an indication of their ire and an unwillingness to be reconciled with la Di's parents; this much was clear. Once again, la Fia's kin would be able to portray la Di's kin as "people who don't keep their promises." But this tactic did not impair the ability of the mediators to conduct their business in a cool and level-headed fashion. This, of course, is precisely why it is appropriate to use mediators in the first place. Ompu Siwe had established an edge by not being present at 7:30, but he was not so foolish as to throw it away by refusing to negotiate or by twitting the other side too much about an insignificant tardiness. Replacing the demand for a buffalo with a demand for wood was also good strategy in that it paralleled the scaled-down demand for monetary compensation. His point—that the wood was not ama Di's to give away—was a valid one and had a better chance of standing up if the claim went to adjudication than the far more nebulous claim of a promised buffalo.

For their part, ama Hamu and ama Kari had a potent threat in the more militant position represented by abu la Rudi's take-it-or-leave-it stance, a position that if taken almost certainly would result in a formal suit brought by la Fia's kin. It was still in everyone's best interest to resolve the conflict amicably and outside of the formal proceedings of a *paresa*, even within the village. Ama Di's position was weak because la Di was breaking off a betrothal of long standing that had been puncti-liously observed by la Fia and her kin and in which they had much to lose. Ama Di was aware of this, and felt badly about it. He knew he was in the wrong and wanted to make amends, but also felt that this had been made impossible by the extravagant demands and intransigent posture of la Fia's kin. Even so, ama Di could not be certain that a panel of *doumatuatua* would not find heavily against him, given la Fia's loyalty and la Di's fecklessness. At the same time, la Fia's kin were in a weak position not only because ama Di had more influence with the headman, but because they had no tangible basis for claiming compensation for labor given freely as part of a betrothal relationship. It was unlikely they could do much better. For both sides it seemed that a mediated settlement was the prudent solution.

There was good precedent for the terms of the settlement, too. Ama Di's side would give up the Rp10,000 they had already put together now and "promise" to share out another Rp15,000 when la Di sent home money. The tactic of promising payment at a later time is a common one when it is infelicitous to declare a clear winner or loser and yet it is desirable to quickly put an end to the dispute; it can, in short, be a face-saving device that allows one side to claim they had been awarded their due without actually making the other side pay anything (cf. Just 1986a:49). In this case the unusual step of making out a written promissory note was proposed, but we thought little of it. We were wrong.

Rather than return directly home, I decided to swing by ama Di's house for what I thought would be a postmortem interview. Most of those present earlier had stayed on and they had been joined by the young Catholic catechist, Guru Markus. The argument had been renewed, and abu la Rudi's position was gaining strength. Again, one participant objected to any compensation paid for *sodi angi* exchange labor. "You don't calculate this on a person-per-person basis," he argued, since la Fia's kin had claimed compensation in part because they had provided more workers for ama Di than vice versa. "One time planting, [is repaid by] one time soy threshing; one time harvesting, [is repaid by] one time transporting the harvest. They've already been repaid: the money we are willing to give them isn't for that, it's an act of generosity, a symbolic peace offering [*imbalan jasa, pahu kataho*]." The catechist countered that they should accept the terms of the settlement: "Look," he said, "the Rp10,000 has already been put together. Money for later is for later and might or might not have to be paid."

Here the promissory note became a problem for many of the participants. If such a note were agreed to, they feared, la Fia's kin would *raho ntuvu*, pester them incessantly, just to give them a hard time. Again abu la Rudi persisted in his counsel that la Fia's kin be given nothing at all, but no one seemed to take his advice seriously. Conversation continued for a time, but no real consensus emerged and I was told that everyone would sleep on the matter and a decision would be made in the morning.

The next morning ama Di told me the terms of the settlement had been agreed to. My wife and I left a few hours later on a trip to the lowlands. Passing through ama Hamu's hamlet on our way we spotted him and I began to congratulate him on having negotiated a satisfactory end to a bothersome dispute. "Oh no," he said. "The deal is off. They're going to get Rp2,000 and the sarongs and that's all. If that's not enough they can sue if they want to." It wasn't clear to me which side was responsible for rejecting the earlier agreement, but I suspect it was la Fia's.

Passing by ama Di's house three days later I was surprised to find him sitting there in the company of abu la Rudi. "What happened?" I asked. He told me the whole problem had been finally laid to rest that morning. La Fia's kin had accepted three sarongs, Rp10,000, and a large timber but that was all. I congratulated ama Di and continued on our way home. Halfway there we encountered ompu Camba, one of the leading *doumatuatua* and *sando* of the community, who also told us that the problem had been solved and that he had been the one to do it. Later that day he came by my house to tell me how he had done it.

At ama Di's request ompu Camba had gone to la Fia's parents and argued that if "compensation" (*ganti rugi*) was to be the issue, then they had no grounds for complaint. They had not, he pointed out, contributed more than a paltry Rp2,000 toward la Di's education, although as prospective parents-in-law, they might have been expected to contribute as much as a parent or parent's sibling— there was certainly precedent for this among other kindreds of betrothed couples. If la Fia's parents and kin were willing to pay la Di's parents Rp200,000 in "compensation" for their expenses in educating la Di, then the marriage could go forward. If not, the money and sarongs offered as a *pahu kataho* ("a sign [literally, "face"] of restoration) were more than generous. This argument was probably a bluff, and at any rate it was unlikely they could muster such resources on short notice, but its cultural and moral logic was unassailable and ompu Camba is among the most persuasive men in Doro Ntika. They accepted the sarongs, money, and wood, and the betrothal was terminated in good order. Ompu Camba was justly proud of his accomplishment. "Ompu Siwe couldn't settle it, Haji Damai couldn't settle it, but I settled it!" he crowed.

As far as I can tell this ended the matter. By this I simply mean that I heard no more of the affair over the next three months. La Fia went on to seek another husband and there were no immediate or obvious sequelae in the relations between la Di's parents and la Fia's parents. Structurally, relations had been restored, although of course there was bound to be a residue of ill feeling and there is no predicting how those personal dispositions might resurface in future political or jural events. But in accepting the *pahu kataho* of sarongs, money, and wood, ina Fia's people were effectively putting an end to their claims and allowing ama Di's people to withdraw from the betrothal honorably and with their moral standing intact. The etiquette of dispute now forbade either side from publicly mentioning the matter again: they were not to carp about it before others. How had ompu Camba succeeded where others had failed?

I suspect that his success was partly due to the fact that in ompu Camba ama Di had finally found a representative of equal stature to ompu Siwe as a *doumatuatua* and *sando*. But ompu Camba's success rested primarily on the moral and cultural merits of his argument. By finding an unfulfilled obligation on the part of la Fia's parents, ompu Camba had effectively canceled out la Di's parents' refusal to fulfill their obligation to wed their son to la Fia. An onus of guilt still lay with la Di's parents; after all, it was they who were breaking their son's betrothal to a loyal fiancee, and they were doing so after many mutual expressions of sincerity in gifts of sarongs and labor exchanges. For this reason it was only right that a gesture of compensation be made. But it was critical that such a gesture be symbolic of a desire to restore relations between the two kindreds to one of amity and not compensation for labor. La Fia's parents were not entitled to a payment specifically in compensation for exchange labor; in this respect, at least, la Di's kin *had* fulfilled their side of the contract and had reciprocated labor with labor. The argument of la Di's kin—effectively that labor provided to "strengthen the asking" of a betrothal was what anthropologists might call a distinct "sphere of exchange" (Bohannan 1959), and reciprocable only with labor (as they had done)—was a convincing argument. The bulk of public opinion in Doro Ntika ultimately sided with la Di's kin over this issue as they did over the justice of the settlement as a whole.

Such was the settlement so far as its superficial, "legal," features are concerned. What is perhaps more interesting, however, is that it was not the failure of la Fia's parents to contribute to la Di's education that was decisive in shaping public opinion; it was their failure to educate their own daughter. "What did they expect?" was the way one of la Fia's kinsmen later put it. "They knew la Di was going to school and would be a policeman. Why didn't they send la Fia to school? If she weren't illiterate, if she didn't have 'village feet,' he would have married her. It's their own fault that he didn't." In this sense ompu Camba's argument about equity in restitution—that if la Fia's people wanted compensation for *sodi angi* labor they should have contributed to la Di's education—was valid on its own merits but also stood as a metaphor for their failure to educate la Fia.

It was this issue that was decisive, and it was decisive because it speaks to a value fundamental to the moral constitution of Dou Donggo society: the equivalence and complementarity of spouses. Dou Donggo married couples are regarded as a sort of unitary social entity, jointly held responsible for one another's obligations, jointly controlling mutually held economic resources, joined together even in their names (Just 1987a) as parents of their children and grandchildren. Dou Donggo feel spouses should be well matched and this is one of the reasons parents are anxious to betroth their children to the children of good friends, hoping that the qualities that have made *vai kata'ari* friends will make their children spouses who are also friends. Indeed, as the reader will have noticed, the imagery of friendship runs throughout the language of betrothal and marriage. In failing to educate their daughter, la Fia's parents had undermined the equality of the marital relationship, allowing an asymmetry between them to arise. Although it was a hard thing to say, la Di was right to reject la Fia as a wife: she was not his equal and her "village feet" would be an embarrassment to him. This makes sense to Dou Donggo because they see spouses as friends and friends as equals. Indeed, at one of the *mbolo* this issue was explicitly discussed and I was quoted the proverb: "*Made mpa rahi mpoka fu'u, made vei, iha kaso laluru mori*" ("When the husband dies, the tree is broken; when the wife dies the very utensils of life are destroyed"). Ompu Camba's argument was effective—and would have been effective before any panel of *doumatu-atua* or the headman—because it spoke to this fundamental moral value, one too deeply seated and ramified to obtain of an orthogenic transformation into determinate rules, but tremendously powerful for its very indeterminacy.

If this case was very much "about" the equivalency of spouses, it was about a good deal more, as well. As a successfully mediated dispute the case lacked the *Sturm und Drang* that sometimes accompany the public displays at *paresa*, but we may still look upon it as a social drama, as an instance of the society talking to itself and reinterpreting social rules in an attempt to accommodate a changing world. For one thing, the nature of contractual obligations between *vai kata'ari* was redefined in a new context. On the one hand, this case established the noncommutability of reciprocal labor: it was in large part symbolic, not commercial, and was to remain so. On the other hand, recognition was now given to the mutual obligation of *vai kata'ari* to help one another educate their children's prospective spouses and to help at a level expected of an elder sibling or parent's sibling: educational expenses were being raised to the level of agricultural labor in the reciprocity of marriage transactions. Furthermore, it was now clearly an obligation to see to it that a betrothed child be educated to the same level as his or her prospective spouse.

This case, particularly viewed in the context of a number of similar cases as everyone in the village did, also brought into question the entire notion of lengthy betrothals. A decision was being made here, in effect, between the value of parental control over their children's marriages and maintaining equality between spouses. The outcome of this case had implications strongly favoring the latter over the former. So long as everyone in the village was a farmer, social equality between spouses was rarely an issue. Only relative wealth was relevant and that was self-regulating through the institution of bridewealth. But with the advent of a new class of salaried, educated civil servants—schoolteachers, nurses, police—one could no longer be assured that two small children betrothed today will remain at a social par when they have reached the age of marriage. If equality between spouses is to be maintained, as this annulment suggests is the preferred course, then the institution of early betrothal, and perhaps of arranged marriages altogether, is far less tenable. Commenting on this case, a good friend remarked that he would not try to arrange a marriage for his younger brother, who like Ia Di had left Doro Ntika for teachers' college in Mataram. "I've told Simon to look for his own wife, even if that means marrying a foreigner from Mataram or what have you. Where am I going to find a Catholic girl of the proper level of education around here? Better he feel free to look for himself." This does not mean that Doro Ntika youngsters are opposed to the idea of arranged marriages per se or that notions of romantic love have replaced sound alliances: one of Simon's classmates in Mataram said he was content to marry a Doro Ntika girl, as his mother was hoping he would. "But," he told me, "I want her to send me the girl's picture and the particulars of her schooling before I agree." He certainly had no intention of being yoked to a wife with "village feet." While not globally decisive, if other cases are settled as this one, it should have a profound damping effect on early betrothals as well as generating important changes in the flow of money in marriage transactions.

The most common alternative to mediation is adjudication by a panel of *doumatuatua*. I have described this process in detail elsewhere (Just 1986a; 1990), so I shall concentrate on a few of the major characteristics of the *paresa*, particularly as they compare with mediated settlements. Like mediated settlements *paresa* involve the presentation of representations of events that in one way or another clarify moral issues, and may be "more true than what really happened." But there are important differences in the forum in which these representations are made and in the way in which they are judged.

From the very outset a *paresa* is a public event, attended not only by kinsmen of both accuser and accused as well as witnesses and neighbors. Especially if it is a notorious case there may also be a large group of onlooking bystanders, who have no fundamental interest in the case per se but who have been attracted by the furor that has been raised or simply out of a reflexive attempt to relieve the boredom of village life. Thus a *paresa*, unlike a mediated settlement, is in many ways played more directly to the public at large; everyone involved in a *paresa* is acutely aware of the audience and is playing to that audience. So it is that when on occasion tempers flare, participants may hurl verbal abuse, may lunge at one another, a questioner may physically threaten or even strike an accused, and from time to time there may be a good deal of posturing. But it is important to understand that while the displays of violence that sometimes accompany a *paresa* are in part real, it is also notable that virtually no one is ever hurt. Such violence may rather be considered as sincere displays of emotion, but displays that are primarily designed to convince the community audience of the actor's seriousness and sincerity.

In this public forum the accuser or a *doumatuatua* presents charges against the accused. Evidence may be presented, and testimony given— or, as sometimes happens, given and ignored—but in most instances the "facts" of the case are already known to the participants. In a sense the facts are almost incidental; as in mediated settlements what will be striven for in the course of the *paresa* is a version of the events that accurately represents the sociological matrix. By this I mean that in the creation of what I have called the "sociological truth" (Just 1986a) there is an opportunity for the status relationships between the disputants and the interests of the community to become part of the judicial calculus, not by modifying the judgment, as is usually the case in Western jurisprudence, but by modifying the account of events to be judged. More immediately than in a mediated dispute, in a *paresa* a consensus on a version of the "truth" emerges through a process of give and take in which accuser, accused, and presiding elders all engage in rhetorical claims and counter-claims. In cases where the dispute does not involve behavior manifestly threatening to the communal peace, or where it is in the communal interest to do so, this process may entail a negotiated settlement that neatly sidesteps the "facts" of the case altogether in favor of a compromise acceptable to all (if need be as a result of prolonged browbeating directed at any recalcitrant parties).

In other cases, however, it may be necessary to strongly censure a person's behavior. Here a second objective of the *paresa* comes into focus: the extraction of a confession. Because a *paresa* is played out before a public audience, it presents an opportunity to publicly chastise the offending party. Similarly, because Dou Donggo jurisprudence often works obliquely—by holding persons liable for crimes they did not commit but might have done, or by using such liability to chasten a person for some other crime (see Just 1990)—it is useful and important to extract a confession as an outward indication that the guilty party recognizes that he or she is guilty of something, even if only symbolically guilty of the crime at hand. A quick act of contrition and humility, as evidenced in a plea for forgiveness and an asseveration that the crime was one of passion or negligence, will almost always result in a rapid resolution of the conflict in which the accused is let off lightly. Conversely, an individual who is recalcitrant and truculent will only provoke the elders trying the case. In such cases the *doumatuatua* and village officials engaged in the *paresa* may take on an aggressive, hectoring style that combines questioning with prolonged admonitory harangues that occasionally fail to stop short of mild physical violence. In such circumstances the concerted diatribes of several of the community's most respected persons may continue for an hour or more, usually enough to reduce all but the most socially self-confident to quivering jelly. Such a procedure, referred to as *ka'a mpori, loa karente wadu* ("burning the grass to expose the rocks") becomes something of a morality play as well, as proverbs and cliches celebrating social values are recited to enlighten the victim and to edify the onlooking audience.[20]

Indeed, the extraction of a contrite confession may be the whole point of the *paresa*. In many instances what the plaintiff is seeking is more a redress of offended *amour propre* than restitution of damages or retribution for suffering; what is wanted is a public admission of the moral asymmetry between the disputants, for this is the real currency of Dou Donggo moral economy. Moreover, because Dou Donggo legal proceedings are primarily concerned with a restoration of appropriate social relationships, there is something of an algorithm at work; younger should defer to elder, those of bad reputation should defer to those of good reputation. A dispute between individuals of equivalent age and community moral standing will be far more likely to be settled on the merits of the case or be resolved by negotiation than a dispute between a young person and an elder or between a known troublemaker and a pillar of the community. In these latter kinds of dispute the disadvantaged party must overcome tremendous prejudice on the part of the *paresa* officiands, and in all but extraordinary cases—or in cases where someone has managed to bribe the headman—such a disadvantaged disputant stands little chance of a successful suit or of exculpation.

It is in this sense that I say, when a person goes on trial in Donggo, he or she goes on trial for his or her total moral character. As anyone who has lived in a small community is aware, a reputation once gained, for good or ill, is hard to shake. Long before a *paresa* begins, interpretations of the events surrounding a particular dispute will have been formed in the context of a general knowledge of each disputant's character. The likelihood that a particular interpretation—one bruited about in an *mbolo* or supplied by local gossip—will be accepted as true, is primarily determined by how well that interpretation conforms to the past behavior of the individuals concerned. It is in this way, too, that a version of events known to be at variance with the phenomenal facts of the case can be constructed and considered "more true than what really happened."

It may or may not be possible to settle a given dispute at a single *paresa*. If tempers flare too hotly or disputants are too inflexible it can become necessary to postpone the final determination of the issue, or to call in other elders who are more adept at either reaching a compromise solution or at extracting a confession. Such in particular may be the case if public opinion about the dispute is profoundly divided; time for such opinion to gel may be needed. The *doumatuatua* of a village have no coercive authority to enforce a judgment when they render one; the headman in theory at least represents the Indonesian government and is backed by the authority of the police, but in practice would only invoke this authority under extraordinary circumstance. A disputant may reject the judgment of a *paresa* and appeal to the hamlet captain or the village headman, if they had not already participated in settling the dispute. In all likelihood, however, the captain or the headman will support a decision of a panel of *doumatuatua* who have conducted a *paresa*. Judgments may artfully contrive to do justice without actually assessing guilt or they may call for restitution or the imposition of a fine. Since compliance with the judgment of a *paresa* is more or less voluntary, only a foolish *doumatuatua* would assess a judgment a disputant could not or would not accept, and *doumatuatua* are, by definition, far from foolish. Compliance may be grudging, but is almost always forthcoming. But the outcome of a *paresa*—particularly if it is a *paresa* whose principal object has been to establish the superiority of one disputant's moral standing over another's—is important well beyond the immediate repercussions of damages awarded or apologies coerced from an unwilling defendant. Just as an outcome in part derives from a disputant's moral character, so does it also become a constitutive part of that moral character.

Considering this, it would seem that Dou Donggo jurisprudence vests tremendous power and latitude in the *doumatuatua* who render the judgments on character that are the outcomes of *paresa*. Such is indeed the case. One of the principal characteristics of Dou Donggo conflict resolution is that justice as a process is very much bound up in the persons of the mediators and adjudicators who oversee its execution. In contrast to our own (idealized) system of jurisprudence, Dou Donggo conflict resolution seems considerably more arbitrary: the "truth," at least as a representation of phenomenal events, is not so much something to be discovered as it is a resource subject to considerable bending and twisting; liability is more than "strict," it seems to extend to crimes one "might have" committed, but did not; and where Western jurisprudence employs elaborate mechanisms for precluding prior knowledge of or personal relationships between litigants and judges/jurors, Dou Donggo law in large part depends on such knowledge and relationships. Yet for all of the flexibility and potential capriciousness that these differences imply, Dou Donggo dispute settlement seems to retain a sense of justice, a sense among the community at large that the outcomes of judicial proceedings are consonant with broadly held, if indeterminate, social norms. Indeed, the citizens of Doro Ntika are conspicuously more satisfied with the justice meted out by their *doumatuatua* than, for example, the citizens of Philadelphia are with the justice dispensed by their lawyers, judges, and juries.[21] What accounts for this?

In part, I think, it is because Dou Donggo notions of justice are quite tightly bound up in the very persons of the mediators and adjudicators who operate the system. The headman and his staff, and most particularly those *doumatuatua* who hold no formal office but nonetheless are the mainstays of village dispute settlement, are not set over the community, they are of the community, indeed, as framers and executors of its values they are the community. Second, they are more than the moral censors of the community: when they act as *sando* they are also guardians of the people's physical and spiritual health and when they act as marriage brokers (*panati*) they are an indispensable means of social reproduction. As such they are so tightly bound up in the daily life of a community already made intimate by the compactness of its physical geography—aware of every sick child, every youthful romance or illicit affair, the fruits of every harvest, the joyous pain of every birth, the grief of every death—that any system of dispute settlement depending on them would have to accommodate their knowledge of human hearts. Next, these people are selected for their role as mediators and adjudicators essentially on two criteria: their reputations for moral rectitude and wisdom, and a demonstration of pragmatic skill at dispute settlement and conflict resolution. As exemplars of the community's value system, something is right largely because they say it is. And the fact that they have past histories of successfully settling disputes confirms them in their (consensual) authority.

This authority is all the more powerful for its absence of enforceable sanctions, because it rests on the collective foundation of communal accord. Dou Donggo justice successfully allows its executors such extraordinary leeway because it and they are part of a cultural tautology, a system of beliefs, values, and institutions that are circular and self-defining: the *doumatuatua* are able to discriminate wisely in creating the "truth" of a dispute because disputes are framed in moral rather than phenomenal terms and because they are the ones who define the community's values. They are entitled to define them because day in and day out they do the hard spiritual work of healing and blessing, protecting and propitiating; it is they who guide, protect, and nurture the community. What completes the circle is that these individuals have the authority they have by consensus, so that someone not able to make the right discriminations would, in theory, never become a *doumatuatua*. Because their legitimacy, slowly acquired, is consensually conferred, recognized, and ratified (for it is usually the disputants themselves who call upon the *doumatuatua*) their decisions carry the weight of the entire community's authority. It is the diffuseness of the *doumatuatua*'s purview—combined with the incrementally gained and constantly reaffirmed legitimacy they hold—that makes Dou Donggo dispute settlement part of either a benignly autocratic gerontocracy or a participatory democracy. In either case, it seems to work to the satisfaction of its constituents.

MAKING REPRESENTATIONS COLLECTIVE: JUSTICE AND MORAL COMMUNITY

I do not claim that there are *no* cases in which *paresa* or other legal proceedings are not used to establish the phenomenal facts of a case, "to which determinate rules may then be applied to decide them" (Geertz 1983:170; cf. Hayden 1984:175). Even in the most closed community, knowledge of (and, more important, *perceptions* of) phenomenal events may differ and be at issue for mediators, adjudicators, and the watching audience constituted by the community alike. But it can be said (and this is more characteristic of Dou Donggo law) that in most situations the phenomenal events surrounding a conflict are not in question for anyone in the community, or a consensus about them may become sufficiently precise and widely held to permit evidentiary and other legal proceedings to become something more: opportunities to construct versions of reality that, if sometimes unfaithful to phenomenal truth, are nonetheless accurate representations of social and moral truths.

Implicit in this analysis has been the notion that Dou Donggo legal proceedings, even at the level of mediation, involve a complex process of constructing, interpreting, and weighing surface representations of deeper moral structures. Thus, for example, la Fia's kin absenting themselves from their house immediately after dark was a surface representation of their claim that la Di's kin were habitual breakers of promises, and thus a statement about the importance to the community of honoring promises. Similarly, ompu Camba's decisive representation about school fees was saying something about a more deeply held, if less determinate, moral statement about equality in relations between spouses.

In mediated disputes the construction of such representations takes place in the kind of *mbolo* described above, as does some of their interpretation and judgment. Most of the interpretation and judgment, especially in mediated cases, is invisible, taking place in part in the communal consensus of public opinion, and in part in the imagination of the disputants, as they calculate the likelihood of success of their arguments before a panel of *doumatuatua* or the headman should the case go to litigation. Here, incidentally, lies one of the principal differences between mediated and adjudicated disputes: both mediated and adjudicated disputes rely on the narrativity of constructed "truths" to represent the moral, social issues at hand, but the authority to select among alternative narratives and to impose an interpretation of the narrative's meaning is differentially distributed. In mediated disputes the negotiators help to select narrative representations and attempt to impose specific interpretations on one another and on the general public. In adjudicated disputes, however, the *doumatuatua* who hear the case assume a more definitive authority to interpret, although they, too, must reflect as well as shape general public opinion about the case.

It is hard to overstate the importance of the plea to public opinion in both mediation and adjudication. At each of the transformational stages—from superficial events to the deep structure of moral imperatives and from moral imperatives to a constructed representation of those imperatives in a reformulated account—the ultimate audience is a general communal one, rather than a specialized institutional one. The *dou-*

matuatua who mediate and adjudicate, who help with the formulation of these representations, choose among alternative representations and finally interpret their meaning through their judgments and settlements, are in an important sense in a dialogue with the community at large, both shaping and reflecting public opinion. And so are disputants, for even when this dialogue is the mute dialogue of imagination, everyone is aware that for the individual any given dispute is but one moral event in a lifetime to be spent in the community and that for the community any given dispute is but one of many in the communal moral landscape. The consequences of a given dispute for the moral standing of individuals, calculated through reputation, reach far beyond its outcome. And the representations themselves, in receiving public approbation, become part of the community's expression of its moral universe, and allow for its dynamic response to changing circumstances.

Dou Donggo disputes and their resolutions offer windows on the dynamics of a society's moral calculus: its creation, maintenance, and alteration. Cases like the one described here are an opportunity to examine the way representations can become collective and the way that collective representations are made concrete in the resolution of disputes, serving as a standard against which outcomes may be judged and a sense of justice achieved.

NOTES

1. The study of plural legal institutions and their interrelationships is one of the most active research fronts in the anthropology of law today. Readers interested in this topic are referred to Tanner 1970; von Benda-Beckmann 1984; Hooker 1975; Kludze 1983; Slaats and Portier 1986; and the various articles in the *Journal of Legal Pluralism*.

2. I am using these three terms in their more or less conventional senses. "Mediation" may be seen as the resolution of a conflict through the good offices of one or more intermediaries, often personally involved in the case, who carry back and forth the representations of both parties to the dispute. The artful presentation of such representations often provides an opportunity for negotiation and compromise. "Arbitration" refers to the resolution of a conflict by a third (presumably neutral) party agreed upon by the disputants to hear out the representations of disputants, and whose proposed solutions may then be automatically accepted or may become the subject for further negotiation, depending on the terms of the arbitration. By "adjudication" I mean the resolution of a conflict by individuals in whom is vested a socially and culturally legitimated authority to review disputes and accusations of misbehavior according to established procedures and to render definitive decisions backed by legitimated sanctions. As will be seen, Dou Donggo legal processes partake of all three kinds of conflict resolution, and the distinctions among mediation, arbitration, and adjudication become blurred and of no great analytical utility. At least so far as

the Dou Donggo are concerned, it would be best to look upon these three means of resolving conflict as a gradual cline.

3. Primary research among the Dou Donggo was conducted between 1981 and 1983 with the assistance of National Service Research Award #5 F31 MH8516 from the National Institute of Mental Health and with the permission and assistance of the Lembaga Ilmu Pengetahuan Indonesia. A detailed description of Dou Donggo ethnicity and social organization is provided in Just 1986b. Out of respect for the privacy of its inhabitants, "Doro Ntika" is a pseudonym; the names of people mentioned have also been changed. I would like to acknowledge with gratitude the hospitality and cooperation of the people of Doro Ntika and the assistance and companionship of my wife, Anne W. Just, who shared with me two years of life in Doro Ntika.

4. This is one of the most important ways in which Dou Donggo society differs from lowland Dou Mbojo society. The latter is featured by an elaborate hierarchy of aristocrats, commoners, and, formerly, slaves, none of which is found in Donggo.

5. That groups of informally constituted and consensually ratified elders form a sort of shadowy, parallel government is not at all unusual in Indonesian villages. See Wessing (1987:163) for a recent description of Sundanese *sesepuh*.

6. The circumstances under which a person becomes involved—"has standing" as it were—in a particular case are highly variable, and will be discussed in greater detail below.

7. I say "spiritual courage" because a *sando* must have truck with spirits who are inherently unpredictable and dangerous.

8. I use the term not in its theological or Weberian sense, but in the more conventional sense of a powerfully persuasive personality.

9. The Batak of Sumatra and the Buginese of South Sulawesi are generally regarded as among the more coarse (*kasar*) of Indonesian ethnic groups. I have heard Indonesian friends compare the refined, restrained Javanese with the coarser more belligerent Buginese by pointing to the different ways the two groups traditionally wear their daggers (*kris*): Buginese wear their daggers tucked into the waistband at the front of the sarong, while Javanese wear theirs at the back. The Buginese are quick to anger and quick to make amends, and just so it is easy to draw the dagger, but easy to put it back in its sheath. The Javanese can unsheathe his dagger only with difficulty and only with difficulty can it be returned to its sheath. Just so is a Javanese slow to anger, but once angered, he will not rest until he has killed you.

10. Dou Mbojo use both "Dou Donggo" and "Dou Manggarai" (the people of West Flores, once under Bimanese suzerainty) as pejoratives.

11. A *sando*, for example, may "*Kidi kai rahasia Ruma*" ("make powerful godly secrets") for the benefit of his patients; but he may also sorcerize his enemies, prey on patients by alternately sickening and curing them, or blackmail them by threatening to sorcerize them if they do not honor his requests. So also in the social world of living human beings, people are regarded as inclined to greed, selfishness, and violence.

12. This point of view is implicit in the " 'might have' principle" of Dou

Donggo jurisprudence described elsewhere (Just 1986a, 1990). In effect, the principle holds that an individual is as accountable for the consequences that might have followed from an action as he or she is for what actually did follow from that action. This suggests a jurisprudential prejudice holding all human behavior to be potentially dangerous and in need of restraint.

13. Indeed, since a person embroiled in a conflict is judged predominantly on the basis of a total moral character, in which case an accumulating reputation for uncivil behavior can be quite injurious, it seems only fair that praise be given when and where it can be most advantageous, that is, so as to add positively to a person's moral standing.

14. These words, like most of the technical terminology in Dou Donggo dispute settlement, appear to be borrowed from the Malay or Indonesian (*masalah* and *perkara*). Those terms, in turn, are borrowings respectively from Arabic and Sanskrit (Winstedt 1965). The precise relationship of Dou Donggo jurisprudence to lowland and Islamic legal traditions is something that has yet to be worked out, although it promises to be a fascinating subject.

15. One might note here that the process of *kataho eli ro nggahi* is something that *doumatuatua* who are *sando* can accomplish through ritual means as well as through legal proceedings (Just 1986b:155).

16. A note on names (see also Just 1987a). Dou Donggo employ a two-generation system of teknonymy in which the particle *la* usually precedes the given name of a child or young adult; hence la Di. His father and mother have taken his name teknonymously and are ama Di and ina Di, respectively. His grandfather and grandmother might be called ompu Di and va'i Di, respectively. Abu la Rudi, another character in this story, uses the Arabic for father, *abu*, as a teknonym connector because he is a haji; his wife takes the Arabic *umi*.

17. "Truck jumping," an exercise in which police cadets rapidly deploy from the back of a moving truck, seems to be the make-or-break test of the academy. Apparently, it is not uncommon for some cadets to break their legs in the attempt and for others to shame themselves by refusing. Truck jumping seems to have made a great impression on la Di and on his father, who reads la Di's letters describing his truck-jumping exploits.

18. At the time of the dispute the rupiah was exchanged at a rate of about Rp980 to US$1. While $40 does not seem like much, it should be recalled again that Doro Ntika has a cash-poor economy. More to the point, a day's wages for agricultural labor was about Rp1,500.

19. This reluctance to refuse requests has its darker side, too. Dou Donggo are afraid that an annoyed requester, especially an old one, may turn out to be a sorcerer who takes out his chagrin on a miserly host.

20. One is reminded of the "self-criticism" sessions of the Chinese Cultural Revolution, another setting in which only a rapid and humble confession to all accusations could secure light punishment.

21. I make this statement mostly on the negative evidence (which of course is no evidence at all) that in my experience Dou Donggo simply do not complain much about the outcomes of *paresa*. To me, satisfaction with juridical outcomes is the best (if naive) measure of justice. I would also point out that Dou Donggo

have the option of access to an alternative system of justice, provided by the
state, yet they conspicuously avoid it.

REFERENCES

Benda-Beckman, Keebet von. 1984. *The Broken Staircase to Consensus: Village
Justice and State Courts in Minangkabau.* Drodrecht: Foris.
Benedict, Ruth. 1946. *The Chrysanthemum and the Sword: Patterns of Japanese Cul-
ture.* New York: Meridian.
Bohannan, Paul J. 1959. The Impact of Money on an African Subsistence Econ-
omy. *Journal of Economic History* 19:491–503.
Bruner, Edward M. 1974. The Expression of Ethnicity in Indonesia. In *Urban
Ethnicity,* ed. Abner Cohen. ASA Monographs No. 12. London: Tavistock.
Geertz, Clifford. 1983. Local Knowledge: Fact and Law in Comparative Per-
spective. In *Local Knowledge: Further Essays in Interpretive Anthropology.* New
York: Basic.
Geertz, Hildred. 1974. The Vocabulary of Emotion: A Study of Javanese So-
cialization Processes. In *Culture and Personality: Contemporary Readings,* ed.
R. A. Levine. Chicago: Aldine.
Hayden, Robert M. 1984. Rules, Processes, and Interpretations: Geertz, Com-
aroff, and Roberts. *American Bar Foundation Journal* 9:469–78.
Hooker, M. B. 1975. *Legal Pluralism: An Introduction to Colonial and Neo-colonial
Laws.* London: Oxford University Press.
Just, Peter. 1986a. Let the Evidence Fit the Crime: Evidence, Law, and the
"Sociological Truth" among the Dou Donggo. *American Ethnologist* 13:43–
61.
———. 1986b. Dou Donggo Social Organization: Ideology, Structure, and Action
in an Indonesian Society. Ph.D. diss., Department of Anthropology, University of Pennsylvania. Ann Arbor: University Microfilms International.
———. 1987a. Bimanese Personal Names: The View from Bima Town and
Donggo. *Ethnology* 26:313–28.
———. 1987b. Recent Structural Change in Dou Donggo Society. Paper pre-
sented at the Conference of the Southeast Asia Summer Studies Institute,
De Kalb, 1987.
———. 1990. Dead Goats and Broken Betrothals: Liability and Equity in Dou
Donggo Law. *American Ethnologist* 17:75–90.
Kludze, A. K. 1983. The Effects of the Interaction Between State Law and
Customary Law in Ghana. Paper presented at the Symposium on Folk
Law and Legal Pluralism, XIth Congress of the International Union of
Anthropological and Ethnological Sciences, Vancouver, Canada.
Slaats, Herman, and Karen Portier. 1986. Legal Plurality and the Transfor-
mation of Normative Concepts in the Process of Litigation in Karo Batak
Society. In *Anthropology of Law in the Netherlands,* eds. Keebet von Benda-
Beckman and Fons Strijbosch. Drodrecht: Foris.
Tanner, Nancy. 1970. Disputing and the Genesis of Legal Principles: Examples
from Minangkabau. *Southwestern Journal of Anthropology* 26:375–401.

Wessing, Robert. 1987. Electing a Lurah in West Java, Indonesia: Stability and Change. *Ethnology* 26:165–78.

Winstedt, Sir Richard. 1965. *An Unabridged Malay-English Dictionary*. Kuala Lampur: Marcian and Sons.

7

Surprised by Common Sense: Local Understandings and the Management of Conflict on Tobi, Republic of Belau

Peter W. Black

Conflict management is only possible in connection with conflict analysis.[1] This analysis may be an explicit, conscious, project; if not, it will be undertaken unconsciously and on the basis of unexamined assumptions. But, willy nilly, an analysis will be made. Just as the participants in a conflict must make it sensible to themselves, so must anyone else who is interested in it. Thus, every outsider involved with the dispute (whether researcher, observer, mediator, facilitator, arbitrator, or judge) carries out some kind of analysis. The question then arises: What prerequisites, if any, exist for a successful third party analysis of conflict? It seems to me that an awareness of the possibility of fundamental differences in deep cultural presuppositions is likely to yield productive understandings. This response raises another, methodological, question: How can the analyst discover the cultural assumptions about being and action at work in a given conflict?

One answer to this question takes advantage of the capacity for introspection and self-awareness that is as much a feature of the humanity that the analyst shares with the parties as is the need to constitute social reality through cultural means. Much can be learned about both sets of cultural presuppositions in use (the analyst's and the parties') if the analyst remains as alert to his or her own internal world as to the actions and statements of the parties. For when the assumptions about being and behavior with which the analyst is interpreting actions or statements are radically different from those that the parties are using in constituting those statements and behaviors, the analyst is bound to be *surprised* at some point in the proceedings. It is this surprise that is the main methodological resource available to the analyst. If it is attended to, that is, if the analyst investigates this surprise, much can be learned.

The surprise that occurs when one's fundamental assumptions are violated results from the predictive, interpretive, or explanatory failure of those assumptions. In other words, the analyst finds that people are saying and/or doing surprising things, things that are unexpected, things that the analyst had not predicted, things that initially at least make no sense. The effort to make sense of those statements or behaviors provides the opportunity to recognize and rethink one's own assumptions and to "question" the parties about theirs through the use of methods developed in the social sciences.

It is very easy, however, to waste such an opportunity. This happens when one's own assumptions remain unexamined and the surprising statements or behaviors of others are "explained" by the kind of ratiocination that does away with all observed difference by forcing it onto a procrustean theoretical or metatheoretical framework. Procrustes, it will be remembered, was the mythical Greek robber who mutilated his guests/victims by chopping off any of their limbs that were too large to fit in the bed he offered them for the night. As an analytic methodology in the explanation of difference, such a maneuver leaves unexamined the assumptions out of which that "bed" (the analyst's theoretical framework) is constructed. It produces statements that are notable at times for the ingenuity with which they translate the seemingly inexplicable into an expression of the analyst's own theory of being and action. Such statements, though, *explain away* surprising variance as often as they explicate it. In this chapter I demonstrate that a less "imperial" analytic maneuver, one that features an inspection of both sets of differing assumptions, can lead to a deeper level of understanding. To do so I detail the dramatic events surrounding a suspected murder attempt on the remote Micronesian island of Tobi.

In 1973 someone apparently attempted to kill the island's nurse. As a result of that event the islanders held a meeting in which an effort was made to identify the guilty party. Despite this meeting it remained unclear whether anyone did learn the identity of the guilty party, or even if there had been an attempted murder at all. Regardless of its "investigative" success or failure, however, in the estimation of the Tobians the meeting worked very well. From my point of view, too, the meeting was far from a waste; I learned much of value. This chapter describes that discovery process; it is part of a more general argument on behalf of a culturally informed perspective in conflict analysis and resolution.

BACKGROUND

Tobi is a small coral island with a total land area of slightly less than one quarter of a square mile. It lies in the extreme southwestern corner of the emerging Republic of Belau in what was American-administered Micronesia. Now a state in the Republic, when these events occurred Tobi formed a municipality within Palau District of the United States Trust Territory of the Pacific and, as such, was administered from Koror, district capital and historic center of Palauan affairs, four hundred miles away. Although closely linked to Palau by political, economic, and (to a lesser extent) social ties, in language and culture Tobians displayed much greater similarity to the inhabitants of the numerous low islands east of Palau than they did to the people of Palau proper. At the time of my studies in the late 1960s and early 1970s there were usually fifty to sixty people residing on the island and another forty to fifty of their fellows living in Eang, the Tobian settlement in Koror.

Political power on the island was split between the traditional chief (who was not present during the events discussed here) and the elected magistrate who was responsible for most government programs and for the collection of taxes. The magistrate's position was created by the Trust Territory government in the 1950s, and the power of the magistrate, as opposed to that of the traditional chief, was usually limited to his official government duties.

Tobi was visited three or four times a year by a government-chartered ship from Koror. This ship was the only way to travel to or from the island. Along with Tobian passengers, it carried representatives of most departments of the District Government, a priest from the Catholic mission in Koror, and an agent or two from a commercial company. During the four or five hours the ship was at the island the government officials attempted to carry out their mandated duties, the priest ministered to this remotest segment of his far-flung flock (all Tobians have been Roman Catholics since their conversion from their indigenous religion in the 1930s), and the commercial agents bought copra from the Tobians and sold them tobacco, rice, kerosene, and other goods not produced locally. Notwithstanding these imports, the Tobian economy was still largely self-sufficient in all essentials, and as such was characterized by relations of generalized reciprocity and a sexual division of labor.

Men produced foodstuffs from the ocean and women grew taro and other crops in their gardens. Social life centered around the household kitchens of married couples where the products of male and female labor were combined into meals to which people living in households without active kitchens were drawn. These people contributed the fruits of their own activities to those meals and constituted a kind of ready-made clique for the owners of the kitchen. Six exogamous, matrilineal clans divided the population while extensive agnatic and affinal ties wove people together.

The field trip was the sole contact the islanders had with the mission, the traders, and all but two of the government departments. These two exceptions were the Education Department, which had hired and trained a Tobian as the principal and sole teacher of Tobi's elementary school, and the Department of Public Health, which staffed Tobi's dispensary with a nurse, a native Micronesian. This nurse, a part-Tobian from one of Palau's other outer islands, was the man someone may have tried to kill.

Word of this event was shocking and frightening to everyone who heard it, including me, but I was less surprised when it happened, I think, than I would have been a few months earlier. For by then I had been associated with the Tobians for some time and had come to be aware of the strong currents of hostility and fear that flowed below the pleasant surface of life on the island.

CONFLICT AND CONFLICT MANAGEMENT

At the time of the attack, I had been living on Tobi for six months while I carried out general ethnographic research. Five years earlier I had lived for a year on the island as a Peace Corps Volunteer and I had also spent a total of six months with Tobians in Koror. By now the Tobians' ability to sustain a harmonious and cooperative tone in their social life had become a matter of some interest to me. The longer I spent with Tobians, the more I understood the depth and extent of the many interest disputes that divided them.[2] The fact that these disputes did not disrupt the cooperative relations upon which social life was built—each person had to, could, and did draw on the labor of everyone else, including his or her worst enemy—was impressive. Further, as I learned of the many antipathies and deep hostilities that characterized the islanders' feelings for one another, I was impressed by the unfailing cheerfulness with which people interacted and the skill with which they used humor and soft words to defuse tense situations. Thus, by the time of the events described here, conflict and conflict-related phenomena had become the main focus of my work. I had collected a large number of stories of past conflicts and had begun to map the dense web of disputes and conflicts to which every Tobian was party.

On Tobi, disputes were generally acknowledged and managed in an extremely indirect fashion. The expression of overt conflict, or even its direct acknowledgment, was resisted because of the Tobian truism that to do so would bring on disaster by endangering the essential web of relationships of mutual support (particularly in the exchange of labor and food) which bound everyone to everyone else. Tobian techniques of conflict management, as might be expected in light of the foregoing, also tended to be very inexplicit and to operate in rather indirect and subtle ways.

Numerous multigenerational disputes over land, political office, and marriage resulted in a network of unacknowledged but universally known alliances and oppositions. The long-term nature of these interest disputes was a result of the lack of finality accorded to outcomes—no victory was ever complete, no defeat ever final. The small size of the population meant that the demographic balance between resource-holding groups (primarily extended families) changed rapidly from one generation to the next. These changing fortunes often led to the inability of victorious families to retain their prizes and the ability of their opponents to reverse their parents' or grandparents' losses. Thus, long-term strategies played a large role in these disputes. This accorded well with a general Tobian attitude toward social life that puts high value on the use of well-thought-out plans for the achievement of goals both large and small. Their "strategic orientation" also helped to explain the characteristic indirection and lack of finality in almost every dimension of the social organization of conflict.

I first glimpsed this culturally constituted stance toward conflict in the way in which the game of checkers had been culturally transformed. In its Tobian version, the game was essentially the competitive display of a comprehensive strategy that, used by a local master, was unbeatable. When two such masters played, the outcome was always a draw unless one of them made an error. When a master played a novice, the novice always lost. The challenge to the novice was to learn the strategy. This was difficult because the only people who could accept direct tuition without losing respect were small children. Unless the novice was a child, therefore, he òr she had to try to deduce the strategy through quick-witted observation. This could take some time; the masters seemed to take as much or even more pride in their ability to keep the strategy secret through various types of mystification as they did in its actual use.

If the master's opponent was a small child, the situation was quite different. In such a case, after the four or five moves necessary to capture all the child's pieces, the master would explain why each of the child's moves was a mistake. The strategy was never unveiled directly, but the child was offered this instruction as part of the generalized role relationship of child to adult. While it is interesting to note that these children had yet to develop the cognitive capacity to master the strategy revealed in this fashion, another feature of this interaction disclosed much more about Tobian attitudes toward contests and disputes. Masters did not at all "play down" to children in the way that would be appropriate in many American contexts.

In the Tobian view of things there was no need to "protect" a child in a competitive game with an adult; such losses were not thought to be painful. This surprising realization led to one of the earliest insights I developed about Tobian interest disputes: Losses (and wins) were thought to be the consequences of the operation of long-term strategies much more than they were thought to be emotionally laden revelations of, or judgments upon, some inner self. The latter stance reflects the unexamined American assumptions about persons, disputes, and competitive games which I brought with me to the island.

This is not to say that Tobians did not, on occasion, feel defeat and victory intensely, but this emotional response was not given the cultural validation that it receives in many other, more individualistic, societies. It was especially neglected vis-à-vis that network of covert multigenerational interest disputes that united all Tobians at the same time it separated them.

Other contests revealed other dimensions of Tobian attitudes toward conflict—Tobian ethnoconflict knowledge. For example, a tendency to shortcut competition when it became clear who the winner would be can be seen in both the tendency of runners to drop out of any foot race once a clear leader emerged as well as in the way in which cock fights were always terminated as soon as one of the roosters (much cossetted pets of teen-aged boys) seemed to dominate the other—almost always before any blood was drawn.[3]

In virtually every Tobian context great emphasis was placed on the maintenance of positive relations with others, no matter what the provocation. And, while a detached cultural stance, one that minimized the emotional component of interest disputes, fit well with this emphasis, it should not be thought that these disputes were, in fact, affect-free. Furthermore, the flow of day-to-day life also gave rise to strong passions, many of them negative.

Marital difficulties, sibling rivalry, intergenerational and cross-gender ambivalence, and the more occasional frictions of everyday life all were evident both to me and to the Tobians. The failure of these passions to penetrate everyday life was for the Tobians one of the great achievements of their collective life. By the time of the attempted murder I had ceased to explain it away as evidence of mass hypocrisy (as my unexamined, taken-for-granted assumptions had led me to); it had become instead an important research problem. As I investigated it I came to believe that this ability of individuals who detested one another (by their own and others' accounts) to cooperate, not only in the day-to-day labor and resource sharing upon which subsistence depended, but also in the creation of a general atmosphere of great good humor and what seemed to be genuine good will, was in fact the major indigenous technique for conflict management.

At the same time, I was learning to see past the easy assumption that the functional requirement of mutual labor exchange, together with the lack of permanent factions due to the ways in which disputes cross-cut each other, somehow "explained" that ability. Instead, I was beginning to understand that this ability rested on a complex combination of a number of factors. These included: (1) the displacement of interpersonal anxiety and hostility onto evil ghosts (Spiro 1952); (2) a continuous use of the all-encompassing gossip network for indirect confrontation and reconciliation; (3) a constant ritual reaffirmation of the sacred character of the community's collective life through twice daily religious services attended by the entire populace; (4) a political system in which the major, indeed almost the sole, responsibility of the chief was to monitor the flow of daily life and to recall everyone's attention to the collective values of nonaggression and cheerful cooperation when they seemed threatened by the imminent surfacing of conflict; (5) the use of recreational and ritual contexts (dances especially) to symbolize enduring structural tensions and the drastic consequences that would flow from their "real world" expression; (6) a complex "conflict vocabulary" that mapped the local typology of disputes and the escalation and management of overt conflict with great vividness; and (7) a large body of customary rules for the minimization of direct competition, the prevention of face-to-face confrontation, and, when all else failed, the rapid defusing and deescalation of overt conflict.

What I had yet to detect at this stage, however, was the underlying cultural logic that made all the various elements of this combination sensible for the Tobians. The meeting that followed the attempted murder provided the occasion for an episode that surprised me into that knowledge.

It is interesting to note that even without "deep" knowledge of the underlying cultural structure, I was increasingly integrated into everyday life on the island. As one of the island's able-bodied men, I took part in many of its collective activities—not just as an observer (with camera and notebook always at hand), but as a participant. My ability to speak a fluent (if still at times inadequate) Tobian helped in this as did the fact that one of the island's main families had become my "family away from my family." The recent departure of my wife and infant son had increased dramatically the amount of time I spent with my Tobian hosts and the depth of my involvement in their activities.

As I gradually grew more proficient at such male skills as roof thatching, canoe handling, and fishing, I played an ever more active role in the domestic economy of the family with whom I lived. Of course, I never achieved the kind of mastery of these activities that a lifetime of practice gave the other men. One thing I never did learn to do was to climb coconut trees. This meant that I was unable to collect the sap used in making coconut toddy. Toddy manufacture required that a man climb twice a day up into the crown of a specially chosen coconut tree to tap its sap. This sap could then either be given to the very old or the very young as a kind of "health food," or fermented into a powerful alcoholic drink and made the occasion for a party. Along with turtle hunting, tuna fishing, and other male pursuits, toddy production was one of the major vehicles for the subtle and unexpressed but, nevertheless, very real competition between men. As a non-toddy maker I had no part in that aspect of this competition. On the other hand, I was considered to be an expert in all things pertaining to the modern world, the mastery of which was another arena for male competition. Given the high value then placed on all things American by the Tobians, this meant that I was continually being asked to give advice on the best ways to deal with that world and its increasing demands on the island. Thus, during the events surrounding the attempted murder I was asked over and over again if there was some special American detective technique that could be used.

THE "CRIME"

Early one evening the nurse's teen-aged son came running over to the house where some friends and I were sitting. Gasping and out of breath, he announced that his father had fallen from his toddy tree. He had been climbing in it when a frond broke. Bruised and shaken he had managed to drag himself back to the dispensary. When he got there he told his son what had happened and that when he had examined the broken frond he could see that it had been partially severed by a knife.

We immediately rushed to the dispensary where the nurse and his family lived. Many of the other adults and children on the island had already arrived and during the next few minutes everyone else appeared. There was a great deal of nervousness as the implications of what had happened became clear. People wondered if someone had gone crazy or if an evil ghost had decided to try to claim a human life. We wondered if others besides the nurse were potential victims and if the culprit would strike again. It was then that a story of an earlier case of attempted murder began to be told and retold. It had happened some thirty years earlier, shortly after the island's mass conversion to Christianity. Like the present case it involved an attack by an unknown person. As the story was repeated, first by the elders and then by everyone else, it assumed the status of a kind of template for action. Therefore, it is necessary to recount it here.

An Attempted Poisoning

As the story was told, a Tobian, suspecting from its appearance that something was wrong with the toddy that he had just collected, tested the sap on his dog, which promptly convulsed and died. Deciding that someone had tried to poison him, the intended victim appealed for help to Perfecto, the powerful, if informal, leader of the 150 people then living on Tobi. Since they were now Christians, the old technique for dealing with such a situation (which relied on the use of spirits to publicly identify the culprit) was no longer available.

At the close of communal prayers later that same morning Perfecto asked the congregation to wait on the steps of the church before going home for breakfast. He told them that something serious had happened. All but one of the people did as he asked and soon a meeting was underway to find the person who had put poison in the collecting cup. The one person who did not participate in the meeting was the old brother of the absent chief who, by prearrangement with Perfecto, had remained hidden inside the church where he could secretly observe the meeting. Perfecto began the meeting by telling the assembled crowd what had happened. He then demanded of each man in turn: "Did you try to kill him?" Each man in turn denied any guilt. But when one man, the husband of the intended victim's lover, was asked the question, he betrayed his guilt to the chief's brother, his intended victim, and the men sitting on either side of him by a nearly imperceptible trembling, by a fractional widening of his eyes, by a darkening of his lips, and by a lightening of his complexion. To these men, and perhaps to others, his denial rang hollow in the face of such obvious signs of fear.

Having completed his questioning of each man, Perfecto, much to the surprise of his audience, called the chief's brother out from the church. "Now do you know who did it?" Perfecto asked. "I know!" the old man answered with a shout that caused the culprit to jump. "Good," replied Perfecto, "this meeting is over, you can all go eat now." Everyone went home to breakfast. The man who had found the poison in his cup said nothing at the time but that night he went secretly to the house of his lover's husband and asked if he had tried to kill him. The culprit admitted his guilt, apologized, and presented his intended victim with some of the gifts that symbolize contrition—tobacco, cloth, and tumeric. Perhaps the intended victim did not believe that he was out of danger even after this customary presentation that, as was appropriate, he reciprocated on the following day. At any rate, he avoided future relations with the man who attempted to kill him by taking the next ship to Koror never to return.

This story (as well as the description of the pre-Christian technique) was repeated constantly during the course of the evening following the nurse's fall from his toddy tree. Initially, the story had been known only to the oldest people on the island. As the evening wore on, it became part of the vast body of public knowledge that all Tobians shared and used in the construction of daily life. Many people did not sleep well that night; several groups stayed awake until dawn speculating and telling stories.

Early the next morning the magistrate, the school teacher, and I (at the magistrate's request) went to investigate. The Tobians pointed out that the frond indeed seemed to have been partially severed, apparently with a sharp knife. Furthermore, the other fronds leading up into the tree as well as those in the crown thirty feet above the ground, where the nurse always sat while collecting his toddy, were also partially cut through. Several conclusions were drawn. We thought that the nurse had been lucky that the lowest of the severed fronds had given way on him. His injuries (a bruised shoulder and a sandy ear) would have been much more severe if he had fallen the thirty feet from the top of the tree and not merely the ten feet from the frond that had given way on him. We agreed that he was lucky that the previous afternoon's spring tide had cleared the beach under his tree of the stones and driftwood that usually littered it. We noted, however, that the culprit was also lucky because that same high tide had eliminated his tracks. Since everyone knows everyone else's footprints, whoever had done this would not have remained unknown but for that tide. The edges of the cut fronds seemed to indicate that a very sharp knife had been used. This led to the belief that the culprit was a man because women do not possess such knives.

The magistrate told us that we would have a meeting to find out who had tried to commit the murder as soon as we had eaten our breakfast and he had finished with his morning chores. So at 9:30 that morning we found ourselves outside the church waiting for everyone to arrive and the meeting to get underway. While we waited the gathering crowd discussed the attempt on the nurse's life. The old people discussed the ways that such situations had been dealt with in the past and, even though they had heard this many times in the hours that had passed since the crime, the young people listened attentively and asked many questions. People also wondered if I knew any special American techniques for discovering the identity of the person who had tried to kill the nurse.

They were disappointed when I had nothing to offer. Several people intimated that as Tobians they did have a technique and that I would be impressed by it. They also made sure that I knew how to tell if someone was guilty. They advised me to look for the same signs of fear that were recounted in the story of the attempted poisoning: darkened lips, widened eyes, lightened complexion, and trembling. They also took delight in quietly asking me, just as they asked one another, if I had any idea who had done it. I replied that I did not (which was true) and listened carefully to the tentatively offered suggestions people were willing to give me. Many such conversations had been held since the news of the nurse's fall had spread. At last the magistrate arrived at the church and the meeting began.

THE MEETING

As soon as he was sure that everyone except the nurse (who was said to be too sore to attend) was present, the magistrate began. He asked the men to form a circle and requested that the women sit apart. Three times he carefully and with exhaustive detail described the events that had led up to the meeting. After each recital he paused, looked around, and made a comment to the effect that it was "bad" to have such a thing occur. He pointed to the fact that there were outsiders on the island (the nurse, his son, and me) and to the possibility that after such an event no other nurse would accept an assignment on Tobi. During this part of the proceedings, the magistrate had what appeared to be the undivided attention of the whole population, including the toddlers and women. He next asked the women if they had witnessed anything the day before that could shed any light on the matter. One by one, the women related what they had been doing the previous afternoon. None of them had seen anything suspicious.

The magistrate then mentioned the fact that only someone with a sharp knife could have sliced the fronds. He turned to the men and asked about some of the teen-aged boys—whom they had been playing with the day before and what time they had come home. As they answered these questions about their dependents (who were all sitting in the men's circle watching and listening), the men started to give details about their own activities during the time in question. None of them had seen anything and all, in effect, denied that they were anywhere near the tree during the time it must have been cut. I took part by recounting where I had been during that time.

The magistrate next let it be known that he had not yet reported the matter to the police and would prefer not to do so. Several of the old women heatedly disagreed with this and he gave way, saying that it would be reported and that he would request that a policeman be sent down on the next ship to investigate. His agreement was only reluctantly given because he was worried that he would have to go to Koror if any court proceedings developed from the case. The old women wanted it reported so that a graphic lesson would be taught to all potential killers. During these discussions, people asked my opinion of the situation and I mostly echoed the magistrate's words. I also took extensive notes of conversations, interactions, and behaviors.

Throughout the meeting, the magistrate used a variety of techniques to alternate periods of focused excitement with periods of relaxed confusion. Following each of the periods of intense discussion and questioning he rather obviously loosened the meeting's atmosphere by ostentatiously rolling a cigarette or asking someone to roll one for him, picking up and tickling one of the small children darting in and out of the group, or some other maneuver that indicated a kind of "time out." Then after a few moments in which people relaxed and discussion began to fragment and go off in various directions, he refocused attention on the issue at hand and began to increase the tension. There were three of these cycles, and each one was more intense than the last.

Each time he called attention back to the meeting's topic he emphatically stated how bad it was that something like this had happened and then went on to make statements about how the fact that there were only a few people on the island meant that we all had to help one another and about how the fact that there was neither policeman nor court meant that we had to take care of our own problems. He also repeatedly pointed out how hard life would be without a nurse on the island. These sermon-like speeches were aimed at the middle of the circle in which the men were sitting; the magistrate seemed to be taking pains to avoid the appearance that his remarks were addressed to anyone in particular.

I sat next to the nurse's son at the meeting. As the discussion about whether the police should be brought in was being resolved, he leaned over and asked if I had found the culprit. When I responded by asking if *he* had any idea, he furtively nodded toward one of the older men who was sitting by himself. This man's face was immobile, his features carefully arranged in the noncommittal expression worn by all the men in the moments when they were not speaking. He had not said a word thus far and he had placed himself apart from the rest of the people. When I walked over to sit next to him, he nodded at my camera and told me to take pictures of all the people—meaning, I thought, that as far as he was concerned they were all equally suspect.

Once again the magistrate turned to the women and asked two of the teen-aged girls if they had seen anything. The girls, who had not previously spoken, replied with detailed itemizations of their activities during the previous afternoon. Just as it was becoming clear that they had seen nothing which directly bore on the issue, an old man interrupted the proceedings, stating that he had been on the beach the previous afternoon and had seen a set of footprints leading toward the nurse's tree.

Amid the gasps produced by this dramatic announcement and before anyone could question him, the magistrate's wife pointed at a naked toddler on the steps of the church. "Stop that baby," she shrieked. "He is going into the church without any clothes on!" I was sitting in the door of the church so it was I who stopped the wayward infant from committing a minor sacrilege. Since I, as well as others around the church door, had spent the better part of the meeting quietly preventing just such innocent desecration, the cry of the magistrate's wife was almost as startling as the old man's announcement.

As I turned back toward the meeting, I saw that she had risen to her feet and was about to strike the torpedo shell that served as a church bell. She rang it twice, everyone stood up, the magistrate led us in a recital of a Hail Mary, and we all went home to eat lunch. I was completely amazed by this sudden termination of the meeting. Why was the meeting being stopped just when it seemed to be getting to the point?

AFTERMATH

Throughout the following afternoon and evening people enthusiastically discussed and rediscussed the events of the meeting. Two or three would gather in an out-of-the-way spot, someone would ask whom the others thought the culprit was, and be met in turn with the same question. Names would eventually be traded off. As the day drew to a close, more and more unanimity was achieved. By the time people started to go to bed everyone agreed that the culprit was the man the nurse's son had pointed out to me during the meeting even though he had shown none of the revelatory signs, nor had he jumped when the old man announced he had seen the footprints.

I was not the only one to watch that man with care in the days that followed. Because his toddy tree was at the opposite end of the village from his home, he had to walk through the village and past the dispensary to reach it. Twice a day he made that trip under the close but disguised scrutiny of one and all. As he passed the dispensary on the first evening after the meeting, he simply kept walking with his head bowed. He did not stop and talk with the nurse as was his usual practice. The following morning he stopped briefly and spoke with some of the people awaiting treatment but did not go in the dispensary for his customary cup of coffee. That evening he spoke with the nurse outside the dispensary in full view of the village. By the fourth day relations between the two men were back on their old footing. They were again spending their evenings drinking coffee, playing cards, and, in general, acting as though nothing had occurred.

Three months later when the next field trip arrived all traces of the incident had disappeared. The policeman who arrived on that ship at the magistrate's request to investigate the crime could find no one who would name a suspect, the severed fronds had grown back, and it was no longer possible to distinguish any alteration in the behavior of victim, suspect, or anyone else that could be linked to the attempted murder. By this time too, an alternative hypothesis had started to gain adherents. When I left the island five months later, most people were saying that it was likely that the nurse, known to be subject to fainting spells, had fallen from the tree by accident and had been so embarrassed at this grossly incompetent behavior that he had climbed back into the tree and cut the fronds himself. Among the factors that led the people I knew best to decide that no crime had taken place were the rock-like normality of the suspect's behavior and his refusal, so far as we knew, to provide an apology to the nurse.

The "decriminalization" of the nurse's fall meant that new explanations had to be sought for the very behaviors that had led people to believe the suspect was guilty in the first place. Everyone could now agree that the reason he had not shown the expected fear signs was that he was not, in fact, guilty. No longer was it necessary to hold to the paradoxical belief that this very lack of somatic evidence of intense fear was an indication of guilt. It had been thought that only someone with something to hide would have acted the way he had acted in the meeting. Adherents of this view had claimed that he kept himself apart and failed to talk because he was concentrating on maintaining a smooth facade. They had claimed that he had not jumped when the old man made his claim to have seen incriminating footprints (a spurious claim the old man later admitted to have been planned by the magistrate and his wife) because too much time had elapsed between the supposed sighting and that dramatic announcement for the claim to have been true. Originally, people had asserted that the suspect had instantaneously deduced that such an explosive discovery could never have been kept secret overnight. After deciding that he was innocent, it was no longer necessary to consider him so quick-witted. The alleged motives for the crime also had to be reassessed. This did not prove difficult because no one had ever come up with a very powerful motive for the crime in the first place.

Initially, the Tobians had seemed to me remarkably unconcerned with the culprit's motivation. For example, very little of the premeeting speculation focused on the question of who among us had the strongest reason to wish harm to the nurse. It was only after the meeting and after consensus had been temporarily reached on the name of the culprit, that people were willing to discuss seriously why he might have attempted such a crime. After a good deal of searching, people did come up with a list of reasons for anger between the nurse and this man. All the items on this list shared one common attribute: they were all minor, petty irritants common to the relations among most adults on the island. It turned out, that is, that these two men composed one of the few adult pairs not divided by antagonisms over resources.

Although the man we all suspected was implicated in a number of sub rosa, long-term interest disputes, none of the disputes involved the nurse. This meant that none of us could find what we viewed as a sufficient objective reason for him to have wanted the nurse's death. No one could see how the nurse's death would have been to his advantage. Furthermore, since the nurse was also a contender in several disputes, it was obvious that there were others whose interests would have been served by his death. It surprised me at the time that the "motiveless" nature of the crime never appeared to be of much concern to the populace.

This surprise, along with my astonishment at the abrupt, seemingly premature termination of the meeting, led me to trace out the differences in the way my Tobian hosts and I were thinking about these events and the people involved in them. It at last became apparent that an important aspect of those differences derived from the contrasting ideas we were using about human nature. And, as I began to grasp the model of human nature with which the Tobians seemed to be operating, I saw, too, the "common sense" assumptions that underlay Tobian ethnocon-

flict theory and praxis. These assumptions are part of a local theory of
the person, or folk psychology.

TOBIAN FOLK PSYCHOLOGY AND THE
MANAGEMENT OF CONFLICT

In common with other Micronesian peoples, Tobians hold a markedly
interpersonal perspective on the self, focusing much more on the relations between persons than they do on the isolated individual and his
or her internal states (Caughey 1977; Lutz 1988). Even when an individual's behavior becomes the subject of intense scrutiny and discussion,
this generally remains the case. Yet occasionally, when forced by the
logic of events, Tobians do talk about what they call "our insides," that
is the private, inner world. When they do they tend to focus on "fear"
and its social uses.

In Tobian opinion, an individual is capable of almost any act. It is
only "fear," they believe, which makes people exercise control over hostile and antisocial urges. Fear, in turn, is closely related to "shame."
Shame at its most intense can lead to such extreme acts as suicide or
murder. This explains the cultural logic that lay behind the magistrate's
(and before him Perfecto's) meeting. Tobian folk knowledge holds that
public recognition of a fault or defect is extremely shameful, the anticipation of great shame is frightening, and fear is always indicated by
certain bodily signs. Given this knowledge, the method used in the meetings for uncovering the culprit is sensible. Furthermore, as long as the
culprit shares the assumptions, the method is bound to work—if only
by making him or her afraid to appear afraid. Also, given these same
assumptions, the lack of motivation for the crime was not a problem. It
could be said, as indeed it was in answer to my inquiries, that the man
we all suspected was a fearless person. A person without fear might do
anything, thus placing the entire society at risk. And the meeting that
resulted from the crime was, in essence, an attempt to teach, or reteach,
fear, not only to the culprit but to everyone else. The entire meeting,
including the way it ended, was built on this set of assumptions.

It took me some time to see this because their perspectives differed
sharply from mine. I was operating with the hydraulic Freudianism
characteristic of both American social science and American common
sense.

In the Freudian view of things, behavior is psychologically determined.
Fear (stigmatized as "anxiety") is largely dysfunctional and should be
overcome; hostility cannot be indefinitely contained by will; a truly motiveless attack is the act of a mad man. Such a view makes the kind of
hearing/trial that I took the meeting to be an occasion to discover important truths about motives so that individual responsibility can be

assigned and justice can be done. These were the assumptions that were structuring my expectations and that led me to be so surprised at the way the meeting ended. From the point of view of the Tobians, though, that ending made perfect sense.

Announcing that footprints had been seen was equivalent to announcing that the guilty party was known. In light of the excitement and fear this announcement was designed to provoke, a rapid defusing of the situation was imperative. This was, in the Tobian view of things, the most dangerous moment in the whole event. A direct accusation at this point, either by one of the more excitable members of the crowd or by one of the nurse's close friends or relatives, could have brought on an even worse situation.

The meeting, like Perfecto's before it, was designed to accomplish three things: the identification of a culprit, the prevention of further disruption, and the enforcement of social control over everyone's behavior. The differences between the two meetings resulted from the different weights the two men gave to these goals and this, in turn, was the result of changes in the Tobian setting. The decline in population and the growth of the settlement in Koror since the time of the earlier meeting clearly influenced the way the magistrate ran his meeting and they provide at least a partial explanation for its differences from Perfecto's.

In discussions during and after the events the magistrate made it plain that his highest priority was the prevention of any direct confrontation that he thought would lead to an outbreak of overt hostility and the departure, on the next available ship, of substantial numbers of people. Given the small size of the population, he feared that were this to happen the remaining community would be too small to sustain itself and would soon be forced to abandon the island.

Although the magistrate placed a different emphasis on the goals of the meeting than Perfecto had, he neither abandoned the old goals nor sought new ones. Both men used similar methods to reach similar goals. This impressive continuity in both methods and goals in the face of drastic change in the sociocultural environment is due to the persistence of Tobian understandings about human nature. Both meetings were designed to trap the culprit into self-identification by the production of somatic indicators of fear. Both Perfecto and the magistrate used the method of creating excitement and tension through the threat of public exposure to trigger those signs. Both intervened at the moment of maximum intensity to terminate the meeting and move the conflict out of the direct gaze of the community. The next steps could only occur privately, as the two individuals involved acted to bring their relationship back to the state in which mutual cooperation and cheerful interaction could be possible.

DISCUSSION

Conceptions of being and action are profoundly implicated in processes of conflict and its management and resolution. Such conceptions,
which are an important element of particular, local cultures are themselves inevitably local. It is possible, and sometimes even analytically
useful, to strip away the "localness" of a conflict. Any thorough understanding of the conflict itself (and thus any possibility for the intelligent
facilitation of its management or resolution), however, is dependent on
coming to grips with the set of ideas, assumptions, values, and beliefs
about human beings and their conflicts that are in play. Such presuppositions are implicated in disputes in two ways.

People use cultural presuppositions to interpret the past as they construct sensible narratives about their own and others' behavior. One way
to think about this retrospective-constitutive use of cultural knowledge
is to imagine social life as a fluid and disordered (or at best, only se-
miordered) stream of interaction and communication. We bring order
to that stream by selecting "events" that can be linked together in culturally appropriate ways. We make sense of, and in, the social world in
which we are so inescapably embedded by creating such narratives. In
a situation of conflict, these narratives become the contested discourse
that makes sensible the various strategies followed by the parties. All the
effort that everyone put into reconstructing the events that led up to
that meeting, and the constant negotiation and renegotiation of different
reconstructions and interpretations, illustrate this point.

The use of local common sense about humans and their conflicts in
this retrospective fashion is complemented by its use in projecting behavior and its consequences into the future. People involved in conflicts
make use of cultural presuppositions in order to predict future states
and actions of the self and others involved in the conflict and to script
behavior accordingly. This prospective-constitutive use of cultural presuppositions underlies the creation of both conscious and unconscious
strategies for behavior and their implementation and modification.[4] The
argument about whether to call in the police was in essence an argument
about the future course of the case, and was predicated on differing
projections of the future state of relations on the island.

Understanding the common sense that is being used retrospectively
and prospectively by disputants is thus crucial for any understanding of
the dispute itself. If and when third parties are involved such an understanding is a necessary prerequisite for any intervention that is to
have more than a random chance of success at resolving the conflict.
When the analyst or intervenor is socially and culturally distant from
the disputants, the first step in this process is to recognize that an un-

familiar common sense about people and their disputes may very well be a crucial component of the conflict at issue.

A difficulty may occur when the intervenor or analyst, unaware of the local nature of his or her own presuppositions, unconsciously assumes that they are shared with the disputants. Attributing universality to one's own cultural presuppositions is probably one of the most common assumptions about assumptions or meta-assumptions made by humans. Such an assumption, even when wrong, may not *always* be a problem since misunderstandings at this "deep" level may be quite irrelevant to either interaction or relationship. For example, as I noted above, I had become relatively well integrated into the community's life even though I had not noticed how differently my hosts and I thought about psychological reality. My unconscious meta-assumption—that they shared my assumptions—did not seriously interfere with this integration. When issues of conflict management arose, however, this meta-assumption proved a serious impediment to understanding what was going on.

This leads to the observation that when issues of conflict management or resolution are involved, an outside intervenor's assumption of universality may have quite damaging results. Changes in behavior (or at least the *interpretation* of behavior) of one or more of the parties is what intervention is designed to achieve. Since cultural assumptions of the type discussed here are one of the most powerful determinants of both behavior and its interpretation, clarity about them in the context of conflict management or resolution is essential. Although my role in the events described here was not that of an intervenor, the many misunderstandings that hindered my interpretation of what was going on (from my continuous misunderstanding of the story of the earlier case to my surprise at the way the meeting ended) are a sobering reminder of how unexamined assumptions of universality can lead one badly astray.

The management of aggression and, especially, interpersonal violence, is a significant problem in small, close-knit groups. The inhabitants of an island such as Tobi live in a world more closed than most, a world in which both space and cooperation are at a premium. In such a world the expression of hostility through violent behavior can set in motion a sequence of events that will disrupt the harmony necessary for communal existence. Based on their indigenous understandings of human nature, the Tobians have created a sociocultural world that allows them to make their ability to cooperate in achieving pleasant, cooperative social relations, their main technique for managing conflict. This case, although not a dispute in the sense we commonly assign to that word—after all, who were the disputants, what was the dispute about?—nevertheless provides a particularly rich example of the mobilization of those understandings. Before I could learn what this case had to teach me, however, I first had to learn from my astonishment at the way it ended.

Surprise can be used as a methodological tool to lead to an awareness of the analyst's own fundamental assumptions, the ways in which they differ from others' assumptions, and then perhaps to a deeper understanding of the cultural presuppositions at play in any given situation of conflict. And it is through such an understanding that conflict can be analyzed so that it becomes sensible to all participants and, hence, at least potentially amenable to management or even resolution.

NOTES

The research upon which this chapter is based was undertaken with support from a NIMH Grant (UPHS 5 TO1 MH 12766). I wish to thank B. D. Webster and my coeditors for their useful suggestions. I have described the events at the center of this chapter elsewhere (Black 1976, 1979). I choose to re-present that case here in order to develop the argument for a culturally informed perspective in conflict analysis and resolution. I will build upon my two earlier discussions of the case in which I used it to illustrate the characteristics of Tobian behavioral routines (1976), and to describe the evolution of a Micronesian dispute-processing procedure as well as to probe questions of conflict management and reconciliation in Tobian society (1979). This case can sustain reanalysis both because it is very well documented and because, like any complex human reality, it resists a complete and final mapping.

1. If one distinguishes between conflict management, thought of as processing of conflict for socially useful ends, and conflict resolution, which involves the transcendence of conflict, the case under discussion here is an example of the former.

2. By "interest disputes" I mean contests over the control of resources. Land is the fundamental resource; marriage and political office provide avenues to its control.

3. In their characteristic pattern these cock fights also demonstrated a high degree of both fascination with and discomfort at possible physical confrontation between men. The high-pitched laughter and near frantic excitement of the teen-aged owners contrasted strongly with the rather apathetic behavior of the roosters as they were pushed at each other. It is also of interest that the bigger boy was always announced the winner (Geertz 1973).

4. See Geertz (1983) for the classic statement of the importance of this kind of knowledge for understanding behavior and interpreting meaning.

REFERENCES

Black, P. W. 1977. Neo-Tobian Culture: Modern Life on a Micronesian Island. Ann Arbor: University Microfilms.

————. 1978. Crime and Culture: Tobian Response to Attempted Murder. *Midwest Review* 3:59–69.

Caughey, J. 1977. *Fa'anakkar: Cultural Values in a Micronesian Society*. Philadelphia: University of Pennsylvania Press.

Geertz, C. 1973. Deep Play: Notes on a Balinese Cockfight. In *The Interpretation of Cultures*. New York: Basic.

————. 1983. Common Sense as a Cultural System. In *Local Knowledge: Further Essays in Interpretive Anthropology*. New York: Basic.

Lutz, C. 1988. *Unnatural Emotions: Everyday Sentiments on a Micronesian Atoll and Their Challenge to Western Theory*. Chicago: University of Chicago Press.

Spiro, M. 1952. Ghosts, Ifaluk and Teleological Functionalism. *American Anthropologist* 54:497–503.

8

Of Nets, Nails, and Problems: The Folk Language of Conflict Resolution in a Central American Setting

John Paul Lederach

"I knew how to connect-in (*entrarle*) with my dad," Carlos said, "but my mother won't let me in (*no me deja entrarle*). I don't know her. She is totally shut (*cerrada*)." It was a typical muggy night in Puntarenas, a Pacific port town in Costa Rica. Carlos perspired as he explained the "situation" in his family to twenty of his fellow *Porteños*. We were all participating in a year-long leadership training course on "social empowerment" with a special emphasis on organizing groups and problem solving. He was in the middle of "sculpting" his family with members of the group, describing them as he went. Around his mother he placed the middle brother and his little sister. "We are six," he explained. "My mother is close with these two. They have their little group." He placed his father across the other end of the room, and then his oldest brother about in the middle of the two parents. The distance between his parents was obvious. At one point he said, "At times I just feel like telling them 'Mama. Papa. *Háblense*! (Talk to each other!).'" Finally, he put himself, the youngest of the brothers, close to his father. "The family is separated," he said. "Not one of the family group gives even a grain of sand to fix (*arreglar*) this situation. Each one is on their own, alone." Now it was the group's turn. "What counsel (*consejo*) would you give me, so that there would be an entry (*entrada*) in my family?"[1]

The two grandmothers in the group did not always speak, but tonight both had thoughts. Doña Fidelia said it simply, "If there is no love, there is no arrangement (*arreglo*). The family needs to be more *sincero* (open, sincere)." Doña Guadalupe gave Carlos a *consejo*, a piece of advice about his *llegarle* mother: "You have to *llegarle suavecito* (connect-in soft and slow). Show her your love," she said. "Go to her with your heart in your hand."

It was Henry, however, who came up with the dominant strategy for the evening. "This is how I explain it. The mother is the trunk. The brothers and sister are the branches. Many times if one wants to get to (*entrarle*) the trunk, one has to go through the branches (*irse por las ramas*). It is not with the trunk that you start. Start with the brothers. Carlos needs moral support (*apoyo moral*). We all need moral support to be able to live. So talk to the oldest brother, *tú a tú* (one-on-one, intimately), tell him that you need it, make him see that you need this love and moral support."

Conflicts are, in every sense of the word, cultural events. They are perhaps one of the most intriguing and complex social accomplishments we humans construct. Situations like Carlos' call forth a lifetime of knowledge about what is right and wrong to do, how to proceed, whom to turn to, when, where, and with what expectations. Like Carlos and the group everyone must make sense of what is happening and decide how to respond. How this social phenomenon is understood and accomplished, however, varies from one cultural setting to another. The study of how people make sense of conflictive situations and appropriate "commonsense" methods of resolving them, including the use of third parties in a particular setting, might be called "ethnoconflictology." The present chapter is one contribution in this discipline, aimed at building our "common knowledge" about conflict in Central America.

The descriptions, ideas, and analyses that follow emerge from data recorded through participant observation, experiences in real-life conflicts, mediations, training seminars, and interviews accumulated during the past several years of travel and living in Central America, particularly in Puntarenas, Costa Rica. The town of Puntarenas sits on a narrow strip of land forming a peninsula jutting out into Nicoya Bay on the Pacific side of Costa Rica. The *Porteños* (people of the port) have known the boom and bust cycles typical of port towns throughout Central America. Like many port towns there are an array of "social" problems: prostitution, alcoholism, drug trafficking, delinquency, and unemployment. The training group known as Genesis was initiated in part to prepare leaders and respond to these community problems. The group was made up of people from the poorer *barrios* of the town, voluntarily participating in a course on social empowerment. Yet Genesis was destined to be more than a course. It was a combination of a "club of friends," a therapy group, and a training seminar.

The majority of the participants knew how to read and write, but had less than a fifth-grade education. There were grandparents, parents, and teenagers who brought their concerns and gifts to the group. Less than half had any steady source of income. In fact most were squatters, living in one form or another of "land invasions." We met twice a week for over a year. The course was based on a participatory design in which members helped create both the goals for the group and the method of study and learning. Over the course of the year the group grew initially to more than thirty and then as the work proceeded decreased to a committed working group of about ten. In the meetings we not only explored the width and depth of personal, family, and community problems, but watched the emergence and management of numerous in-group conflicts. Genesis was a living laboratory of families, friends, and neighbors working on community problems.

This chapter describes native understandings of the conflict process through a study of their everyday "conflict-talk," permitting insight into folk ways of resolving problems and expectations of third party involvement. To clarify further, in most instances the specific language-variety-in-use is "talk about conflict" more than the actual talk used in conflictive exchange. Study of this type of talk is particularly useful to discover their ways of understanding and conceptualizing conflict. While the most detailed and in-depth observations of this "talk" came from the experience in Puntarenas, this language is common to many of the Spanish-speaking peoples of Central America, and this chapter will also draw from that wider experience to illustrate key points.[2]

TALK ABOUT CONFLICT: THE FOLK VISION

For some time I have been interested in the intersection of language and conflict behavior. As a mediator I was trained in "communication" problems and skills. As a sociolinguist I am convinced that language is not merely a "means" of communicating but an essential feature of the conflict experience. Discovered and carefully observed in everyday usage it can serve as a window into how social reality is constructed and understood.

Early on in my research in Central America I paid particular attention to how people, in their everyday language, talked about conflict. I began to notice that virtually nobody, and certainly nobody in our Puntarenas group, used the word "conflict" to describe their everyday disputes. As one *Porteña* noted, "Ah, no, here we don't have conflicts. Conflicts are what they have in Nicaragua. Here we have *pleitos* (disputes), *líos* (messes), *enredos* (entanglements), and *problemas*." "Conflict" is perceived as an academic term, and when used at a folk level refers primarily to violent, armed, intergroup struggles. At the same time a wealth of other terms and phrases describe the more common daily experience of conflict.[3]

CONFLICT: THE "NET" OF LIFE

Perhaps the term that best indicates and describes the folk concept of conflict is *un enredo*, or *estamos bien enredados* (we are all entangled). A simple translation, however, does not transmit the full significance of the term. This is a fishing metaphor in its roots. It is built around the Spanish word *red*, a fisherman's net. To be *enredado* is to be tangled, caught in a net. The image is one of knots and connections, an intimate and intricate mess. A net, when tangled, must slowly and patiently be worked through and undone. When untangled it still remains connected and knotted. It is a whole. A net is also frequently torn leaving holes that must be sewn back together, knotting once again the separated loose ends. Nothing describes conflict resolution at the interpersonal level in Central America better than this folk metaphor.[4]

"Interpersonal conflict" is perhaps a misnomer in this context. It leaves the impression that individual persons are in conflict. It fits a Western conceptualization permitting focus on individuals and their issues, often in isolation from their network. In Central America issues and people, and therefore conflicts, are always viewed holistically, as embedded in the social network. In my observations, the single most important characteristic affecting both the understanding and resolution of conflict is a person's network. *La red* is also the word for network, although in Puntarenas they more naturally would refer to it as *mi gente*, my people. Broadly this covers people who are well known to a person, usually friends, fellow workers, neighbors from the *barrio*, and most important, the extended family.

People here think in terms of families. For example, refugee camps, *barrios*, and housing projects are always counted in families, not individuals. They would rarely say, "one thousand people live in this neighborhood." It is almost always, from government officials to the person in the street, "two hundred families live here." The extended family often lives in close proximity, occupying various houses on the same block. The first time I had the car tuned, my mechanic and new found friend wanted me to see his house. As we walked down the block he pointed, "Here is where my brother lives. Here, my cousin. Here my mother with my sister. Here my uncle." When we got to his house he turned and smiled, "This is your house. You'll never get lost. Just make it to the neighborhood and asked for the Morales. Everyone knows which street the family is on." Time and again, little pieces of evidence underscore that Central America is familial in social construction, not individualistic.

Families and *mi gente* are the context in which conflicts, or the daily "entanglements" develop, are understood, and are managed. Around the experience of being in and dealing with these "entanglements" a

rich folk language had developed, characterizing both the conceptualization of conflict and the native processes for managing them. These
terms are evidenced in the short description of Carlos' family and the
group's response to him to which we now turn as a basis for our broader
discussion.

THE "INS AND OUTS" OF CONFLICT

Recognition that a person is "in" a conflict usually comes with some
form of the verb *meterse*. "I have been *metido*," that is, placed, put, introduced, or forced "into" a tangled net. In popular usage people often
accuse others of "putting me in this problem." As Ruth said, in telling
a story about a problem she had with a friend, "I told her, *vos me metiste
en chisme* (you put me in gossip, got me in trouble)." It is not unusual,
however, to hear that "I put myself in." *Meterse* also has the connotation
of meddling and interfering. For example, before one of our meetings
I was talking with Carlos and Minor, another member. We started discussing how we would "enter" Carlos' family to help. Minor shook his
head. "It wouldn't work here, because here, the family is the family and
nobody interferes (*se mete*). The family is closed (*cerrada*). It is very *porteño*
to not *meterse* in family problems. That is the family's job." In all the
cases, however, to be *metido* carries the recognition that one is now a part
of, inside a larger whole.

Once *metido*, the search begins for "how to enter into the problem and
the person" (*cómo entrarle al problema, y a la persona*). These concepts are
more complex than simple "entry." The verb invariably is used in the
form *entrarle*, and it is the *le* that points to the effort to get "into" or
"inside of." *Cómo entrarle al problema* seems to be used in two ways. First,
it is the question of how to gain access to the problem. This is foremost
a search for the right connection, that is, for *la entrada*, which invariably
is a person. In the description above Carlos' question about *entrada* invited discussion around whom to start with. Henry, for example, suggested that the entry with the mother (the trunk of the problem) is
accomplished by entering first with the brothers (the branches). Notice
here two important characteristics in this folk wisdom. First, the suggestion is to proceed indirectly, by going through other people and
channels to reach one's objective. Underlying this is a sense that too
direct an entrance may upset the balance and "close" the person. It is
important to proceed in the initial phases "soft and slow" (*suavecito*). We
then add the natural insight of *who*, in the family, is the correct person
to approach first. In this case Henry, as did others in the group, suggested the older brother, who in many families has special responsibilities
as a go-between and trouble shooter. The *consejo* offered here is based

on a sense of what is proper and traditional, both in terms of who is sought and how they are approached.

Second, *cómo entrarle al problema* is also the question of how to get "inside" in order to understand. Another common term accompanying *entrarle* is *compenetrar*, to penetrate into the other's world. In this conception if problems are to be understood they must be felt and seen from the "inside out." *Cómo entrarle a la persona* runs parallel with this latter idea. The basic question is both how to approach and then connect-in successfully with the other. Used interchangeably is the phrase *cómo llegarle*: how to arrive in the world of the other. Viewed in context, successful entrance into the person means we have spoken and understood, we have seen each other from the inside.

This understanding helps explain the prevalence and importance of the typical conflict "person-description" that someone is *cerrado*. Carlos' problem with his mother, and the difficulty the group experienced in giving him advice repeatedly came from the "closed" nature of his family. *Cerrado* is not so much that a person is stuck in a position, hard to negotiate with, or hardheaded, the term reserved for that is *duro* (a hard guy). It is specifically that they will not let you into their world, there is no entry, you cannot get inside. Notice how Carlos says his mother is "closed" and in the following breath, "I don't know her." If you cannot get inside people, you do not know them, you do not feel their world, nor do they feel yours. In the folk view, a closed person means that there is no way to "get into the problem" and no way out of the entanglement.

Accompanying this notion of how to "get into the problem" is the other side of the coin: how to get out. A common expression of the *Porteño* caught in a problem is the simple phrase: *"Cómo voy a salir de eso?"* (How am I going to get out of this?). "Resolution" involves the task of "getting out" (*salida*) of the entanglement. Consider, for example, another much used phrase for conflict that illustrates this point: *"Ay, el clavo que tengo"* (What a nail I've got). "Having a nail" could mean pain, something hard or sharp. As it has been explained in their terms, a nail, once driven "in," is very hard to get "out." The fundamental folk understanding: conflict is a process of "ins and outs."

"Getting out" usually has one of two meanings. It can mean pursuing a variety of avoidance tactics so that one is not forced to directly confront the problem or, more important, the person. The most common tactic is to simply cut off contact and not talk (*no se hablan*). This is experienced as separation, distant and painful, leaving holes in the net. Here people are "closed"; it is no longer possible to reach into the other's world. There is no entrance. This is Carlos' case, where, in his words, each is on their own, alone, denoting the feeling of isolation and incompleteness.

Or, it can mean the pursuit of "putting things back together" through an *arreglo*. It is to this latter process that we now turn our attention.

THE ETHNOMETHODS: GETTING FROM "IN" TO "OUT"

Getting from "in" to "out" involves three basic processes, the internal ethnomethods of "getting into the problem": *ubicarse* (get my bearings); *platicar* (talk, dialogue); and *arreglar* (manage, arrange, and fix). We might call them "ethnomethods" to highlight their taken-for-granted nature.

Ubicarse is to locate or situate something or oneself. For example, an advertisement will often give the *ubicación* of its business by listing the street address, or where it is located in relationship to other important buildings. It is not uncommon to hear someone say, "We are *ubicados* (living) in such and such a neighborhood." When people are lost in the city, they are *desubicado* (disoriented). "*Tengo que ubicarme,*" they will say. "I have to get located, get my bearings." The same feeling and terminology are used in social and group settings. For example, one of the *Porteñas* once talked about her experience in San José with a group of professors and diplomats. "*Me sentí bien desubicada,*" she reported. "I felt out of place." In the Puntarenas group we regularly made group decisions by using *la ronda*. In *la ronda* we went "around" the circle and each person in the group made a brief statement of how they saw the problem, what decision they wanted, or how they were going to vote. It was not unusual for people to struggle to understand what was being asked of them, what they should say, or how they should vote. We would often hear, "*Es que no me siento bien ubicado. De qué se trata?*" (I'm not sure what is going on. What are we talking about here?).

In an ethnomethodologist's terms, *ubicarse* is the process of "making sense" of something. *Ubicarse* is a folk term for the crucial process of "framing" something in order for it to become some "thing" meaningful. It is a particularly appropriate term given its metaphoric image of "locating oneself." For example, the "meaning" of an event, like Carlos' mother not greeting him when he comes home for a visit, is accomplished by "locating" it in a frame of reference along with other events and behaviors. "*Tengo que ubicarme*" (I have to get located) indicates a sense-making procedure is under way. The event at hand needs to be located so that I know where I am and can, therefore, decide where I should go. In this folk understanding, dealing with social interaction and particularly conflict, is like looking for a new address or being lost in the city.

The single most important way to *ubicarse* is through *la plática* (talk, chat). *Platicar* is more than simply "talking"; it is a way of sharing, exchanging, and checking things out. It cannot be reduced to a technique because it is a way of being with the other. As an example, consider an experience with our landlord's hired hand in San José. Manuel is a Nicaraguan refugee, one of thousands undocumented in Costa Rica. He makes a living doing odd jobs, and has built a good reputation for being honest, which puts him in demand for housesitting when people go on vacation or travel. Soon after moving into our house, we went on a short trip and had Manuel housesit. Upon our return, I told him we would be traveling again and several weeks later he came by, as I would soon discover, to raise his nightly wage for housesitting.

He arrived at about 8:00 in the evening. We went through all the customary greetings as I invited the unexpected visitor in. Our conversation wandered through a variety of subjects: family, work, religion, and politics. He was curious about our religion. He listened patiently as I explained Mennonite theology. We talked at length about Nicaragua. We drank coffee. He spoke about his distrust of all politicians, the life of a "Nica" in Costa Rica. The conversation lasted more than two hours. Finally, Manuel stood and said, *"Me gustó la plática"* (I liked our talk), and we headed for the door. As he went out into the garage he turned and said, "Don Juan Pablo, look, if you need my services for watching the house it will be 300 colones a night." That effectively doubled his earlier price. We then proceeded to negotiate for another half an hour until we reached an *arreglo*.

In this instance, as in many others, *la plática* is a way of being with, of reaffirming the relationship, of preparing the way for dialogue. It is open-ended, and feels roundabout in nature. As Henry said, "Go through the branches" not directly to the trunk. *La plática* permits one to test the waters and *ubicarse*. It is through *la plática* that all important contact is made, and one "penetrates into" the world of the other.

La plática lies at a very important border in folk categorization of conflict: talking and not talking. For example, note Carlos' deep felt need to just say, "Mama. Papa. *Háblense*" (talk to each other). It emerges from the folk recognition that the conflict has reached a level where people *no se hablan* (do not directly talk to each other). "Talk" must now travel through a *tercero*, a third person. It is *la plática* once removed. Or it can happen through *indirectas*, a peculiar form of speaking about someone in their presence without addressing them, or without addressing the subject directly.[5] Subtle forms of confrontation take place through inferences, skirting the risk of more volatile direct fighting. They may live in the same house and not talk, as Carlos' family, or they may separate and have no contact: *no se hablan, y no se ven* (don't talk and don't see each other).

Dialogar, another "talk" term, implicitly refers to the movement back from *no se hablan* to *se hablan*, that is, the movement of conflict from one qualitative level to another. Consider, for example, Roberto's *consejo* to Carlos: "You are the head now. You have the *confianza* (trust) of your father, but not your mother. You have to *dialogar* with your father, and then later your mother." Or, as Máximo told him, "You have to carry them (*llevarlos*) to dialogue." *Dialogar*, by implicitly recognizing separation and distance in the relationship, is conceived as a bridge for reconnecting. It carries with it a sense of connecting, an entrance into a space in which it is possible to exchange, a contact that permits restoration of a broken or entangled whole.

One common way that conflicts are resolved is through *un arreglo*. This is a multifaceted concept. Consider, for example, different contexts in which forms of the term are used. "*Arreglo de llantas*" handpainted on a sign hanging on a garage denotes a common form of self-employment: fixing flat tires. Florist shops make flower "arrangements" (*arreglos*); children are *arreglados* for school; accounts are "settled" (*arregladas*). To the question of surprise, "How did you pull that off?" a common response may be "I've got my ways" (*yo me las arreglo*). Or looking more directly at a particular arena of conflict, in Costa Rica negotiated settlements arranged directly between workers and management as a way to avoid strikes and that do not use arbitration, court, or government intervention are called *arreglos directos*, a direct agreement.

In folk usage as it refers to conflict, *arreglo* seems to combine three primary meanings. The first we see in Carlos' statement that nobody in his family gives "even a grain of sand to *arreglar* this situation." Here, the conceptualization is that of repair. Viewing his explanation in its broader context, Carlos understands an *arreglo* for his family as a way of fixing, of putting back together that which is broken and separated. We see an underlying and implicit recognition that the network is not as it should be and must be restored. Notice also that this way of thinking evolves through holistic problem conception.

The second and third meanings we see in Doña Fidelia's comment, "If there is no love, there is no *arreglo*." That is, without the basis of mutual caring, there is no possibility of creating an "arrangement" that permits restoration. In other statements she added that the family has to be more *sinceros*, in the sense of being more open, and have to know how to "understand" and "carry each other" (*hay que saberlo comprender y saberlo llevar*). "Arrangements" seem to be based on permitting mutual entry into the world of the other: "We understand each other." From understanding comes the possibility of "carrying each other": we mutually recognize our part in the whole. An *arreglo* is conceived as a combination of "understanding" and "arranging." Through an arrangement and an understanding, we fix the broken and undo the tangled.

In Figure 8.1 we can visualize the folk understanding of the conflict

Figure 8.1
The "Ins and Outs" of Conflict

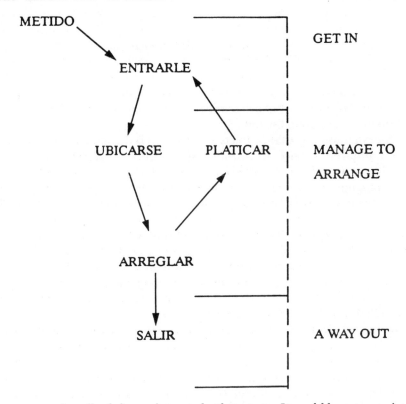

process as described through everyday language. It could be summarized in the following phrase: "We get in, so we can manage to arrange a way out." In short, *metido* is a recognition that we are caught. *Entrarle* is a set of social processes for moving fully "into" the problem through the people involved. Once inside, it is necessary to "get located." This evolves through some form of "talk." If it is not directly between those involved it will come through the "third," who, talking with both sides, formulates the "arrangement" and "understanding." An "arrangement" then becomes the *salida*, or the "way out." While a *salida* can often be a form of escape using avoidance tactics, an *arreglo* is a "way out" that restores the relationship through mutual comprehension resulting from dialogue. As such, *arreglar*, based on *"ubicarse"* and *"la plática,"* is a folk term for "conflict management," but not in the sense of explicit strategies for controlling the expression of conflict, but rather in the implicit, taken-for-granted sense of "managing to work it out." There is, throughout, the recognition that one is a part of a wider whole, which has to be entered and restored. Further, the visualization helps us perceive the process as circular rather than linear, as a constant movement back and forth between these taken-for-granted yet crucial aspects of getting in and out of a conflict.

CULTURAL PATHS OF CONFLICT ACTION

The actual, real-life workings of these ethnomethods result in three significant and appropriate paths of cultural conflict-action: *el consejo, la confianza*, and *las patas*. A Western mind would be tempted to call these techniques. It is hard, however, to reduce a way of being and relating to a technique. It is preferable to consider them cultural paths, which essentially are folk categories of appropriate ways to respond to a conflict. These are, therefore, more akin to general strategies than specific tactics.

In exposing his problem to the group Carlos was seeking a *consejo*, a piece of advice. To ask and give *consejos* is the first and most common path of response to conflict. It is the intersection between *ubicarse* and *platicar*: I talk with others to get my bearings in this situation. Or to put it in the words of the pop song, "I get by with a little help from my friends." While this may sound facetious, the underlying phenomenological importance of a *consejo* in the process of conflict should not be lost, that is, "how" and "why" a *consejo* makes its appearance.

We can understand the reasons and process behind a *consejo* by considering another typical folk expression for conflict: *"Qué problema!"* "What a problem!" It is often said with a sigh, or with special emphasis added through the Latin finger slap. The message is understood. Conflicts are experienced as a jolt in the flow of everyday life. The folk vision understands that in conflicts, events and peoples' behavior surrounding those events are literally problematic, that is, the "meaning" is not readily apparent and cannot be taken for granted. In other words, special attention must be paid to these things. Likewise, the appropriate response to those people and events is problematic, and thus poses the need to *ubicarse*, to locate oneself and "things" in a frame that make them and one's action meaningful. A first step involves explaining those "things" and the problem to oneself. To seek a *consejo*, however, is a process that moves the explanation from a subjective and individual to a social and intersubjectively shared level. This process is simultaneously the entry of the "third" and the social construction of meaning. We create and tie ourselves to a reality beyond the personal. This seemingly simple process represents the very basis of constructing social reality, and merits further description from the folk perspective.

Superficially and with a Western individualistic bias, a *consejo* feels like one person is telling the other what to do. For example, take the group's *consejos* given to Carlos. In virtually every instance, people told him, "You have to (*vos tenés que*)." Careful study of the broader context and the more complete transcript, however, highlights a key observation. A wide variety of *consejos* came out, and in some cases the same person gave different and even somewhat contrary opinions. This seems to back up what I have seen in other settings where *consejos* were being offered. While framed in what appears to be an imperative grammatical structure, the *consejo* is not interpreted as an order but rather an option, a possible way out, a possible view of the situation. From the perspective of all involved, the most important thing is participation; spontaneously give your view, your advice. And virtually everybody has an opinion, something to offer. Rarely, if ever, do you hear, "Boy, I don't know what I'd do." It is a little like giving directions in Central America; even if I do not know where it is, it is improper to not respond with an idea. Nobody will be necessarily tied to this *consejo*, but by giving it, we are part of, we participate, we create better understanding, we find an appropriate frame. We have fulfilled a network task. We participate in creating our shared social reality, in reaffirming and tying ourselves to it. In this example from the Puntarenas group, the *consejo* represented a way of "thinking together," of being with the other, of sharing, of not only situating the problem in the network, but more important, of once again reconstructing our shared sense of the whole, of the reality we create and live in.

At a second level of investigation and considering observations made throughout Central America, when asked about "asking advice" peoples' responses identified several key terms that indicate a variety of purposes and expectations. "Orientation," for example, parallels the idea that a *consejo* helps to get one situated and discover an appropriate frame. On the other hand, people may seek *ayuda* through the *consejo* indicating more involvement: action and intervention on the part of the third party in behalf of the person is expected. Further, *ayuda* is often specifically related to financial problems. *Apoyo* (support) through *consejo* is indicative that a person needs a safe place to share a problem and a friend to listen and talk with. Its purpose may simply be to reaffirm and show "moral support" for the person.

In this latter idea we introduce the second major path: It is not possible to ask a *consejo* of just anybody, only those who "inspire" *confianza*. This complex and profoundly cultural idea cannot be captured in a single English term, although most often it is translated as "trust." To have *confianza* denotes a special quality of relationship, a bond of mutuality and understanding. Within the folk conceptualization there are levels of *confianza*, each with different expectations and requirements.

Confianza is a process, something that is built over time and accumulative. It moves from the level of "knowing someone" (*nos conocemos*) to "friendship" (*nos conocemos bien*, we know each other well), to the ultimate, "a person with whom I can share a personal problem." The three verbs—

to have, to inspire, and to deposit—that most regularly accompany *confianza* illustrate this further. Through contact and time I know if a person "inspires" *confianza* in me, that is, whether I have the sense that I can safely "deposit" my trust with them. As a group of social workers in San Jose decided, "With time we arrive at personal knowledge that permits us to ascertain their sincerity, the base for friendship and *confianza*." It is a process by which I evaluate if and how many of my intimacies I can safely place with the other. Take, for example, the phrase *la confianza que rompió el saco*. This refers to an abuse of trust, that someone has taken advantage of our friendship by asking for too much. Such an abuse "broke the sack"; the accumulated contents spilled out.

We can understand more clearly these levels of *confianza* by looking at it in the context of folk networking. *Confianza* and the network are resources for problem solving. At the first level, "to know someone" makes that person a potential contact, at the periphery of our network but not in it. Here there is not sufficient *confianza* to ask for a *consejo* or *ayuda* in solving a problem. If that person was determined to be in a special position to be helpful, perceived as a *entrada* into our problem, then we would look for a "friend of a friend." In other words, we go to someone in our network, with whom we have more *confianza* and who, simultaneously, has *confianza* with the other targeted person, who will in turn serve as an "entry" into the problem.

This carries us to the second level of *confianza*, friendship. Friendship comes with time and more intimate knowledge. Friends are "in" my network, part of *mi gente*. Here we can expect more and expect to give more. The type of problem solving that emerges at this level can be seen through the type of *consejos* sought and given. They will often be related to what might be called "external matters": how to deal with a financial problem, how to get through bureaucracy, how to handle a community problem.

"Internal problems," *problemas personales*, are saved for the third level, the *entre nos* level. *Entre nos* means "just between you and me." Here we can talk as if we were "family." In some instances it is an opening for sharing a piece of secret gossip. But it always carries with it a sense of intimacy, of openness and trust. This is similar to the *consejo* offered by Henry. "Talk to the oldest brother *tú a tú*, tell him what you need." *Tú a tú* is a folk category for a type of talk. It will be intimate. I will reveal myself, my needs. I will open myself and expect openness from you. What is said will be respected and kept to ourselves.

The *Porteños* have a special word for these type of friends, *huevitos*. The origin of the image, in their explanation, is picturesque if a bit vulgar. In most of Latin America, *huevos*, or eggs, is a slang term for testicles, or "balls" as we might say. In port town talk, *huevitos* are the closest of friends, like "two balls in the sack." Where you find one, you will find the other. *Huevitos* are not family members, but are friends who know each other "like family." They are *compenetrados*, they know each other from the "inside out." It is with one's *huevito* that one has the surest sense of *confianza*. It is *confianza entre nos*.

Confianza entre nos takes place between only a select few in the network. It is reserved for intimate friends and family. It is distinguished above all by the ability to share and talk about a "personal problem." *Confianza* at this level can be recognized by the fact that two interpersonal relational norms can be broken without consequence. The first involves "talk about the other." *Tú a tú* permits open, frank talk about the other. As one group in Guatemala said, "We can *decirlo todo* (say it all), without that affecting our relationship. We are still friends." In other words, we can confront directly, face-to-face, without paying the "normal" consequences. For example, in many cases, the consequence of direct confrontation is the movement to "not talking." The second norm involves "talk about self." *Confianza entre nos* permits me to *ventilar*, "air out" my personal problem, to reveal my hidden world, to let another into my world.

Confianza entre nos is problem solving based on a mutuality of trust, and rare, intimate self-revelation of problems, hurts, and weaknesses. It is a form of peer therapy, of healing through a trust relationship, of restoration of the network through the healing. It was with considerable insight that when they decided to launch out into the community and offer themselves as "counselors," the group in Puntarenas hung a sign in front of their room that read: "*Centro de Confianza: Orientación y Consejería*" (The Trust Center: Orientation and Counseling).

A third path for problem solving is to have *patas*, or connections.[6] *Patas* literally are feet. Metaphorically it is "networking." It views people in our network as resources who can, because of their position, abilities, or connections, accomplish something that we need to resolve our problem. *Patas* is the conflict-action of knowing people in the right place who can effect the action desired. Close examination of the "talk" that makes use of the "connection" reveals the purpose is not self-revelation but rather getting action from the other on our behalf. It is based on accumulated knowledge about people, their functions, their relationships and connections, and, most important, the inner net-workings. It is knowledge about who to turn to in order to accomplish what kind of task. It is important to describe the relationship and differences between *confianza* and *patas*. This will be best accomplished by describing a specific example.

During about six months I worked off and on with a conflict in a Nicaraguan Mennonite congregation of refugees in Costa Rica. As a backdrop to this description I should clarify that I worked for a North American Mennonite relief agency collaborating with the Costa Rican

Mennonite Convention in a resettlement project for the Nicaraguan congregation, made up of about forty families. The convention leadership was made up of almost entirely Costa Rican Mennonites, although it still received a good portion of its budget from a different Mennonite mission. Although we were organizationally separate and I had nothing to do with the inner workings and decisions of the convention, in the view of the refugees there was little distinction and I was viewed as a missionary, working with the convention.

These refugees had originally come from the same region in Nicaragua, although not all of them had been members of the same congregation there. On the way down others from a variety of denominations joined them, the majority from a pentecostal background. Once in the refugee camp the congregation grew and as the possibility of resettlement became a reality, a conflict emerged that threatened to split the group. It evolved around leadership issues, membership and adherence to "Mennonite" doctrine, and access to resources, primarily who would get to go to the farm. I met with the two major groups and their leaders on numerous occasions. Given the circumstances and events I spent considerable time alone with Javier, a Mennonite pastor who, through the long journey by foot out of Nicaragua, had become intimate with and was the unspoken leader of the non-Mennonite, pentecostal group. We began to develop *confianza*. They eventually created an *arreglo*. Javier decided to stay and give leadership to the congregation that would remain in the camp. The Mennonites, over the course of the year, would move to the farm. Before separating a "reconciliation," as they called it, took place between the two groups, restoring their relationship.

That was not, however, the end of my participation. Over the course of the next five months I got numerous phone calls from and had several meetings with Javier. Shortly after the "reconciliation" I received a call inviting me to come and meet with the pentecostal "brothers," to hear their "expressions." Curious and a bit uncertain about the invitation, I asked if he wanted me to bring along other leaders of the Mennonite Convention, who were responsible for administering funds, directing the refugee project, and providing spiritual leadership to the churches. Javier responded, "No, it is better for you come alone, first." I went and met with Javier and the group of five pentecostal brothers. Over the course of a morning they explained their view. They had two primary concerns: not to be left alone and outside of the convention after the others left for the farm; and whether there was any chance they could eventually get back on the list to go to the farm. They were interested in my *consejo* and in my "helping" them with the convention. I was their "entry" and their *patas*. I promised and did contact the convention leadership, although nothing happened in the next few weeks.

A month later Javier called again. He reiterated their concern about getting *apoyo* from the convention. In my awkward *gringo* style I probed the question of why he did not call and talk to them directly. He responded, clarifying the unspoken knowledge that he assumed we all knew but which I was struggling to make explicit: "No, brother, you are the channel *(canal)* that can help us *(ayudarnos)* with them." I was, I discovered, the ongoing go-between. I again spoke at more length with convention leaders and we agreed to set up a meeting and invite Javier the following week, *si Dios quiere* (God willing). God did not provide that opportunity. Among trips, conferences, and work, the meeting got lost in the shuffle.

Several months later I received a call from Javier. He was in the San Jose area and wanted to know if we could see each other and *platicar*. As I was soon to discover he had made the four-hour bus trip to see me, personally. We did speak and he again underscored their needs, especially as related to *apoyo* from the convention for the congregation in the camp. This time his view and concern became clearer. As he explained the most frustrating aspect: "I do not know how things are set up, who I should talk to when I have a problem." Javier was concerned that his network was falling apart. Now that the Mennonites were going to the farm, his congregation would be left without contacts in the Mennonite world. A Mennonite pastor, leading a congregation of pentecostals, in a refugee camp in a foreign country: They were a people without a net. He was engaged in a mission to put the network together. I was the entry, the first step in getting that accomplished.

What is of particular interest in this example are the steps leading down the path of *patas* as problem solving. First, there is recognition of the problem. In this case: how to get *apoyo*, and assure that we are in the convention network, which will provide us with a variety of resources. Second, there is accumulated and implicit knowledge of the networkings. This necessitates a response to two questions: Deciding who, in the end, can effect the results we desire, and what the best way is to reach that person to assure action. The response to the first was the leadership of the convention; the response to the second involved a search for an entry and an evaluation of contacts and *confianza*.

Javier had numerous options. He knew each of the members on the council, including the president. He had the number of the convention as well as those of several individuals on the council. We even met in front of the convention offices when he came the last time. But he did not call them, he called me. He looked for and decided on the person with whom he had the most *confianza* and who was connected to the people who could effect the desired action. Finally, he chose the most appropriate way of assuring action: personal contact. Get into the problem by getting into the right person. This is not necessarily *confianza entre nos*; it is friendship *confianza*. He was not pursuing this path to work on a personal problem, he pursued it to get action on his behalf as a way to resolve an external problem. His knowledge of us, of conventions, of mission boards and missionaries suggested at least a working, if not intimate relationship between the convention and myself. He had made an evaluation of me and our relationship, as compared to his relationship with others. In his mind, our time alone "inspired" enough *confianza* to make this a reasonable and expected request. He could "deposit" his trust. I was the logical entry. I became the channel. He contacted me to contact them. *Patas* is an appropriate image: you get "feet" to enter in where you do not have access.

IMPLICATIONS FOR INTERVENTION: CROSS-CULTURAL CONSIDERATIONS

Our discussion thus far both invites and permits us to consider the implications for intervention within this setting and cross-culturally. As a point of departure let us consider the case with Javier and our discussion of the "ins and outs" in reference with the continua of cultural expectations (Figure 8.2). This classification originally emerged through an earlier study of the assumptions taken for granted in the North American, Anglo, and professional model of mediation (Lederach 1985). It is based on cross-cultural literature and common characteristics identified by social scientists to distinguish "modern" and "traditional" societies. I have adapted it to fit the basic folk language and vision described above. In brief, the continua suggest several basic aspects with important components that must be accomplished as third parties enter a conflict. How these specific components are accomplished varies from one cultural setting to another. This "variance" can be conceived as a continuum between a "pure formal" and "pure informal" model of intervention. The continua suggest that as third parties enter a dispute they must use knowledge about what are appropriate ways of responding to the conflict and the disputants. For example, they must decide what setting or forum is most appropriate for the resolution procedures to follow, they must decide what form of contact and communication should be used, they must determine what kind of outcomes are desired and appropriate, and they must use knowledge about what is expected of them and their relationship to the disputants. For example, in the case of Javier, broadly speaking, the intervention was very informal. My role and the expectations about my role were never formalized, but rather were assumed. It is precisely the assumptions that Javier took for granted but that I did not necessarily share that highlight intercultural differences. Consider these other items the continua contemplate.

First, in essence I was a surrogate for direct communication between

Figure 8.2
Continua of Assumptions Affecting Conflict Process and Intervention

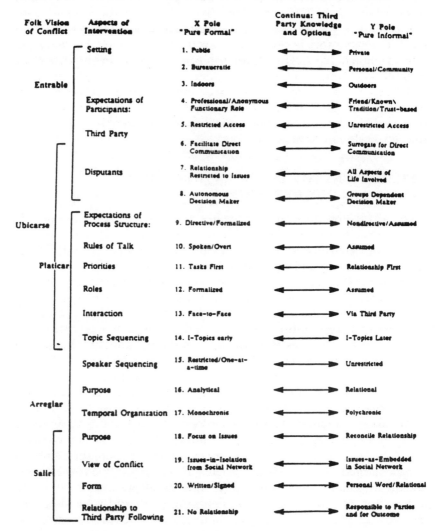

the convention and Javier, a broker of sorts, but not a decision maker. This was based on an evaluation of *confianza* and "connections." From the beginning until this writing we progressively reached higher levels of *confianza*, which meant I was increasingly a part of his network. I was viewed as a friend within, not a professional outside of the network. Correspondingly, I became a more effective go-between, but one who was in the flow of their expectations.

Second, given this basis there were fewer limits on access to me as a resource. As a *gringo*, at times I felt like it encroached on my "private space." This, of course, never even crossed their minds. Increasingly, the broader aspects of their lives were a part of our discussions. I was not expected to merely concentrate on "mediating" the congregational split: I was pulled in on personal problems, on what to do with the youth, about connections to the convention, about communications back to Nicaragua. There was no simple "in and out" of their lives; the connection was translated into an ongoing relationship. I was, in their taken-for-granted view, responsible to them and for the arrangements reached, not simply negotiating a settlement on isolated issues.

Third, problems are conceived in the context of the network. Even when they seemingly fell outside, it became necessary to expand the network, to locate the connections that permitted Javier to get "in" and "out." Correspondingly, as a third party I was sought out because I was connected. Legitimacy of the go-between was established not through distance and neutrality, but rather through knowledge and trust. As such, there was no "dropping-in" to resolve the problem and then "getting out." At the folk level, "once in, always in": I was, after all, increasingly a part of his network, more like a godparent than a professional mediator. The "third" becomes the hand that knots and sews the net together. Their connection is based on personal relationship, not professional function or written contract.

It is perhaps appropriate at this point to mention briefly what it feels like to mediate and serve as a go-between in another culture. The few accounts I have read of international and intercultural mediations have tended to present their interventions as the work of competent "anthropologist-politicians" who deftly make their way through the cultural meanings and mazes, understand what is going on, and press forth to reach agreement. Quite frankly, I felt more like a bull in a china shop. A sensitive bull perhaps, but nonetheless a bull who with each step ran the risk of crashing through a delicately arranged social structure. The reason, I think, is clear. The understandings, the process, and the expectations for dealing with conflicts were based on the people's implicit knowledge that they assumed operative but which I had not fully accumulated. It is a little like trying to make your way through the china shop without knowing where the aisles are located. I, too, was in a constant process of trying to *ubicarme*.

In many instances, while I had a good command of the language and I understood all the words I struggled to capture the meaning. With Javier I repeatedly found myself trying to break things down, specify what exactly the concerns were, and make a list. Often he would give me a smile, a look of puzzlement, and then tell yet another story explaining what he meant. I would ask things that were obvious to him, like "What do you expect from me?" To which he would respond: "Be the channel, talk to them, arrange it with them." *Connect, talk,* and *arrange*—the words are loaded with years of accumulated meaning.

My work was not based on a sense of professional intervention but rather a slow process of discovering meaning, expectations, and hopes as a basis for knowing what action on my part would be appropriate and useful, and how, exactly it should be accomplished. Time and again, it was not a set of techniques but rather the simple effort to be with Javier in person that seemed to produce results in this setting. I have found this to be true in the majority of the many disputes I have mediated in Central American settings.

This discussion based around the continua suggests that accomplishing the basic aspects of intervention in a conflict can vary broadly in different settings. It highlights the need on the part of intervenors who are not from the setting to be both sensitive and flexible. Personal experience suggests we should recognize that our premises and assumptions about the conflict process are not necessarily shared by those who we are attempting to help, and that we may, inadvertently, break a lot of china in our attempts to find the aisles.

I have outlined the folk understanding of the conflict process as described through everyday language in several Central American settings, particularly that of Puntarenas. As a conclusion we can identify several important characteristics that affect the understanding and resolution of conflict.

First, conflict is viewed and understood as evolving in an ever-present social network. Within the broader network, the most important connections will be those of the extended family. Untangling and putting the network back together is perhaps the single most pursued purpose of conflict management activity. Likewise, the network itself is the most used resource for resolving problems.

Second, conflict is viewed holistically, not analytically. That is, understanding takes place, not by breaking down the problem into parts, but rather by viewing it as embedded in the "net-workings." Understanding the conflict is a process of "getting inside it" through entry into the others' world and through the right connections. Successfully accomplished it reaffirms that we are part of a larger whole.

Third, the process of getting "in and out" of conflict is circular rather than phasic in its inner workings. It is not, therefore, linear or "rational" in nature. In other words, it is not based on an evaluation of what is the most direct, time-efficient, or effective manner of resolving this problem. It is based on what is proper and traditional, on evaluating the subtleties of trust and the intricacies of relations and connections. It is a process of "locating" and "relocating" oneself, involving taken-for-granted knowledge about who to turn to, when, and for what reason. Often that will involve an intricate decision about how to go through the branches to get to the trunk.

Finally, the entrance of the "third" is both natural and constant: through this person people are reconnected, the net kept integral. The third party is regularly someone from within, not outside the network. Persons who are too far removed are viewed with reservations, because of the lack of *confianza*. Often they will be the bridge, the channel through which messages and negotiation flow. The expected purpose will be to reconcile the relationship, create an arrangement, not necessarily to isolate and resolve issues. As will the people involved, the "third" will tend to focus on the problem holistically, as embedded in the social network. In the end they are a part of the network, and thus are responsible to the parties for what happens and for the quality of the arrangement made, both based on the ebb and flow of relationships, not written contract.

NOTES

1. There are always certain tradeoffs when one writes in one language about another language and ways of talking. I have opted in this chapter to include the original Spanish for the most important phrases and words. To the uninitiated in Spanish this may appear cumbersome. For the students and native speakers of the language it provides at least a minimal view of the exact language-use-in-context.

2. Central America is made up of many varying cultural settings. There is tremendous variety between the more isolated areas of the *campo* and the city; between Ladinos and Indians; between the slums and squatter villages and the more established *barrios*. Personally, I have worked with numerous indigenous groups, refugees, and a variety of religious groups. It is, of course, difficult if not erroneous to generalize across such broad populations. To avoid this trap, I will identify as clearly as possible the specific group I am referring to as I make my points.

3. Curious about this I designed a simple exercise in my workshops on conflict management in which people were asked to list all the synonyms for conflict they could identify. I have carried out this exercise over a dozen times in seven countries in this region and to date nearly two hundred words and phrases have collectively been identified. They indicate a wealth of accumulated folk knowledge about levels and types of disputes, as well as providing metaphoric insight into folk conceptualization.

4. It should not be lost that this folk vision closely parallels and lends support to the work of Georg Simmel (1955), who consistently viewed conflict, as one of his titles suggests, as the "web" of group affiliation. Lewis Coser (1956) would later discuss this as a function, the "cross-stitching" or "binding" effect of conflict.

5. This folk tactic seems prevalent throughout Latin America. In Brazil, for example, they call it *intriga*. When I am *intrigado* with a person I do not talk, or

address that person directly, nor does that person talk with me. While leading a seminar in Recife, a North American friend described to me the case of his two employees who became *intrigado*. One morning they had a number of errands to complete but the car was broken. The three of them were together in the room as they discussed what to do. Employee 1 had certain tasks that morning and did not need a vehicle. My friend then suggested that employee 2 take the bike that belonged to employee 1 to complete his errands. He said he could not do that. When asked why he responded, "We are *intrigado* and I cannot ask him to use the bike." They could not directly address "the word," that is, could not talk to each other, much less make requests. It could only be accomplished through my friend, even though all were in the room together and engaged in the discussion.

6. *Patas* is a word that seems specific to a Costa Rican setting. *Cuello* is perhaps more broadly understood in most of Central America although it is Honduran in origin. In Spain they would say *enchufe* (plug-in); in Mexico it is *palanca* (leverage).

REFERENCES

Coser, Lewis. 1956. *The Functions of Social Conflict*. Glencoe, Ill.: Free.
Hall, J. 1983. *The Dance of Life*. New York: Anchor.
Lederach, John Paul. 1985. Mediation in North America: An Examination of the Profession's Cultural Premises. Akron, Pa.: Mennonite Central Committee.
Simmel, Georg. 1955. *Conflict and the Web of Group Affiliation*. New York: Free.

9

Rhetoric, Reality, and Resolving Conflicts: Disentangling in a Solomon Islands Society

Geoffrey M. White

While conflict is an established interest of social scientists, the narrower focus of this volume—conflict resolution—is a more recent preoccupation. Among anthropologists, interest in conflict resolution is related to two distinct developments. First, the call for ethnographies of "the native point of view" leads quickly to the recognition that one of the things that people think and talk a great deal about is interpersonal conflict. Second, theoretical disquiet about looking only at symbols and cognitions has spawned renewed interest in praxis, in the ethnography of performance (Ortner 1984). It is in events and practices aimed at managing or resolving conflict that people in many societies enact or negotiate some of their most significant social, political, and moral understandings. This chapter analyzes a specific conflict discourse on the island of Santa Isabel in the Solomon Islands. In so doing, it presents an approach to the cultural analysis of processes that people use to create and transform the realities in which they live.

As in any comparative project, problems of definition loom large at the outset. These problems need to be addressed through a close sifting of local understandings in relation to the actions, relations, and situations where those understandings are produced. The analysis that follows applies diverse but complementary perspectives to the problem of determining the meaning and force of conflict talk in particular cultural contexts.

CONFLICT DISCOURSE

In many Pacific Island societies metaphors of disentangling and straightening are used to signify deliberate efforts at ameliorating interpersonal conflicts (Watson-Gegeo and White 1990). The people of Santa Isabel in the Solomon Islands discussed in this chapter invoke images of entanglement in their efforts at dealing with interpersonal conflicts. The label "disentangling" and its local meanings point up problems with simply referring to these efforts as conflict resolution or dispute management. To begin with, the notion of disentangling signals a process rather than an end-product, indicating that engagement in moral negotiation itself may be more significant than specific decisions or outcomes. Second, the image of a tangled net or a knotted line suggests a blockage of purposeful activity, reminding the members of a community that the problem at hand requires attention lest it impede normal social life that everyone has a stake in. Finally, disentangling presumes a conception of an unmarked, background state of affairs in which the strands of people's lives do not become snarled and ineffective. Whether spoken or implied, models of "straight" or correct relations may themselves be subject to negotiation in the disentangling process.

This chapter examines conceptual and interactional processes through which a people produce moral accounts within the constraints of a particular sociocultural universe, even attempting to redefine that universe as they do so. The aim of the analysis is to articulate the structure of a discourse that works to transform problematic events into a more desired social reality. The discussion examines the culturally constituted means used to achieve these desired transformations.

Anthropological writers have frequently observed that small-scale, non-Western societies employ a range of means for handling interpersonal conflict and managing contentious or divisive issues. If formal "courts" are present at all, they may be narrowly limited in the types of cases they take up, possibly to events involving conflict defined in terms of Western-style laws. In their place, diverse practices varying from gossip to informal village meetings and highly ritualized ceremonial activities function as conflict-regulating and order-maintaining mechanisms. In this spectrum of events, Western observers have noted what seems to them a blurring of genres, of dispute procedures with therapeutic functions (Gibbs 1963), and of religious ceremonies with overtly political messages (Gluckman 1955; Norbeck 1963). Instead of asking just what people themselves think they are up to on these occasions (and how one could decide), the dominant approach has been to explain this multiplicity of forms by imposing theoretical dichotomies such as rational versus irrational and practical versus ritual. For example, in works that have been widely influential in social anthropology, R. Turner (1957) and Max Gluckman (1955) suggested that societies deal with "surface" interpersonal conflicts through rational dispute procedures aimed at resolving decidable issues, whereas problems arising from irresolvable structural contradictions (such as between matriliny and virilocal descent) tend to be dealt with through ritual practices that evoke strong emotions in the service of social integration.

Oppositions have their place in exploring cross-cultural reality, but they are also susceptible to oversimplification when opposition becomes dichotomy, where one term excludes the other. One of the difficulties with the opposition of "law" and "ritual" is that lurking just behind the scenes is the evolutionary claim that "we" have rational law, whereas "they" have emotive ritual. In line with Andrew Arno's (1979) observation for Fiji that all dispute processes climax in ritual activity, practical and ritual moves frequently comingle in conflict discourse, as do rational and emotional appeals to moral judgment. By focusing on local concepts of person and specific strategies of conflict talk, it is possible to determine the significance of practices that are at once social, emotional, and political.

When James Gibbs (1963) observed that Kpelle moots dealing with marital disputes exhibit features of Western therapy (citing Parsons 1951), he had uncovered a highly significant property of many informal procedures for conflict resolution: they explicitly invoke a rhetoric of emotions. Many other examples could be cited, such as the Tolai *varkurai* or moot described by A. L. Epstein (1984:29), which comes "to a climax in an emotive appeal to certain highly cathected norms," or the Bunyoro *rukurato* portrayed by J.H.M. Beattie (1957) as a type of "informal judicial activity" held to "finish off people's quarrels and abolish bad feeling" (cited in Gibbs 1963:9).

Such cases arouse interest because they combine meanings and activities usually kept apart in the more neatly dichotomized Western conceptual world where the political-legal-rational is separated from the psychological-moral-emotional. These parallel oppositions rest upon the edifice of Western concepts of the person as a highly individuated, autonomous actor. In the prototypical Western case, the major lines of social discord are typically drawn between the boundaries of individual persons, with moral dilemmas reflecting the problems of reconciling individual desires and community norms. Dispute resolution and psychotherapy become mirror images of one another: the former a process whereby individuals or factions attempt to impose their own preferred models of reality upon wider collectivities, the latter a matter of replacing a disordered personal experience with a more coherent normative vision. It follows that, in political disputes where the intended outcome is an authoritative vision of reality, individual desires and emotions are ideally suppressed and controlled. And, in Western psychotherapy, where the desired outcome is a new personal integration, the individual is sheltered from the inhibiting constraints of social norms and relations so that emotions may be more freely explored, felt, and expressed (Parsons 1951; Pande 1968; Scheff 1979).

The disentangling practice examined in this chapter presumes that the person is embedded in a matrix of social relations. Rather than extricate the person from that milieu, as in the legal persona represented in Western courts or the "real inner self" revealed in psychotherapy, the context examined here involved persons as moral actors engaged in interaction with significant others—usually the very same others involved in the precipitating conflicts. Whether the aim of the activity in question is an authoritative statement on contested issues or an emotional rapprochement among family members, a collective vision of social reality is constructed through the mutual involvement of participants in the activity. The case examined here shows that the process by which collective statements are jointly enunciated is itself a product (in some cases, the primary product). It is an enactment of identities, relations, and emotions that reproduce a desired state of social reality.

To outside (Western) observers, the rationale for activities that involve discourse on interpersonal conflicts but neither aim for nor achieve specific decisions is problematic. The cultural significance of the activity examined here lies primarily in the rhetorical construction of social reality. Seen in this light, particular conflict episodes are part of an ongoing community dialogue in which events and relationships are continually shaped and reshaped in the moral "negotiations" of everyday life. The disentangling event is significant because it is distinguished from the stream of ordinary interaction as a situation overtly concerned with interpersonal problems. It is marked as a speech event that permits a type of discourse not possible in other contexts. As recent studies of political language make clear (Brenneis and Myers 1984), much of the genius of such events is in providing a context for communication about topics that are not only problematic in themselves, but frequently cannot even be talked about in ordinary ways.

The activity that the people of Santa Isabel refer to as "disentangling" is defined as a situation for talking about bad feelings and interpersonal conflict. This chapter takes an event-centered approach to understanding how such situations are defined and enacted. The situational focus has both advantages and disadvantages. On the one hand, it necessitates a certain myopia with regard to related activities and contexts. It does allow a more careful examination of the question, What do actors think they are up to when they engage in "disentangling"? The fact that the overt definition of the situation frames actors' discourse gives greater leverage in tackling problems of interpretation.

The discussion proceeds by asking two related questions: What is the

local model or ideology of disentangling that gives the activity its pub-
lically avowed purpose? How is the event organized interactively so as
to achieve this purpose? Convergences in the answers to these questions
yield interpretations of social process linked to both ideology and social
practice.

THE SETTING

Santa Isabel is one of five major islands in the Solomon Islands. According to the last national census in 1986, the population at that time
was about 14,600. Four distinct languages are spoken on the island. It
is the largest language group known variously as Maringe, A'ara, and
Cheke Holo that is the subject of this chapter (White et al. 1988). The
people of Santa Isabel engage primarily in subsistence gardening, and
in recent years have initiated a variety of agricultural schemes to produce
cash crops. While economic changes have been slow in coming, cultural
transformations associated with colonization and Christianization have
been more dramatic (White 1988). During the first half of this century,
the most significant agent of change was the Anglican Melanesian Mission (now the Church of Melanesia), which completed its work of con-
verting the island population about sixty years ago. The work of the
mission at the end of the nineteenth century was received eagerly by the
Isabel people who had been severely victimized by marauding head-
hunters from the Western Solomon Islands (White 1979). Conversion
entailed major changes in residential patterns in which people formerly
scattered throughout the bush migrated to coastal villages of unprece-
dented size (one to two hundred people), with ceremonial life centered
on the village chapel.

Prior to these changes at the turn of the century, social organization
was based largely on kinship relations and regional alignments in which
local leaders (*funei*) were the focal point for intergroup feasting and
raiding. The idiom of descent is distinctively matrilineal, with descent
groups identified with territorial regions and sacred shrines where pro-
pitiatory offerings were once made to deceased ancestors. Since conversion, ceremonial life has been almost entirely recast in the framework
of Christian activities and contemporary social and moral ideals expressed in terms of Christian ideology (White 1988).

DISENTANGLING: MODEL AND METAPHOR

Disentangling (*gruarutha*, from the verb *rutha*, "disentangle, undo") is
recognized as a distinct type of activity in which people talk among
themselves about interpersonal conflicts and bad feelings in their community. The avowed purpose of disentangling is to "talk out" (*cheke*

fajifla) bad thoughts and feelings that pose a danger to personal and community well-being if they remain hidden. Such dangers come in the form of illness, injury, or failure of important activities such as hunting and fishing. Disentangling may take two forms: as a therapeutic activity aimed at the psychosocial causes of illness or misfortunate, and as a preventive measure used to dispel bad feelings that could interfere with collective projects such as turtle hunting.

At first glance, disentangling bears some resemblance to Western notions of both psychotherapy (or group therapy) and dispute resolution. Yet it is neither. To label disentangling as either therapy or dispute procedure is to gloss over the more fundamental question of what it is and what it does as a culturally constituted activity. Somewhat like Western psychotherapy, disentangling can be used to ferret out social and emotional sources of illness. In both cases, persons are urged to review their feelings associated with past events. But unlike psychotherapy (Pande 1968), disentangling is eminently social, conducted in a community milieu, usually with the very same others who figure in the entanglements under review. While both entail the revelation of personal thoughts, the "therapy" of disentangling lies precisely in the telling, in the act of giving a certain kind of public account, and only secondarily in the reorganization of mind or personality.

The preventive type of disentangling usually takes the form of a village (or intervillage) meeting. In this setting, the activity resembles other types of village meetings aimed at discussing (*roghe*) or managing disputes (*fapuipuhi*, from *puhi*, "action" or "way," literally, "make a way"). Meetings called to air (if not resolve) community disputes also involve the public recitation of accounts of interpersonal conflict. Yet the accounts voiced in dispute meetings attempt to influence village leaders who formulate authoritative versions of reality. For disentangling meetings, the culturally prescribed outcome is simply the production of a certain kind of narrative. At least in the normative model of disentangling, what you say is what you get. No comments, evaluations, or judgments from third parties are necessary. Perhaps more like the Fiji Indian *pancayat* described by Brenneis (1990) than other, more deliberate forms of conflict resolution, disentangling manifests an emotional aesthetic.

The difference between disentangling meetings and the more straightforward dispute meetings is best indicated by the fact that Isabel people themselves do not see them as comparable. When I asked one informant about disentangling, he compared it to a communion service.[1] At first glance from an outsider's perspective, this seems an odd comparison. Both, however, are a kind of moral cleansing—an instrumental means of expiating personal conflicts that could prove injurious. Being allowed to receive the sacrament presupposes that one is free of serious moral transgression, and hence may participate in church-sponsored ritual that helps to ensure well-being and avoid misfortune. Similarly, disentangling puts a symbolic seal on old wounds and conflicts, certifying that social relations and personal thoughts/feelings are in an expressed state of solidarity, thereby threatening neither self nor community (White 1985a).

The functional similarity between disentangling and communion services should not, however, obscure the obvious differences between them. First of all, disentangling is far less scripted than the highly ritualized and formulaic quality of communion services (which require only passive involvement of participants). Second, disentangling is primarily an interpersonal activity, with spirit forces in the background, if present at all. The issue of a supernatural component of disentangling (such as the belief that failure to disentangle could invoke ancestral or godly retribution) is an open question (Watson-Gegeo and Gegeo 1990). Most evidence points to a fundamentally interpersonal activity that has been Christianized in some respects (such as the now customary presence of a priest to listen as people speak their minds). Because of our own assumptions about causal agents mediating cause and effect (Needham 1976), there is a tendency to insert supernatural beings in the chain of reasoning that links socioemotional conflict with misfortune, even though there is little evidence that the indigenous model posits such connections.

In the local theory of disentangling, personal thoughts and feelings have explanatory efficacy. Like the Western theory of psychosomatic disorder, which attributes psychosocial causes to maladies that show no obvious somatic cause or do not respond to conventional cures, the disentangling theory attributes socioemotional factors in cases of illness that persist despite the application of usual treatments. For example, in the case of a woman suffering from uterine pains and bleeding who had been treated without success by a variety of traditional remedies over a period of six weeks, a village leader finally said that he could see that ordinary treatments were not working because of problems between the woman and her husband. In the leader's words, it was "their thinking which blocked the work of the other treatments," and thus they needed to disentangle their thoughts and feelings.

The most significant difference between the disentangling theory and Western theories of psychosocial disorder is the distinctly interpersonal or social character of the Isabel model. For example, the disentangling theory includes the premise that one person's socioemotional entanglements may cause illness or misfortune for third parties—for significant others or for the community as a whole. In the words of one informant, "If two people, husband and wife, are always arguing, then their child will continually be sick." Such reasoning appears to be extremely wide-spread in non-Western models of illness (Harris 1978; Ito 1985; Turner 1964; Strathern 1968; Watson-Gegeo and Gegeo 1990).

The explanatory efficacy of emotions extends beyond illness to various kinds of collective misfortune. The failure of an important community enterprise such as fishing or hunting may be attributed to some lingering, bad feeling that has obstructed or blocked success, similar to a "curse" (*tibri*), which could have the same effect. One of the most common examples involves lost pigs. Domestic pigs are often not penned, but are allowed to forage in the forest where they establish well-known feeding places and can be located and retrieved when needed. On occasion, however, a pig cannot be found, despite concerted efforts to do so. If after one or two days the pig is not located the searchers will conclude that something is "obstructing" their attempt to find it, just as something was "obstructing" the medical treatment of the woman's illness mentioned above.

In one case where two brothers and their sister were preparing (together with their respective households) to host a memorial feast for their father who had died a year earlier, one of their pigs could not be located after a day and a half of searching. So they decided to hold a disentangling meeting in which the three siblings, their spouses, and their mother gathered to "talk out" any bad feelings that might be blocking their efforts. The topics discussed at the meeting included: (1) the mother's regrets about her children's failure to take good care of their father in his old age; (2) a previous argument between the brothers about their responsibilities in preparing for the feast; and (3) a dream by the sister that her father's ghost was playing tricks on the party searching for the pig. Since the pig was located the next day, it was generally inferred that this airing of bad feelings served to overcome the obstructions.

The preventive uses of disentangling can be seen as an extrapolation of the premises of this theory of illness and failure. Given the premise that bad feelings can cause misfortune or obstruct social activities, disentangling before important social ventures is a way to avoid accidents or injuries and help insure success. Hence before undertaking the fishing or hunting required for a major feast, a series of intervillage disentangling meetings may be held to air bad feelings.

Emotions play a mediating role in local reasoning about misfortune: they are both caused *by* and causes *of* problematic social events. It is not just emotions in general, but negative, conflicted feelings harbored within the person that are believed to be most dangerous as possible causes of illness, "accidents," or failure. In this way, the unexpressed disappointments and resentments that accrue from everyday conflicts (the "tangled feelings") take on a culturally constituted significance that requires a culturally constituted remedy: disentangling. How, then, is disentangling conceptualized so that it is seen to provide an antidote to such problematic emotions? Clues are to be found in the language, particularly the figurative language, used to talk about such things (Lakoff and Kovecses 1987).

"Entanglement" is a key metaphor in local understandings of mind and emotion, with a number of entailments indicative of understandings about social-emotion and process (White 1985a). Both emotions and interpersonal relations may become "entangled" (*fifiri*) because of conflicts in everyday life. This ambiguity of reference, both emotional and social, is significant. It reflects a perspective on social life that consistently draws linkages between personal experience and interpersonal relations, rather than boundaries between the psychological worlds of individuals.

The notion of "tangled" feeling subsumes a variety of specific negative emotions such as anger, sadness, and shame.[2] To talk of "tangled" emotions is to say something more complicated than would be conveyed by any one of the more particular terms. Specifically, to describe feelings as "tangled" (*fifiri*) or "knotted" (*haru*) is more evaluatively ambiguous than describing them as, say, "angry" (*di'a tagna*). It is particularly in relations with significant others, between persons closely related through kinship or residence, where negative emotions are most problematic, that feelings are said to become "entangled" due to disagreements or transgressions.

The metaphor of entanglement is not just a vague cover term. In the terms of George Lakoff and Mark Johnson (1980), it is "productive" insofar as it entails an array of specific propositions and images used to conceptualize social reality. Consideration of the range of conventional metaphors related to entanglement reveals a set of images linked to an underlying "theory" of conflict and what to do about it (Quinn and Holland 1987).

Troublesome feelings and damaged relations in need of repair are variously described as "tangled" (*fifiri*) or "blocked" (*nagra*). Each term is part of an opposition that implies the need for efforts at resolution, calling up images of movement toward a solution: tangled→untangled (*krutha*) and blocked→clear (*snagla*). These oppositions represent the beginning and ending points of scenarios of activity aimed at alleviating conflict. Extending the metaphor of entanglement, persons who do not straighten out their affairs are likely to become further snarled, in the sense of "snared" or "caught in" (*khale*), just as a turtle gets tangled in a net. By representing socioemotional conflict as a state of affairs that impedes normal purposeful activity, like a path blocked by a fallen log, these images imply that some sort of deliberate attempt at removing the problem or impediment is required. It is against the backdrop of these scenarios that the verbs "disentangle" and "clear away obstruction" (*fas-*

nasnagla) acquire their meaning as active attempts to move from one side of the opposition to the other, from a problematic state to one which is "untangled" or "clear."

How then is disentangling or clearing away obstruction accomplished? Put simply, it is by talking about one's feelings and thoughts in the presence of significant others. By making the personal public, and doing so in accordance with prescribed formats (described below), disentangling provides a culturally prescribed discourse for constituting desired forms of social reality. In line with some of their most basic social values (White 1985a, 1985b), the people who engage in disentangling describe its social aim as being of "one mind" (*kaisei gaoghatho*) or "being together" (*au fofodu*) in community thought and action. This aim is rhetorically fulfilled in the enactment of disentangling, through the process of articulating personal thoughts and feelings and thus creating a jointly enunciated sense of community solidarity.

The notion that certain experiences manifest themselves as thoughts and feelings within the person as an individual is basic to local conceptions of psychology (White 1985a). Troubled thoughts and feelings about which one does not readily speak are described as "hidden" (*phoru*) from others, unless they are "revealed" (*thakle*) or become "visible" (*kakhana*). The movement of thoughts and feelings from within the person to the social arena is described as "revealing" (*fatakle*) or "making visible" (*fakakhana*). In addition to the sight metaphor, the movement of thoughts and feelings in the social world is also conceptualized with an up/down orientational schema. Problematic experiences may be kept "down" (*pari*), "buried" (*fruni*) or "covered over" (*plohmo*) (and hence out of sight), or they may "rise up" (*hnaghe*) or "surface" (*thagra*), just as a turtle becomes visible when it comes up for air.

The terms and images used to talk about disentangling indicate an indigenous view of knowledge and emotion as dynamic processes that traverse personal and public realms of experience. The movement of thoughts and feelings from personal to public reality is conceptualized as a process of revelation, as metaphorically making enclosed objects visible. Revelation is thought of in a variety of specific ways. Reflecting some of our own figurative language for knowledge control, one of the speakers in the case described below says that he learned of his brother's attitudes after they "leaked out" (*suplu*) in gossip. Disentangling, however, is a more deliberate, purposeful process. Two primary means of revelation are "opening up" (*tora*) and "putting outside" (*fajijifla*) thoughts and feelings, just as one might open a box to remove its contents or allow others to see inside. Participants in disentangling sessions invoke images of "talking out" (*cheke fajifla*) and "opening up with talk" (*cheke tora*) to urge one another to engage in the type of talk that fulfills the public agenda of the occasion, of making thoughts and feelings public.

This type of talk is not only seen as efficacious, it *is* efficacious in transforming that which is hidden, inside, and under to that which is visible, outside, and on the surface, thus clearing away impediments to desired social ends.

This discussion is intended to illuminate the ways disentangling is conceptualized as a culturally defined and socially acknowledged activity. As a public occasion for talking about interpersonal conflict, however, it is inevitable that disentangling sessions will also be used as a forum for moral negotiation in which competing interpretations of problematic events are posed and counterposed. Indeed, interlocutors play upon the overt definition of the situation as one aimed at a simple public accounting of emotions to assert more indirect claims about moral liabilities connected with past events. This covert agenda, then, creates certain problems for maintaining the normative definition of the situation (Bailey 1983). There is always the possibility that the assertion of moral claims will evoke counterclaims, and possibly lead to confrontation and animosity—just the type of entanglement that would be anathema to the avowed aim of disentangling. To counter these potentials, participants work cooperatively to frame their discourse by voicing the purpose of disentangling and by jointly managing the course of conversational interaction. How is a context constructed so that it produces "straightening" rather than disputing? Some of the conversational and interactional devices used to create and sustain the disentangling context are considered briefly-below before looking more closely at an excerpt of disentangling discourse.

CREATING A CONTEXT

My understanding of disentangling is based largely on information derived from four specific meetings, two of which I tape-recorded.[3] The tape-recorded sessions were village-level meetings held in anticipation of a major Christmas feast. Meetings were held in four villages where people were involved in preparations for the feast. Each meeting drew people from more than one village and some individuals participated in more than one of the sessions. It was the need to plan and prepare for the feast that occasioned these meetings, rather than any specific conflicts to be disentangled (although most people probably anticipated which events would be raised in the meetings). Both of the recorded meetings began with disentangling but finished as planning sessions discussing feast preparations.

The two recorded disentangling meetings, then, are of the preventive type, concerned with clearing away emotional obstacles that might block the success of upcoming hunting and fishing expeditions. I cannot say what aspects of the analysis that follow might be extended to the smaller type of family disentangling usually aimed at the treatment of illness.

For the preventive purposes of the larger disentangling meetings, the very fact that a meeting occurs goes a long way toward fulfilling its aim. By just staging a session, and getting the protagonists of past conflicts to coparticipate, villagers implicitly certify that there are no lingering social rifts that would prohibit them from talking or working together. This, however, implies that participation itself may be problematic. To participate in a disentangling session is to be prepared to offer an open account of one's responses to conflictful events—an account that is supposed to be in line with the harmonizing goals of the occasion. Those unprepared to do so simply do not show up. Indeed, in one of the incidents taken up in a recorded meeting, some of the key principals were absent—a fact noted and criticized by others present. Given that knowledge of interpersonal squabbles is widely circulated in gossip, it is likely that most participants have a reasonable idea of which events will be discussed and who should discuss them. Extrapolating from topics raised in the recorded sessions, it appears that events taken up in disentangling sessions are located far enough in the past (by a matter of weeks or months), that they are unlikely to give rise to unexpected challenges or outbursts.

Both of the meetings I recorded took place in the late evening, after people from several villages had gathered in one of the larger village houses (most of the people who attended would later be engaged in cooperative activities preparing for the Christmas feast). In each meeting, floor space inside the house was completely occupied by people sitting on mats, attending to the casual activities of rolling and smoking cigarettes or chewing betel nut. With only a few small kerosene lamps inside the house, most people (about thirty in number in each case) were only barely visible in the shadows at the periphery. In addition, an indeterminate number remained outside the house, some of these occasionally speaking through the thatched walls. In this manner disentangling meetings situate participants so that anyone who speaks can be readily heard by others, while at the same time avoiding or minimizing eye contact. The physical separation of speakers imposed by darkness and seating arrangements facilitates talk about conflict without evoking confrontation and argumentation.

These features of the physical setting are consistent with the mode of speaking most characteristic of disentangling sessions. Most of the talk consists of long, uninterrupted narratives in which speakers recount past events. Each narration may take five, ten, or even twenty continuous minutes. The narrative mode permits a speaker to develop an account from his or her point of view. This format is consistent with the purpose of disentangling to provide an occasion for people simply to talk out their thoughts and feelings. Indeed, in the disentangling discourse analyzed below the major speakers introduce their turn at speaking by saying that they are going to "tell a story" (*toutonu*).

In addition to the contextual features of physical setting and narrative mode, the meaning or intent of disentangling is underscored by overt statements about the aims of the occasion. Explicit statements about the purpose of disentangling punctuate transitions between narratives, framing their significance as talking out, rather than challenging or arguing. Senior men in the village take the lead in initiating opening remarks (see below), but statements aimed at defining the situation and managing the course of interaction are contributed by many. Disentangling sessions have no single person who assumes the role of group leader to direct interaction and control speaking rights. Instead, participants collaborate in constructing a context conducive to the aims of disentangling.

The opening of each of the recorded sessions is marked by explicit statements about its purpose. The direct, focused quality of these statements index the opening of disentangling through their contrast with the unfocused talk that precedes them (cf. Turner 1972). The conversational sequence shown below illustrates the way in which four different participants jointly initiate a disentangling session through four successive turns at speaking:

Arnon: Go ahead and disentangle at this time because it is nearly time for one group to go out (fishing). It's only how many days (away) already?

Basi: Maybe Bilo and Pala should disentangle in order to go to the work, the hunting, that would be good.

Chaku: The man who died at Mosu didn't follow the doctrine, collections, didn't stay in the church. He just followed his own ways. And then he went pig hunting and died. People just accused Fada, saying that Fada made sorcery. That is what they said about that. That's what is strong (hot) with the church: collection, prayer, and disentangling before going out fishing, pig hunting and so on.

Dofu: There are always things that bite in the ocean and forest.

This exchange effectively accomplishes a number of pragmatic ends. First of all, the first speaker signals the beginning of disentangling by referring to the upcoming turtle hunt that has occasioned the meeting. The first case to be discussed is then evoked by the next speaker who calls upon two people, Bilo and Pala, to disentangle so that the collective work of turtle hunting may proceed. It is likely that most people present at the meeting expected that Bilo and Pala would discuss their entanglement in the incidents that make up the case discussed below. And, indeed, immediately after the quoted sequence, Pala begins his narrative account of the events in question.

The other opening remarks frame the purpose and importance of disentangling by reminding everyone about the harmful consequences of not doing so. The third speaker, Chaku, does this by referring to a recent incident in which a man out hunting by himself was gored by a wild pig and died from his wounds. Although the death was commonly attributed to sorcery, Chaku suggests that it may have resulted from moral failure, from failure to adhere to Christian doctrine and practice. He lists disentangling along with Christian practices of collection and prayer—practices regarded as essential for maintaining a mantle of spiritual protection against accidents and misfortune. The comparison is consistent with the functional analogy noted earlier between disentangling and communion. Chaku thus reminds those present that disentangling is a way of remaining "strong with the church" before venturing out on risky ventures such as hunting or fishing. Dofu makes the same point somewhat more succinctly by simply noting that "There are always things that bite in the ocean and forest."

These opening statements articulate the "official agenda." But this is by no means all that goes on in disentangling. In addition to the stated goal of talking about bad feelings, disentangling narratives promote a speaker's interpretation of events—events in which that person has been personally involved. It is not surprising then to find that disentangling discourse is aimed in part at rationalizing such involvement. The ambiguity between the two agendas, overt and covert (i.e., attempting to achieve community rapprochement and asserting a preferred interpretation of conflict), creates a conceptual tension that is deftly manipulated by participants. Even though the acknowledged definition of the situation is that of an occasion for airing bad feelings without engendering further conflict, disentangling is inevitably concerned with competing interpretations of contested events.

When the mode of interaction drifts too far into the realm of challenge and riposte, however, it is likely to be directed back on course by other participants. So, for example, in the case taken up below, one of the participants attempts to signal the end of the exchange between the two brothers, Pala and Bilo, after each has completed an extended narrative:

The two of them are finished. All right, very good.

But when Pala and Bilo continue to exchange further remarks, another participant attempts another closing:

So, it's gone all right, you two.

The younger brother, Pala, however, persists in rationalizing certain aspects of the case until yet a third participant interrupts to assert that they are wandering from the relevant subject, and someone else should quickly initiate a new topic:

You two are going to other talk. Someone else go ahead, quickly.
It is not unusual for participants in these sessions to call for others to
initiate disentangling. In this instance, however, calls for the transition
to a new topic are evoked when Pala and Bilo slip out of a narrative
mode of speech into a more confrontational style, marked by a more
rapid sequence of turn taking in which each is responding directly to
the other.

A CASE OF DISENTANGLING

In the remainder of this chapter we will focus on one segment of talk
in a disentangling meeting that pertains to an incident in which a teen-
age boy was beaten by other boys, causing their parents and other villagers to become embroiled in disagreements about how to deal with the
offenders. In this case the process of disentangling consisted primarily
of narrative accounts of what happened by the two main principals: the
victim's father, Pala, and the father of one of the attackers, Bilo. As in
most cases of disentangling, the principals are closely related (in this
instance maternal cousins, classificatory brothers living in neighboring
villages). Discussion of this case at the meeting came to a close when
others present intervened to shift to another topic.

Nearly one year prior to the disentangling meeting, three teen-age
boys ganged up on Pala's son, Rubin, and beat him up either as a prank
or to settle a score of some kind. In itself, this incident was not contro-
versial. Everyone agreed that it was a somewhat serious example of
adolescent misbehavior. The incident became a problem for the wider
community when relatives of the boys disagreed about how to deal with
the matter. It appears that Rubin's mother's brother, Mark, reported
the attack to the police who then discussed the matter with various people
in the community, including Pala, who agreed to take the attackers to
court. The three boys were ultimately given fines of up to five dollars,
a substantial amount of money in a cash-poor society where many people
have difficulty raising the eleven-dollar annual tax.

It was this response, reporting the matter to the police and pursuing
it in court, that upset the parents of the attackers and others, leading to
a more serious rift with repercussions for people in several villages. As
a result of the police intervention, Bilo, father of one of the accused,
said that he would withdraw from the upcoming Christmas feast that
was to be staged in his village. Furthermore, he said he would rather
leave the island for wage labor than have to interact with the people
who had taken his son to court. This threat affected a wider network
because Bilo had been raising pigs contributed by Pala and others for
the feast. Once the rift occurred, Bilo let it be known that Pala and the

others might just as well come up to his village and cook and eat their pigs.

And so it was that a fight among teen-age boys had reverberations that threatened to disrupt a major Christmas feast being prepared by several villages. It is in fact the repercussions that are most at issue in the disentangling narratives. The accounts related by Pala and Bilo are concerned essentially with how people responded to the fight incident and what those responses imply about their relations with one another. By describing events in a certain way and imputing feelings and motives of a certain sort, speakers construct interpretations of the episode, focusing especially on the nature of their relations with one another.

Both Pala and Bilo are concerned with rationalizing their past actions. Pala must defend his taking the boys to court and Bilo his threat to withdraw from community activities. In doing so, both construe their motives in ways that highlight their concern for community values and solidarity. These concerns are stated explicitly but are also implied in the speakers' talk about the way they responded to the events in question.

The opening segment of Pala's narrative is translated below as a basis for analyzing more closely the cultural assumptions and rhetorical strategies used in disentangling discourse.[4] As already discussed, disentangling meetings are not led by any single individual who sets topics or regulates turn taking. Villagers come to the meeting with expectations about what events will be reviewed. In this case, all that was required to initiate discussion of the beating incident was for someone to utter, "Maybe Bilo and Pala should disentangle." Two turns later, with Bilo sitting quietly across the room (and Mark not even present), Pala began as follows.

"Perhaps the two of them should disentangle," you all say. But for myself, the sort of thing that happened is already finished. Perhaps it is still with my older brother Bilo. But I will go over that story again about the two of us going to court so all of you and my brother Bilo will know "Oh, so that's how it was!" even though I'm now finished with that. I don't have any more thoughts about that which is now gone, finished.

All right, that incident that we all know about is the way of all the young men. When the three young men fought, they were still mine, not someone else's. My boy also came to play. I didn't know about them, didn't see them. I don't know about their playing around, the wrestling of the young men. . . . It was from (the police) that I heard about it. "Your boy was choked by them until he almost died, man" was the news that reached me here. Because of that I was sad for my son (Rubin). They are all really my children. . . . Bilo's children are my children. The children of other men at Molana (Bilo's village) are also like mine. Since I am not ashamed of these places, when passing by I can just go and reach for food in their baskets at those places. I am not ashamed; they are all my children, to my way of thinking. I was sad about my child who almost died, that is what I was sad about. It was when they came to take Rubin that I realized, "So the police have taken (the boys) because of the fight these young men had!" Because of that I thought, "Oh, that behavior will get them in prison."

As can be seen in this portion of Pala's narrative, he weaves talk of emotion into the early part of his narrative, framing his interpretation of the beating and its aftermath. Specifically, he says that he was sad (di'a nagnafa) for his son "who almost died." By speaking of sadness rather than anger, Pala draws attention to the nature of his close relations with the transgressors rather than with the transgression itself. The local concept of sadness (di'a nagnafa) pertains to the loss or damage of relations with significant others, whereas anger signals a reaction to transgressions against the self or community. The implied meanings of sadness are also evident in more overt remarks that Pala makes about his relationship to the offenders at this point in his narrative. Immediately following his talk of feeling sad about the beating, he goes on to describe his relation with the attackers and others in their village, Molana, as one of diffuse solidarity.

Pala's characterization of social relationships draws upon two powerful idioms: kinship ("Bilo's children are my children") and shame. The kinship metaphor, which occurs throughout the narrative, is commonly used to signify enduring ties marked by mutual interest and reciprocity. To buttress this characterization, Pala talks about the absence of shame (mamaja) in his interactions with the people of Molana. In its affirmative form, talk of shame marks a failure of social definition in which appropriate distance has not been observed (Epstein 1984; Fajans 1985; White 1990b).

By negating shame in situations involving distant relations that would normally evoke it, Pala implies that his relations with Molana people are of the familiar sort unencumbered by distance-maintaining rules of etiquette or avoidance. He does this by stating that he is accustomed to going into people's houses to help himself to leftover food, and does so without shame. The image of entering a house for food is a common symbol of solidarity.[5] In Pala's narrative, the food-sharing scenario exemplifies familiar behavior that would certainly evoke shame in the wrong context, that is, one characterized by more distant relations. Since in this instance shame is *not* evoked, the listener is led to infer that the relations in question must in fact be close and enduring.

If all Pala is trying to accomplish in his narrative is to reaffirm his relations with Bilo and others, this sort of talk might be sufficient. Yet, he must also give an account of the problematic events surrounding his taking Bilo's son and others to court. The images of kinship and absence of shame are in the service of Pala's overall assertion that he acted out of sadness (that others so close to him could so undervalue their relationship). The sadness attribution, however, is also an effective way of making a claim about Pala's intentions in responding the way he did to the beating incident. According to the indigenous model, sadness typically leads to efforts at reconciliation rather than retribution given the value placed on close relations and the need to restore them. To underscore this concern in the passage above, talk of shame with its connotations of closeness is embedded between references to the sadness evoked by the beating.

Each emotion attribution is a partial "filling-in" or instantiation of a general schema (White 1990a, 1990b). Once the emotion portion of a scenario is stated, the listener may draw inferences about how the events leading to or following from that emotion are to be interpreted. The rhetorical role of emotion talk is especially significant for disentangling meetings with their need to avoid provocation and confrontation. Talk of emotions allows speakers to make *indirect* moral claims. By relying on shared models of the person and action, the speaker hopes that the listener will fill in unspoken portions of the model with information available in the narrative or elsewhere, even though the speaker has not been explicit about those aspects of the events.

By saying that a particular emotion arises in relation to a certain event, the speaker implicitly characterizes that event as a specific instance of a general class of events known to evoke that emotion. Thus, when Pala asserts that the beating of his son made him sad he is implying, in this context, that the beating is an instance of damage to close relations, that is, the sort of thing that evokes sadness. And, even more important for his portrayal of the incident, his taking the offending boys to court can be recast as an attempt at "teaching" his fictive sons rather than as some kind of angry getting-even, which would be inappropriate between close kin, especially (fictive) parents and children.

The fact that both anger and sadness could plausibly be said to follow from the same event involving transgression creates the possibility of ambiguity as to which aspects of the event participants are attending to. It is just this ambiguity that Pala and others in disentangling manipulate in their talk of sadness as a response and as a motive.

Immediately following the passage quoted above, Pala raises the matter of how and why he went to court over the incident. He describes his participation in the court procedure and the issuance of fines as motivated by an interest in seeing that the boys be led to repent (*tughuhehe*; literally, "change their minds"); and he further rationalizes that participation by saying that he arranged for the fines to be lowered from a potential thirty dollars to five dollars and three dollars because the attackers are "my boys, like my children."

Prior to closing his narrative, Pala asserts that he would have preferred dealing with the matter of the fight in the "way of togetherness, the way of discussion," but that once the police intervened, that was not possible. In this way, Pala brings his interpretation in line with the avowed goals of disentangling to reassert solidarity in significant interpersonal relations.

Immediately following Pala's account, his older brother, Bilo, gave his account of the contested events. The structure of his narrative mirrors that of Pala's account. Like his younger brother, Bilo prefaced his remarks by distancing himself from the actual fight involving his son. Instead, he addresses the act of reporting, referring to the man (Mark) who reported the matter to the district constable, noting that this action bypassed village discussions, which would have been the best way of handling the affair. Following this, Bilo agrees with Pala's account of his threats to leave the island prior to the planned feast, but goes on to rationalize these actions by describing the way in which Pala and Mark bypassed village-based solutions in favor of the police and court. He describes this use of the court with ironic references to getting "burned" in the "live fire." With these events as a backdrop, he refers again to his talk of leaving, characterizing it as a response of sadness to the actions of those who went to the police:

I did say those things that you, Pala, are talking about. Those were the words that I spoke, the words which you speak about. Yes, they sent the pigs to me, and I was here (tending them) when I heard about those actions (reporting to the police). Then I was sad. "Maybe I should go out, go away." That's what I said when we had our meeting there at Kolobanga which you (Pala) did not attend.

So, just as Pala was sad about his metaphorical children beating up his son, Bilo is sad in response to the fact that his relations took him and his son to court, rather than work things out as would be done in the customary ways of being sympathetic and talking well before trying more severe measures.

This episode not only illustrates the use of emotion rhetoric in the discourse of moral claims, it also shows that the exchanges are concerned as much with the ground rules for managing conflict as with the particulars of the case at hand. The narratives seem concerned as much with negotiating the premises of a moral system as with applying them to the evaluation of a particular incident. Analysis of disentangling discourse suggests that it is in the application that moral assumptions are either reaffirmed in their enactment or diminished by their failure to achieve evaluative force.

As stated at the outset, the narratives in this exchange were directed at the discrepant ways in which a problematic event (the beating of a young boy) was handled by people in the community. A key point of disagreement concerned the entry of the local police into the matter, symbolizing a widening of the conflict event beyond the villages involved to include the district government apparatus. Just how the police were drawn in was a point of contention that remained ambiguous in the narratives. But all of the speakers acknowledged the fundamental opposition of tradition and government as two distinct arenas through which to deal with interpersonal conflict. In this instance, the traditional means of engaging in face-to-face discussions led by chiefs was seen as preempted by the Western-style bureaucratic mode once the police stepped in. As Pala put it:

If when the boys did that you, older brother Bilo, had acted and James Muno (catechist of his village) had just come straight to me and said, "The boys have done this, made it difficult for us (exclusive), man."[6] If that is what had happened when the news of the fighting first arrived, maybe we (exclusive) could have finished it in the way of togetherness, the way of discussion. But when the police came in, we (exclusive) were finished. No way could that be.

Bilo also elaborated on this point in his narrative, since it was his son and nephews who were taken to court and fined. As he put it,

In my thoughts about these things we (inclusive) ourselves should have handled them first. We should take care of them ourselves before saying, "O.K., this matter is bad, it is appropriate for that place over there (the District Court)." But what actually happened was just charging by in order to do that. The other kind of thinking could have easily gone ahead. Chiefs, men for doing these things, for deciding these ways for us, are still here. It would have been best if we ourselves (inclusive) had done those things, gotten to the bottom of it, before saying "Oh, all right, this fits that place (the court)." . . . This is the present (modern) kind, the modern way, the modern life. The way before would have been to be sympathetic with a person, to talk well before going and doing something. . . . So you two (Pala and Mark) went right by, you two did that first, you two went right into the live fire (court).

For Bilo the disentangling session afforded him an opportunity to articulate a perceived injustice by invoking shared understandings about the value and priority of traditional modes of resolving conflict. It is inevitable that ambiguities and contradictions in the wider political system in Santa Isabel will surface in disentangling narratives. In this instance, problems arising from the intrusion of a modern bureaucratic system into small communities based on diffuse ties of kinship and face-to-face morality are played out in the narratives of Pala and Bilo, each seeking to frame his own actions in terms of ideal models of social reality.

As an activity aimed at "conflict resolution," this case of disentangling does not seem to have accomplished very much. The two protagonists,

Pala and Bilo, both had their say, with two somewhat discrepant accounts of contested events produced, and the narratives allowed to stand with little comment or reflection on their relative merit. Furthermore, the disentangling meeting occurred only after the legal issues had been resolved in local court, so that the disentangling is ritualistic at best, an aesthetic device designed to "smooth over" ruffled feathers. Rather than draw dichotomizing distinctions between the "instrumental" and the "expressive," or between the "practical" and the "ritual," I would argue that the rhetoric of disentangling is concerned with the highly practical activity of constituting an intersubjective social reality within which people create their mutual relations and coordinate their lives. While Pala and Bilo may disagree in their interpretations of the contested events, the assumptions they use to construct those interpretations—assumptions about the ideals of solidarity among kin and about the desirability of teaching correct behavior to the young—are implicitly acknowledged by both. Hence, in addition to the culturally recognized need to talk out hidden grievances and avoid possible calamities caused by bad feeling, engaging in disentangling presupposes and reaffirms taken-for-granted understandings about social relations that make up the fabric of community.

The act of disentangling itself pragmatically realigns relations that may have been left askew by prior conflict. In this case, the mutual involvement expected between fictive brothers is indexed by the simple fact of their joint participation in disentangling. The disentangling event creates a context for enacting an idealized model of ongoing relations and shared interest among kin. In this case, the public performance of disentangling creates a collectively acknowledged basis for Pala and Bilo to cooperate in preparing for the Christmas feast. Indeed, when the feast was held three weeks after the disentangling session, both of them took part, with the pigs that Bilo had threatened to withhold making up a notable portion of the food distribution.

In this chapter we have looked at an account of the activity of disentangling in a Solomon Islands society such that it may be understood in its own terms. This has involved paying attention to how disentangling is practiced as a culturally conceived and socially implemented form of discourse. Disentangling relies upon shared conceptions of person and emotion to indirectly advance moral claims at the same time that it fulfills the overt agenda of talking out bad feelings.

In the small villages of Santa Isabel, it is usually regarded as improper, if not dangerous, to talk casually about interpersonal conflict, especially in the presence of those with whom one may be "entangled" (White 1985b). In Santa Isabel, as in many Pacific Island societies, people embroiled in conflict experience shame (*mamaja*) and actively avoid one

another—a task that may be highly burdensome in small island communities. Disentangling provides a culturally constituted means of restoring relations and dispelling shame. As Lamont Lindstrom (1990) has
noted, meetings that appear to be about "conflict resolution" in Pacific
societies may actually be more concerned with "avoidance resolution"—
with reestablishing a subjective basis for everyday interaction.

As a somewhat unique occasion for constructing social reality through
talk, disentangling meetings are a key site for the reproduction of so-
ciopolitical structures and a sense of community (Brenneis and Myers
1984).[7] To the extent that a disentangling session establishes some degree
of convergence in the models that are presumed or asserted in speakers'
interpretations of events, the activity succeeds in externalizing those
models as social reality. At the same time, however, each time a given
moral premise is invoked it raises the possibility of its own revision or
restructuring to accommodate disquieting events. For example, in the
case examined above, the discussion of alternative ways of handling
conflict in the community revealed differing conceptions of the relevance
of "tradition" and "chiefs" as a resource for dealing with disputes in a
modern world where government courts and police play a powerful and
often ambiguous role. While both Pala and Bilo appear to subscribe to
the desirability of traditional ways of resolving conflict by talking with
village chiefs, those ways take on meaning only in opposition with the
"modern ways" that both speakers implicitly acknowledge as the dominant political reality. In this manner, disentangling narratives rework
concepts of person and community coded in images of "tradition" to
accommodate the novel situations and challenges of contemporary society. Seen in this light, the rhetoric of disentangling is also the reality
of changing lives.

NOTES

This chapter is based in part on previous publications by the author on related
topics (White 1990b; White and Watson-Gegeo 1990). Research for this chapter
was carried out in Santa Isabel in 1975–76 and in 1984. Support of that work
by the Social Science Research Council and the Wenner–Gren Foundation is
gratefully acknowledged. Francis Kokhonigita, a friend and informant who has
since passed away, gave invaluable assistance at all stages of data collection and
provided the keys to many of the doors that have opened since. I am grateful
to numerous people for comments and suggestions on previous papers related
to this topic. I especially wish to thank (without holding them responsible) Peter
Black, Edwin Hutchins, Karen Ito, John Kirkpatrick, Naomi Quinn, Melford
Spiro, and Karen Watson-Gegeo.

   1. In addition to the comparison of disentangling and communion, there is
an analogy between disentangling and Anglican confession. Unlike the former,

the latter does involve divulging transgressions in an act of verbal expiation. An important difference, of course, is that disentangling is ideally done in the presence of those with whom one is entangled. In both cases sheer participation signifies good standing in the moral community. I was told by more than one informant that the confessional provided an important innovation that allowed people a way to fulfill the cultural "requirement" of divulging transgressions (rather than keep them hidden, where they may be dangerous to self and others) without the sorts of public revelation that could lead to further entanglements. At least one priest I talked with saw his role in taking confession as providing an alternative to customary disentangling. There is today a continuum of moral events in which priests play a major role, ranging from confession to family disentanglings (which may sometimes be convened by a priest) to the larger village meetings (where priests frequently sit in as listeners and facilitators). The participation of priests in the latter type of meetings follows primarily from their role as representatives of the moral order rather than their role as mediators of the spirit world, although both roles are probably relevant.

2. My gloss of vernacular emotion words from one of the Santa Isabel languages (Cheke Holo) with English terms raises important translation issues. Obviously, the use of English glosses assumes some overlap in meaning, but at the same time simplifies and distorts understanding in those areas where the two languages diverge. Much of this chapter is concerned with the problems of representing indigenous emotion concepts with English words, and the reader should be aware of the inadequacy of glosses such as anger, sadness, and shame as translations (see also White 1990b).

3. The two tape-recorded sessions were transcribed in their entirety by a local assistant who had himself been present at the meeting. I then checked the transcripts and reviewed their contents with him to fill in gaps in my translation and knowledge of the events discussed. Given the amount of presupposed knowledge in the meeting narratives, this expansion is an essential part of the analysis. Unlike many of the detailed studies of therapy discourse in more familiar settings (Labov and Fanshel 1977), this expansion draws upon a wide range of ethnographic background data.

4. The narrative excerpts are given in English translation prepared by the author in consultation with a local informant. No strong argument is given for the validity of paragraphing, offered as an aid to readability. For a full transcript of the meeting from which this case is drawn see White 1990b.

5. This image relies on the understanding that people customarily place leftover potatoes in a hanging basket inside the house. Not only is food an important symbol of relations characterized by reciprocal exchange (Fajans 1985), but easy movement across house boundaries is usually reserved for members of immediate or extended families.

6. Like most Pacific languages, Cheke Holo makes a distinction in first person plural pronouns (we, us) as to whether or not the collective "we" includes ("inclusive") or excludes ("exclusive") the listener. In a context such as disentangling, the choice of pronouns is a clear political act, indexing the nature of relations between people in the meeting.

7. Given its symbolic and practical significance in shaping social reality, the practice of disentangling is itself a contested subject—a site for debate about the

meaning and value of cultural practices for dealing with conflict. The role of disentangling in contemporary Santa Isabel society—thoroughly Christian and embedded in a newly independent nation—is uncertain at best. It is my impression based on observations over about fifteen years that disentangling as a distinct activity is on the wane. Eroded on the one side by church practices of confession and communion, and on the other by expanding government courts, disentangling meetings appear to be less and less common. While it is likely that the long history of Christianization on Santa Isabel has already affected the goals and practice of disentangling, the highly egalitarian and participatory social structure of disentangling has struck some church leaders as inconsistent with their role in regulating their society's moral discourse. One district priest suggested that his consultations with families are a form of disentangling, but one that must remain private and directed by him. And, in a recent conversation with the retired (indigenous) bishop of Santa Isabel, I was told that "the idea alone is not very good. So in some cases I tried to discourage it. I mean, from the church point of view, we have the general confession. At that time you can say anything in the general confession in church. But general confession in public is not very good. I mean, you break custom and there is no privacy. The church doesn't accept that."

REFERENCES

Arno, Andrew. 1979. Conflict, Ritual and Social Structure on Yanuyanu Island, Fiji. *Bijdragen Deel* 135:1–17.

Bailey, F. G. 1983. *The Tactical Uses of Passion: An Essay on Power, Reason and Reality.* Ithaca, N.Y.: Cornell University Press.

Beattie, J. H. M. 1957. Informal Judicial Activity in Bunyoro. *Journal of African Administration* 9:188–95.

Brenneis, Donald. 1990. Dramatic Gestures: The Fiji Indian *Pancayat* as Therapeutic Event. In *Disentangling*: Conflict Discourse in Pacific Societies, eds. K. Watson-Gegeo and G. White. Stanford: Stanford University Press.

Brenneis, Donald, and Fred Myers, eds. 1984. *Dangerous Words: Language and Politics in the Pacific.* New York: New York University Press.

Epstein, A. L. 1984. The Experience of Shame in Melanesia: An Essay in the Anthropology of Affect. London: Royal Anthropological Institute of Great Britain and Ireland, Occasional Paper No. 40.

Fajans, J. 1985. The Person in Social Context: The Social Character of Baining "Psychology." In *Person, Self and Experience: Exploring Pacific Ethnopsychologies*, eds. G. White and J. Kirkpatrick. Berkeley: University of California Press.

Gibbs, James. 1963. The Kpelle Moot: A Therapeutic Model for the Informal Settlement of Disputes. *Africa* 33:1–11.

Gluckman, Max. 1955. *Custom and Conflict in Africa.* Glencoe, Ill.: Free.

Harris, Grace. 1978. *Casting Out Anger: Religion among the Taita of Kenya.* New York: Cambridge University Press.

Ito, Karen L. 1985. Ho'oponopono, "To Make Right": Hawaiian Conflict Resolution and Metaphor in the Construction of a Family Therapy. *Culture, Medicine and Psychiatry* 9: 201–17.

Labov, William, and David Fanshel. 1977. *Therapeutic Discourse: Psychotherapy as Conversation*. New York: Academic.

Lakoff, George, and Mark Johnson. 1980. *Metaphors We Live By*. Chicago: University of Chicago Press.

Lakoff, George, and Zoltan Kovecses. 1987. The Conceptualization of Anger in American English. In *Cultural Models in Language and Thought*, eds. D. Holland and N. Quinn. New York: Cambridge University Press.

Lindstrom, Lamont. 1990. Straight Talk on Tanna. In *Disentangling: Conflict Discourse in Pacific Societies*, eds. K. Watson-Gegeo and G. White. Stanford: Stanford University Press.

Lutz, Catherine. 1988. *Unnatural Emotions*. Chicago: University of Chicago Press.

———. 1987. Goals, Events and Understanding in Ifaluk Emotion Theory. In *Cultural Models in Language and Thought*, eds. D. Holland and N. Quinn. New York: Cambridge University Press.

Lutz, Catherine, and Geoffrey White. 1986. The Anthropology of Emotions. In *Annual Review of Anthropology*, ed. B. Siegel. Palo Alto: Annual Reviews.

Needham, Rodney. 1976. Skulls and Causality. *Man* (n.s.) 11:71–88.

Norbeck, Edward. 1963. African Rituals of Conflict. *American Anthropologist* 65:1254–79.

Ortner, Sherry B. 1984. Theory in Anthropology Since the Sixties. *Comparative Studies in Society and History* 26(1):126–66.

Pande, S. K. 1968. The Mystique of "Western" Psychotherapy: An Eastern Interpretation. *Journal of Nervous and Mental Disease* 146:425–32.

Parsons, Talcott. 1951. *The Social System*. Glencoe, Ill.: Free.

Poole, F. J. P. 1985. The Surfaces and Depths of Bimin-Kuskusmin Experiences of "Anger": Toward a Theory of Culture and Emotion in the Constitution of Self. Paper given at the 84th Annual Meeting of the American Anthropological Association, Washington, D.C.

Quinn, Naomi, and Dorothy Holland. 1987. Culture and Cognition. In *Cultural Models in Language and Thought*, eds. D. Holland and N. Quinn. New York: Cambridge University Press.

Scheff, Thomas J. 1979. *Catharsis in Healing, Ritual and Drama*. Berkeley: University of California Press.

Strathern, Marilyn. 1968. Popokl: The Question of Morality. *Mankind*: 553–62.

Turner, R. 1972. Some Formal Properties of Therapy Talk. In *Studies in Social Interaction*, ed. D. Sudnow. New York: Free.

Turner, Victor. 1964. An Ndembu Doctor in Practice. In *Magic, Faith and Healing*, ed. A. Kiev. New York: Free.

Watson-Gegeo, Karen, and David Gegeo. 1990. Shaping the Mind and Straightening Out Conflicts: The Discourse of Kwara'ae Family Counseling. In *Disentangling: Conflict Discourse in Pacific Societies*, eds. Karen Watson-Gegeo and Geoffrey White. Stanford: Stanford University Press.

Watson-Gegeo, Karen, and Geoffrey White, eds. 1990. *Disentangling: Conflict Discourse in Pacific Societies*. Stanford: Stanford University Press.

White, Geoffrey M. 1979. War, Peace and Piety in Santa Isabel, Solomon Islands. In *The Pacification of Melanesia*, eds. M. Rodman and M. Cooper. Ann Arbor: University of Michigan Press.

————. 1980. Social Images and Social Change in a Melanesian Society. *American Ethnologist* 7:352–70.

————. 1985a. Premises and Purposes in a Solomon Islands Ethnopsychology. In *Person, Self and Experience: Exploring Pacific Ethnopsychologies*, eds. G. White and J. Kirkpatrick. Berkeley: University of California Press.

————. 1985b. "Bad Ways" and "Bad Talk": Interpretations of Interpersonal Conflict in a Melanesian Society. In *Directions in Cognitive Anthropology*, ed. J. Dougherty. Urbana: University of Illinois Press.

————. 1988. Symbols of Solidarity in the Christianization of Santa Isabel. In *Culture and Christianity: The Dialectics of Transformation*, ed. G. Saunders. Westport, Conn.: Greenwood.

————. 1990a. Moral Discourse and the Rhetoric of Emotion. In *Language and the Politics of Emotion*, eds. C. Lutz and L. Abu-Lughod. Cambridge: Cambridge University Press.

————. 1990b. Emotion Talk and Social Inference: The Case of Disentangling. In *Disentangling: Conflict Discourse in Pacific Societies*, eds. Karen Watson-Gegeo and Geoffrey White. Stanford: Stanford University Press.

White, Geoffrey M., Kokhonigita, Francis, and Pulomana, Hugo, 1988. *Cheke Holo Dictionary*. Canberra: Pacific Linguistics.

10

Ho'oponopono: Straightening Family Relationships in Hawaii

E. Victoria Shook and Leonard Ke'ala Kwan

Ho'oponopono, which means "setting to right," refers to the process used by Hawaiian families to restore harmonious relationships through prayer, discussion, apology, and forgiveness (Pūku'i et al. 1972). It is a process guided by a member of the extended family, the *haku*, who is not usually involved in the conflict, but is intimately known to the parties and often a respected elder. *Ho'oponopono* also seems to be a concept and practice that attracts the attention of non-Hawaiians, perhaps because it suggests patterns, associations, and nuances about conflict and conflict resolution that are not easily translated. Howard Rheingold has written a book entitled *They Have a Word for It: A Lighthearted Lexicon of Untranslatable Words and Phrases*. Although the book is, as the title suggests, mostly entertainment, Rheingold admits a more serious purpose for the lexicon: "Although it's great fun to read about strange and curious words, unless those words also happen to match semantic niches in our culture—a real social need for a specific attitude, object or behavior—they are no more than amusements. But a book of useful, heretofore untranslatable words for attitudes, objects or behaviors that we don't have but might need in America could become something more powerful than an amusement. It could become an instrument of change" (1988:4).

It is not too surprising that Rheingold "discovered" *ho'oponopono* and featured it prominently in the book.[1] What is so intriguing about this concept?

A HAWAIIAN VIEW: THE WEB OF RELATIONSHIPS

In a recent book exploring traditional and contemporary Hawaiian values, G. H. S. Kanahele (1986:19–20) lists the following values as most important to Hawaiians today: *aloha*,[2] humility, spirituality, generosity, graciousness, keeping promises, intelligence, cleanliness, and helpfulness. These attributes suggest a relational view of the world, a worldview that rests firmly on a spiritual foundation. Before the coming of Westerners to Hawaii there was not a specific word for religion. Spirituality was not separate from life, but permeated all aspects of it. Why name it? As in many other Pacific societies the Hawaiians perceived the cosmos as sacred. All things were related in a web of life and possessed *mana*. About *mana* Kanahele (1986:74) says: "Basically it represents the most primordial force in the universe that animates or gives life or power to all things." It was important for a person to know how to relate to the varieties of life force, whether of rocks, fellow humans, animals, or the gods, in a beneficent way. Wrongful or disrespectful actions could have negative reverberations throughout the web. M. Mossman and P. Wahilani (1975) adduce a triad of relationships among the major forces: the gods, nature, and man. Contemporary examples also testify to the understanding that spiritual concerns pervade the social order.[3]

One example illustrates this triad relationship clearly. In a recent continuing land-use dispute on the island of Hawaii, Hawaiian activists were opposed tõ geothermal energy development because it would violate the *'āina* (land). The development site on the Kīlauea volcano is believed to be the home of Pele, a Hawaiian goddess. "Some individuals believe that the area of active volcanism is, in fact, *Pele*'s body and therefore any exploration and development would remove her energy. This, in turn, would threaten the continuance of ritual practices and therefore inhibit the training of ritual practices and of young Hawaiians in traditional practices and beliefs" (Edmunds 1987:109).

The Nexus of the Web: The *'Ohana*

The triad of relationships among humans, nature, and the gods is primary, but the family (*'ohana*) is the nexus of the relationships according to M. K. Pūku'i et al. (1972:166). The word *'ohana* is derived from one of the root words for a stalk of taro, *'oha*. The taro plant (*kalo*) is a staple food and linked to myths about the origin of the Hawaiian people. Metaphorically, the family is also likened to taro: many shoots arise from a single root. Pūku'i has described the qualities of the *'ohana* as "a sense of unity, shared involvement and shared responsibility. It is mutual interdependence and mutual help. It is emotional support given and received. It is solidarity and cohesiveness. It is love—often; it is loyalty—always. It is all this, encompassed by the joined links of blood relationship" (Pūku'i et al. 1972:171).

The family is made up of multiple generations: parents and children, grandparents, aunts, uncles, cousins, and so forth. The family also extends to the past and to the spiritual world through its ancestors. The *'aumākua* were the ancestor spirits. "The concept of *'aumākua* was a nearly ideal one. The Hawaiians lived within the close relationships of the *'ohana* (family or family clan); the *'aumākua* remained members of the clan. The *'ohana* invested family authority in its senior members; the *'aumākua* as spiritual ancestors were certainly seniors. With one's *'aumākua*, a human-to-spirit communication was possible" (Pūku'i et al. 1972:35).[4]

The family's structure is hierarchical, with guidance and authority residing in the seniors or *kūpuna*. The *kūpuna* are respected for their wisdom and experience and as teachers of younger family members. The following Hawaiian proverb extols the value of the elders:

E mālama i ka makua, he mea laha 'ole; o ke kāne he loa'a i ka lā ho'okahi.
Take care of parents for they are choice, a husband can be found in a day.
("Parents should be cared for, for when they are gone, there are none to replace them. One can marry again and again.") (Pūku'i 1983:42)

Traditionally, the *kūpuna* have also had a key role in resolving conflicts in the family and are frequently the leaders of *ho'oponopono* sessions.

Children have an important role in the family and are highly desired. Infants are generally indulged and are often the focus of attention in the family. A toddler is expected to begin assuming some family responsibilities (Gallimore et al. 1974). Older siblings are involved in caring for the younger children. The child development process fosters interdependence and increased opportunity to exercise adult-type roles by working and contributing to the family's economic and social welfare.

Children learn family tasks through observation and experience. They learn to be unobtrusive. If they do otherwise they risk rebuff and punishment. Children may seek help and approval from adults, but in a subtle, nonintrusive manner. Rewards and punishments in the family are often meted out to a group rather than to an individual. R. Gallimore et al. (1974) suggest that this fosters one of the two primary strategies used by children to get along in the family: sibling cooperation. The other strategy is avoidance of conflict with adults. As we shall see in the Kealoha example later, *ho'oponopono* provides an outlet for children to express conflicts in ways that do not violate general family norms.

These socialization practices underscore a predominant value pattern of affiliation. Many writers have emphasized the affiliative nature of Hawaiian social order (Whitney 1987; Ito 1985b; Howard 1974; Gallimore et al. 1974). This value is expressed in local Hawaiian social interaction in terms of concepts such as *laulima* (cooperation) and *kōkua* (help), words that reinforce interdependence.[5] Hawaiian culture requires an individual to cultivate the ability to perceive and attend to others' needs, often without being asked.

An Extended Concept of Self

The Hawaiian concept of person or self is relational. K. L. Ito (1985a:320) points out that "self is a socially interactive concept tied to correct social behavior (*hana pono*) between self and other." She also describes the self as extending genealogically to ancestors, ancestor gods (*'aumākua*), and major gods. This self-in-relationship is manifested in daily life through *kino lau*, the various natural forms of gods and goddesses.

Pele, the volcano goddess, had *kino lau* of not only volcanic activity and lava flow but of a young, beautiful girl, an old hag, red-colored earth, fire, and tiny lava pebbles called *Pele*'s tears. Belief in *Pele*'s *kino lau* is much alive on the Big Island of Hawai'i where volcanic activity remains vigorous. Adults and children tell of encountering *Pele* as an old woman on the road and children explain that *Pele* is still in the lava rocks they pick up on the ground (see also Ciborowski and Prince-Williams [1982]). In Honolulu, Hawaiians frequently cite *Pele* as an ancestor because they have a hot temper: a type of personality *kino lau*. (Ito 1985a:305).

An expanded version of the triad model would now show a self embedded in family relationships that include manifestations and relationships in the spiritual and natural world. The key operating principle in this network is reciprocity. "Reciprocity . . . may be compared with a gigantic spider web whose threads represent the mutual obligations that each society bears toward others" (Kanahele 1986:80).

The Nature of Conflict

Conflict is perceived as a disturbance that reverberates throughout the system; if serious and unresolved, it has such consequences as natural disturbances, physical illness, misfortune in the family, or diminished interpersonal and intrapersonal functioning.[6]

Interpersonal conflict is perceived as a blocked pathway. People are connected via emotional channels and conflict blocks the flow of affection. A colloquial expression for this condition is the exclamation that a relationship is "all jam up!" The web, channel, or "conduit" (Ito 1985a:307) metaphor is apparent in the Hawaiian concept of *hukihuki*, which literally means "pull, pull."

Hukihuki describes a total, damaging situation that exists when opposing individuals or groups tug, pull and pressure to gain emotional ascendancy over another individual or group. Often it affects children. Mother and father are rivals for their children's affections. Divorced parents battle for child custody....

When the one-in-the-middle becomes involved in the struggle, *hukihuki* becomes harmful. Adults who are forewarned, experienced or naturally wise can escape such involvement. Others cannot. Children are almost always caught. Children are almost always hurt. (Pūku'i et al. 1972:88–89)

Conflicts, or negative blocks in the pathways, can be present even when individuals are unaware of them. This lack of awareness does not prevent negative repercussions. Misfortune or unexpected occurrences can be understood as evidence that "the way had not been clear," that forces in the larger field impinged on human activity. Recently, one of the authors was scheduled to do a presentation on *ho'oponopono* for a group of inmates at a local correctional facility. The presentation was to be co-led with a Hawaiian woman who was a counselor. We met together a few times to plan the presentation and a date was set, but the presentation was cancelled and rescheduled several times due to illness and conflicting work commitments. Finally we were able to do the presentation. Afterwards, while talking about the cancellations and rescheduling, she explained to me, as if it were obvious: "The way wasn't clear for us to do the presentation before today."

It is also a common Hawaiian practice to "clear the way" through prayer, fasting, or "mental cleansing" before any significant undertaking, such as a first birthday feast (*lū'au*), surgery, purchasing a home, or a birth. The Hawaiian counselor mentioned above "clears the way" through mental self-examination to "purify" her thoughts and attitudes before beginning a *ho'oponopono* session. She believes this preparation enhances the likelihood of a favorable outcome.

Another conflict metaphor central to *ho'oponopono* is *hihia*, or entanglement. When a conflict between two or more family members is unresolved others tend to be drawn in, which multiplies the number of *hihia*. This confuses the issues and compounds the atmosphere of tension. It becomes necessary to bring in someone else to help unravel the problems and restore harmonious relations.

These expressions about conflict reinforce the belief that people need ways to straighten things out, to restore and maintain harmony (*lōkahi*). *Ho'oponopono* is a sophisticated, yet straightforward mechanism for achieving this aim in the family.

HO'OPONOPONO

A Description

A number of variations of *ho'oponopono* exist and it is difficult to determine the prevalence of any of them. One 1976 report by a Hawaiian agency, Alu Like, indicated that 38 percent of Hawaiian and part-Hawaiian households surveyed said they used *ho'oponopono* (Boggs and Chun 1987:1). How the respondents defined the practice is not known. Pūku'i reported that the use of *ho'oponopono* had fallen off dramatically by the mid-nineteenth century due to the rise in influence of the Christian missionaries (1972:69). The version of *ho'oponopono* that she had learned and practiced while growing up was later published in *Nānā I Ke Kumu*. This publication codified definitions of her version, and it became the model for many contemporary practitioners.

Various descriptions of the purposes of *ho'oponopono* are found in the literature. M. P. Mays (1973:2) describes two aims: "to solve interpersonal disputes, and to resolve conflicts and bad feelings; and to restructure the family, reintegrate members, and to foster individual role socialization performance." S. T. Boggs and M. N. Chun (1990) review a number of descriptions and discuss four elements common to all: 1) discovering the cause of the trouble; 2) curing or preventing physical illness, depression or anxiety by means of 1); 3) resolving interpersonal problems...; and 4) untangling or freeing agents from transgressions against spirits and gods as well as humans. Boggs and Chun conclude that apology and forgiveness are central elements in all the variations.

The form of *ho'oponopono* described here is one based on Mary Kawena Pūku'i's accounts published in *Nānā I Ke Kumu* (1972). This is the form that is most widely described and the one most familiar to the authors.[7] (A few Hawaiian social workers, who were students of Pūku'i's, have trained others to use this version in their families or in agency settings.[8]

Traditionally *ho'oponopono* was a family conference to straighten out problems, although today it is used with other kinds of groups as well. In the past the sessions were led by a respected senior family member, of if necessary, by a respected outsider, perhaps a traditional healer. Today the leader may not be a family member, but a social worker or minister instead. The process is complex and potentially lengthy. It includes prayer, a statement of the problem, discussion, confession of wrongdoing, arrangement of restitution when necessary, forgiveness, and a formal release of the problem.

The Steps

Ho'oponopono is opened with *pule wehe*, prayer conducted to ask God and/or the *'aumākua* for assistance and blessing in the problem-solving endeavor.[9] *Pule* is usually led by the senior person conducting the session, known as the *haku*. Prayer signals the family to shift to a more serious tone and reminds everyone that sincerity and truthfulness are necessary conditions for participation.

In the beginning phase there is a period of identifying the general problem, known as *kūkulu kumuhana*.[10] During this initial phase the *haku* outlines the whole problem-solving sequence in order to reacquaint all participants with it.

Once the proper climate is set, the leader begins the discussion. This is the most lengthy part of the process because its purpose is to uncover the core problem. This process of working through the many layers of the problem is called the *mahiki* and may be repeated a number of times if there is more than one problem. The *haku* asks questions and interprets responses at this time in order to identify the *hihia*, or negative entanglements. This leads to a clearer understanding of what created the negative repercussions in the family network and what the initial transgression, or *hala*, was.

The *haku's* role is to skillfully question the participants and to monitor the nonverbal and verbal content of messages. The *haku* also draws on past knowledge of and experience with the family to understand what led to the present situation. The *haku* prods the family to gain a full cognitive and emotional understanding of the problem, and may also use his or her status and authority within the family structure to remind members about correct behavior.

All discussion of the problem is led and channelled by the *haku*. Family members speak to the *haku* rather than directly to one another. This indirect communication design keeps individuals from confronting one another, a situation thought likely to provoke further emotional outbursts and misunderstandings. Traditionally, Hawaiians believed that such outbursts would only escalate the problem and hinder resolution.[11] Each person affected by the problem in some way—directly or indirectly—is asked to share thoughts and feelings, or *mana'o*. There is an emphasis on self-scrutiny and maintaining an attitude of humility, or *ha'aha'a*. When participants speak they are encouraged to do so honestly, openly, and in a way that avoids blame and recrimination. If tempers flare or other strong emotions surface, the leader may declare a *ho'omalu*, a cooling-off period of silence. Participants are directed to consider what prompted the outburst and to reflect on the original intention of the process—the restoration of family harmony and goodwill.

Once the discussion has uncovered the *hihia* and *hala*, the *haku* checks to see if the individuals are ready to forgive one another. If anyone is not ready, there are a number of alternatives. A *ho'omalu* can be declared on that particular problem until the person is no longer resistant. In the meantime the group discusses other *hihia*. An unwillingness to move on to the forgiveness stage can also indicate that more discussion is needed. In this case the leader could return to *kūkula kumuhana*, restate the problem as it is now understood, and resume the discussion. In some situations the group may come to a true impasse, where resolution seems unlikely or impossible. The *ho'oponopono* may have to be concluded with a summary of what was uncovered—the entanglements and problems—and then a prayer. Although ideally *ho'oponopono* is considered complete when resolution is achieved, it is also seen as a useful way to understand the extent of family conflict when resolution has not occurred.

In the past this truncated *ho'oponopono* was rare because holding a grudge or failing to forgive was considered a grievous offense that threatened the spiritual, physical, and emotional health of the family.[12] To persist in a state called *ho'omauhala*, or holding fast to the fault, could result in *mō ka piko*,[13] or severing the family's relationship to that person. This practice is not usually used today.

In most sessions when all family members are prepared to proceed, the resolution stage of *ho'oponopono* begins. This is the time for confession, mutual forgiveness, release of the negative emotional bonds, and laying the problem to rest. If appropriate, restitution is discussed and arranged. The interlocking steps of resolution are called *mihi, kala,* and *'oki*. The *haku* may encourage individuals to speak directly to one another, since at this stage direct communication is likely to reinforce a positive emotional connection.

Mihi is the sincere confession of wrongdoing and the seeking of forgiveness. It is expected that forgiveness will be given whenever it is asked. *Mihi* is followed by *kala*, or loosening of the negative entanglements. Both the person who has confessed and the person who has forgiven are expected to *kala* the problem. This mutual release is an essential part of the process and true *ho'oponopono* is not complete without it. The *kala* indicates that the conflicts and hurts have been released and are *'oki* (cut off). The *haku* announces that the problem is now finished, or *pau*. The family is instructed to avoid any future discussion of the problem that might resurrect the *hihia*.

If the group has other unresolved issues the *haku* initiates another *kūkulu kumuhana* and *mahiki*. If time has run out, or if all the problems are resolved, the group proceeds to the closing phase, or *pani*.

The structure of the closing is the same whether for a single session or series of sessions in the resolution process. The *pule ho'opau*, or closing prayer, summarizes the session, gives thanks for the resolution, and reaffirms the family's strengths and enduring bonds. The problems that have been worked out are declared closed, never to be brought up again. The prayer may also include a *mihi, kala,* and *'oki* between the family and the spiritual forces. If other layers of the problem need to be worked out, arrangements are made for other sessions. Sometimes *ho'oponopono* takes many sessions. After the session the family and leader traditionally share a meal to which all have contributed. This is a transition time for the group to reenter more normal daily routines and to relax and enjoy one another. As one leader aptly put it "Food is important. . . . When you have a full stomach, you feel a lot better. So I think it lends to the process!"[14]

In summary, *ho'oponopono* is a highly structured process with four distinct phases: an opening phase that includes the prayer and a statement of the problem; a discussion phase, in which all members are asked to speak about their thoughts and feelings in a calm manner and to listen carefully to others; a resolution phase, when mutual forgiveness takes place; and a closing phase that summarizes what has transpired, gives thanks, and reaffirms the spiritual and emotional ties of the family. Figure 10.1 is a simplified model that represents how these elements fit together.

Ho'oponopono with a Hawaiian Family

The description and chart of *ho'oponopono* should be considered a model of an ideal type. The example given here is also "ideal" in the sense that it is taken from a videotaped performance that was produced to educate various audiences about *ho'oponopono*.[15] Abbreviated transcripts and a videotape of the "Kealoha family *ho'oponopono*" have been studied by a number of researchers (Shook 1983; Ito 1985a; Boggs and Chun 1987). This case is particularly striking because as the unrehearsed role play proceeded the family members became emotionally engaged in the session, perhaps because they had chosen a situation that they had dealt with in the past.

The precipitating event is a disagreement between two sisters (Kalau and Kili) about who is supposed to cook Sunday breakfast. The bickering continues at breakfast and leads to a lot of commotion among all family members—mother, father, three daughters, and a son. Finally Mr. Kealoha, the father, intervenes. When his few questions and chiding remarks fail to settle the affair, he suggests that the family "go *ho'oponopono*" after breakfast.

With everyone seated in a circle on the living room floor, Mr. Kealoha opens the session with a lengthy prayer.

After the prayer Mr. Kealoha begins to question Kili and Kalau. It becomes obvious that there is more going on than just a disagreement over chores. Kalau alludes to longtime difficulties with Mrs. Kealoha that have not been aired. This issue is tabled until the problem between the two sisters is resolved. After more questioning and discussion Kili and Kalau are ready to forgive one another. Each recites their confession and forgives the other. A tearful embrace seals this *mihi, kala,* and *'oki* sequence.

Next, Mr. Kealoha directs his questions to the youngest daughter, Ka'ai'ai, and son, Kekumu, to uncover their parts in the morning fracas. Both of them had joined the bickering at breakfast. This round of dis-

Figure 10.1
A *Ho'oponopono* Session

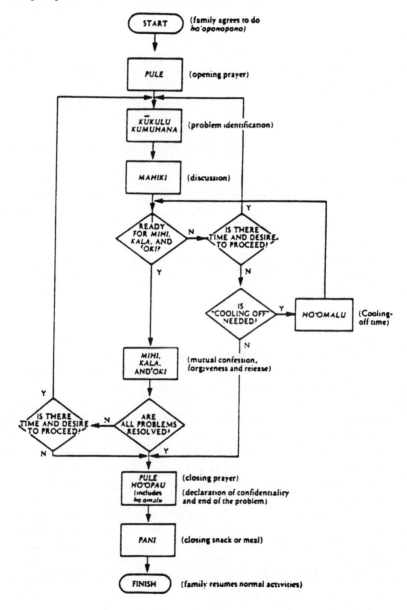

cussion quickly leads to sequences of confession and forgiveness. With all of the immediate entanglements resolved the family returns to what now seems like the most resonating hurt—the pattern of misunderstandings between Kalau and Mrs. Kealoha. When Mrs. Kealoha begins to speak she starts to cry and says, "Let me pull myself together." Mr. Kealoha explains this *ho'omalu* to the others. "Mommie needs to pull herself together because she feels—" (Kekumu:) "Sad!" (Mr. Kealoha:) "But also so that she can say things in a way that doesn't create more *pilikia* (trouble). O.K.?"

All but Mr. Kealoha weep silently as mother and daughter recount their understanding of how the strain developed between them. Mrs. Kealoha admits that she "digs in" on the kids about the chores and that she does not always check things out with them to make sure they understand the agreements. She admits sadly that she realizes Kalau has had a hard time talking with her. Kalau admits that she does not listen very well and often argues with her mother. She knows that she takes her frustrations out on the others. After a while the two forgive one another and share a lengthy embrace.

Before the session concludes Mr. Kealoha steps out of his role as the *haku* and asks Mrs. Kealoha to take over for a few moments. He admits that he has also contributed to the family's problems by failing to make sure that everyone understood the cooking agreement, and by getting angry with Kalau. Mr. Kealoha returns to the leadership role to conduct the closing prayer. He states that "problems are laid to rest not to be brought up again" and reminds the family of the spiritual dimensions of conflict and reconciliation.

Dear Lord...As we hurt one another...we also hurt You, and we ask for Your forgiveness. Please forgive us. Please release and please set into the depths of the ocean our *pilikia*, never more to rise...

At the prayer's conclusion the family members hug and kiss one another, then rise.

EMERGING ISSUES

Contemporary Adaptations

The current popularity of *ho'oponopono* testifies to its virtues as a useful, practical process and as a potentially transformative idea that changes the way that people perceive, understand, and address conflict. As an idea, *ho'oponopono* is familiar to many in Hawaii. Yet only a small number of individuals actually know the specific features of it; fewer still use it. The publication of *Nānā I Ke Kumu*, with its section on *ho'oponopono*, stimulated new applications of the process. Several Hawaiian social work agencies began to use it with families. In these settings a social worker or counselor was the *haku*, instead of a family member. Also, since the majority of families seen by the agencies either were experiencing crises, or had multiple, often long-standing problems, the kinds of problems addressed in the *ho'oponopono* sessions were more complex.[16] Families presented problems of divorce, delinquency, domestic abuse, and mental illness, as well as less dramatic issues. Often these problems were exacerbated by the political, economic, and social realities in the Hawaiian community whose way of life had undergone dramatic dislocation since Western colonization. As a result of these social forces many Hawaiian families have become culturally pluralistic, incorporating Asian and American beliefs and practices into their life. *Ho'oponopono* leaders today have to be multiculturally competent so they can unravel "Hawaiian" beliefs and issues from Western and Asian ones, translate concepts and terms, and use multiple cultural frames of reference as needed. Fortunately, *ho'oponopono* "translates" well. E. Haertig, a psychiatrist who was part of the group whose work resulted in the publication of *Nānā I Ke Kamu*, remarks: "*Ho'oponopono* may well be one of the soundest methods to restore and maintain good family relationships that any society has ever devised" (Pūku'i et al. 1972:70).

Ho'oponopono is also being used outside the Hawaiian community and family setting, perhaps because others see its elements as universal or pan-cultural. During the 1970s the Pūku'i model was used by non-Hawaiians in at least two agencies.[17] One was a residential substance abuse treatment program for adolescent boys. The program director described their use of *ho'oponopono* as "a primary spiritual element, as well as our major therapeutic counseling tool" (Shook 1985:47). It was also one way the boys learned more about Hawaiian cultural traditions. Many of them were part-Hawaiian, although most of the counseling staff were not. *Ho'oponopono* was also used in a wilderness program that offered one- to three-week courses on the island of Hawaii. The backpacking, shifting climate conditions, rugged terrain, and tensions of group living made the courses physically strenuous and emotionally demanding. The rigor and intensity led to group conflict. Course instructors used *ho'oponopono* as a way to alleviate pressure and to resolve issues that got in the way of safely proceeding on schedule. The sessions also reinforced the group's identity as an *'ohana* since, like a family, the individuals were dependent on one another in very concrete ways during the course.

Other organizations have shown interest in *ho'oponopono*. The Department of Education distributes information about it in curricular materials. They recently produced a videotape on *ho'oponopono* that demonstrated an uncle settling a conflict among teenagers.[18] D. Nishimura

(1978) reported on his own use of *ho'oponopono* as a high school counselor on Maui. In a different setting a newly formed mediation program invoked *ho'oponopono* in its first brochure. The text stated that the opening of the center "Brings to Hawaii a new way of resolving disputes but at the same time it is also a return to an old way; the traditional Hawaiian way of *Ho'oponopono*; a way of resolving disputes by talking them out in the family or extended family setting in the spirit of *'ohana* and *aloha*" (Honolulu Neighborhood Justice Center 1980).

The state correctional system has sponsored educational forums for inmates on conflict resolution, including *ho'oponopono*. One of the authors once did a presentation at a facility that led to a "shuttle diplomacy"-style *ho'oponopono*. At an inmate's request he attempted to smooth out some difficulties between the inmate and his family. Recently the governor of Hawaii convened a task force of mostly Hawaiian community leaders to study and recommend ways to intervene in emerging complex community disputes using approaches that are "more Hawaiian," that is, harmonious and collaborative rather than confrontational and adversarial. The group is taking a close look at *ho'oponopono* to get ideas.

Cautions and Concerns

These examples illustrate an enthusiasm and optimism about contemporary uses of *ho'oponopono*. Those who want to learn and apply the process quickly, however, discover that there are very few practitioners available to instruct and guide them. Also, while some advocates remain unabashedly in favor of more widespread use, others are more cautious and concerned about the implications such "adaptations" imply. Many questions are raised. What happens when this Hawaiian process is taken out of its traditional family setting? How does the meaning change? What happens when English words or theoretical constructs are used to describe *ho'oponopono*? It is this last question that we believe is particularly germane to researchers and practitioners who adapt the process beyond its traditional context. If this chapter had been written in Hawaiian the meaning would be different—probably more precise, certainly more evocative and contextually familiar to the Hawaiian-speaking community. Recently during a presentation on *ho'oponopono* one of the authors was asked: "What is the equivalent of 'negotiation' in *ho'oponopono*?" The response was: "There isn't one." While some social scientists might disagree with the response, the point bears consideration. If particular behaviors or interactions look similar to one another, are they equivalent constructs? For example, is the *haku* simply a culturally specific example of a "mediator" who "facilitates" family "disputes," or a "therapist" who conducts "family therapy"? Is the *mahiki* a "discussion," or something else? Do we do justice to *ho'oponopono* when we call it a "conflict resolution process," or overstate the case when we call it a "therapy"? These are familiar and knotty issues in cross-cultural work. We urge caution in setting up these equivalencies. While writing this chapter we struggled with our English descriptions and remain uncomfortable and unsure about some of the compromises we made. Geoffrey White and Karen Watson-Gegeo (1990:35–36) also make a case for using more precise language when discussing Pacific island disputing processes:

We prefer the label "disentangling" over "conflict resolution" or "dispute management" because disentangling points to elements of local meaning that seem to organize and guide the activities we examine. To begin with, the notion of disentangling signals a process rather than an end product, indicating that management in moral negotiation itself may be more significant than specific decisions or outcomes. Secondly, the image of a tangled net or a knotted line suggests a blockage of purposeful activity, reminding the members of a community that the problem at hand requires attention lest it impede "normal" social life. It is in this sense that many of the activities examined in the following chapters are considered therapeutic for individuals and collectivities alike. Finally, disentangling presumes a conception of an unmarked, background state-of-affairs in which the strands of people's lives do not become snarled and ineffective. Whether spoken or implied, models of "straight" or correct relations may themselves be trans-figured in the disentangling process.

Despite our cautions and uncertainty we remain grateful that there is indeed "a word for it," as Rheingold celebrated in his book. *Ho'oponopono* is one example of a fairly sophisticated, metaphorically rich, and practical way of dealing with disrupted human and spiritual relationships. If it also gives conflict resolvers, therapists, and cross-cultural researchers an "ah ha!" of recognition and some new ideas about their own work, then that is a bonus.

NOTES

Financial support for this paper was provided in part by the William and Flora Hewlett Foundation through the University of Hawaii's Program on Conflict Resolution. The authors also wish to thank Neal Milner for insightful and good-humored editorial comments on an earlier draft; Jan Matuseski for research assistance; to the staff of University of Hawaii Program on Conflict Resolution, particularly Patricia Shields for her speedy word processing and great patience. We especially would like to thank our teachers in *ho'oponopono* and all the people we have worked with to straighten relationships for opening their hearts and minds to us.

1. *Ho'oponopono* appears on the cover, is used as an example twice in the introduction (pp. 4, 6), and has a separate entry in the chapter on human family affairs (pp. 13–15).

2. *Aloha* means love; a greeting of hello or good-bye; compassion. The word summons up a pattern of many Hawaiian values that are difficult to pin down in a single definition.

3. The recent popularity of traditional forms of *hula* has brought back a strong spiritual element to dance. Blessings of work endeavors, social gatherings, and opening and closing ceremonies are commonplace. The love of nature is demonstrated in various ways. A popular phrase, *aloha 'āina* ("love of the land"), is used to support many Hawaiian concerns, including highly political development issues. There also has been a resurgence of *Makahiki* festivals in recent years. These yearly celebrations, traditionally held in the fall, were a time for sports and religious activities and were a tribute to Lono, the Hawaiian god of agriculture. Today's festivities usually combine spiritual tribute with an opportunity to build community strength and conduct community fund-raising activities.

4. Dreams, visions, portentous symbols, and precognitive messages (extrasensory perception) are also experienced by many Hawaiians and accorded prominent value in providing interpretations of past events and for giving guidance regarding future actions. See Pūku'i et al. 1979, chapters 4 and 7.

5. These values apply to many areas of endeavor, including work. For example, *ukupau* is still used by some businesses in Hawaii. The word literally refers to "piece work," or paying someone by the job rather than by time. On some jobs everyone pitches in and works quickly together so the work is finished early. For example, trash collectors in Honolulu help each other finish their routes. Workers then have more time for hobbies, social activities, or to take second jobs to help support their families. This contrasts with the predominant American work pattern of adhering to a strict time clock system and requiring workers to be on the job for a specified period of time regardless of task completion.

6. See Ito 1978 for a fascinating study of Hawaiian women's beliefs regarding the "retributive" nature and consequences of negative thoughts, feelings, or acts toward others.

7. Shook has conducted research; Kwan is a trained practitioner. Both conduct educational presentations on the subject.

8. See Shook (1985:7–10) for a description of how Pūku'i's model became resurrected and later used by a number of practitioners, mostly in social service settings.

9. In pre-Christian times the *pule* would be offered to the *akua* (major gods) and *'aumākua* (family gods). Today the prayer is addressed in various ways to the "powers that be," the Christian God, the *'aumākua*, or a combination that fits the family's beliefs.

10. This term has two additional meanings that are part of *ho'oponopono*. *Kūkulu kumuhana* is the pooling of strengths for a shared purpose, such as solving the family's problem. It also refers to the leader's effort to reach out to a person who is resisting the *ho'oponopono* process to enable that person to participate fully.

11. This is an interesting contrast to conflict resolution or therapeutic situations in other cultures, where emotional catharsis is believed to be beneficial and is encouraged as a means of "letting go" of the hurt, anger, or resentment.

12. Pūku'i et al. (1972:74) report that retribution from the *'aumākua* would befall an individual who did not forgive when asked.

13. *Mō ka piko* literally means to sever the umbilical cord, an obvious reference to severing family connections.

14. Quote from a case study respondent named "*Keola Espiritu*" in Shook 1985:88.

15. This videotape was produced for use by the Sub-Regional Child Welfare Training Center, School of Social Work, University of Hawaii. A videotape discussion guide (Shook 1983) was also produced.

16. This complexity may be a significant factor explaining why there are so few practitioners (at least those who are known to the general community). See Shook, 1985:100–101 for more on barriers to the use of *ho'oponopono*.

17. See Shook 1985 for case study treatment of these and other examples.

18. This videotape, entitled "Nā Ki'i Hana No'eau Hawai'i, Ho'oponopono: Problem Resolution," was produced by the Hawaii State Department of Education in 1986.

REFERENCES

Boggs, S. T., and M. N. Chun. 1990. Ho'oponopono: An Hawaiian Method of Solving Interpersonal Problems. In *The Discourse of Disentangling: Conflict Discourse in Pacific Societies*, eds. K. Watson-Gegeo and G. White. Palo Alto: Stanford University Press.

Edmunds, S. 1987. Geothermal Energy Development in Hawai'i: A Decade of Conflict. Honolulu: University of Hawaii Program on Conflict Resolution Working Paper Series 1987–4.

Gallimore, R., J. Boggs, and C. Jordan. 1974. *Culture, Behavior and Education: A Study of Hawaiian Americans*. Beverly Hills: Sage.

Hawaii Department of Education. 1986. Nā Ki'i Hana No'eau Hawai'i, Ho'oponopono: Problem Resolution (a videotape). Honolulu.

Honolulu Neighborhood Justice Center. 1980. Program brochure.

Howard, A. 1974. *Ain't No Big Thing: Coping Strategies in a Hawaiian-American Community*. Honolulu: University of Hawaii Press.

Ito, K. L. 1978. Symbolic Conscience: Illness Retribution among Urban Hawaiian Women. Ph.D. diss., University of California, Los Angeles.

———. Ho'oponopono: "To Make Right": Hawaiian Conflict Resolution and Metaphor in the Construction of a Family Therapy. *Culture, Medicine and Psychiatry* 9:201–17.

———. 1985b. Affective Bonds: Hawaiian Interrelationships of Self. In *Person, Self and Experience: Exploring Pacific Ethno-psychologies*, eds. G. White and J. Kirkpatrick. Berkeley: University of California Press.

Kanahele, G. H. S. 1986. *Kū Kanaka: Stand Tall*. Honolulu: University of Hawaii Press.

Mays, M. P. 1973. Coming Together: A Conflict Resolution Theme in Hawaiian-American Families. Honolulu: Governor's Office, State of Hawaii, 299 Task Force Report.

Mossman, M., and P. Wahilani. 1975. Kūlia i ka lōkahi i ke ola! Mimeograph.

Nishimura, D. 1978. Culture, Counseling and Ho'oponopono: An Ancient Model in a Modern Context. *Personnel and Guidance Journal* (May):56–62.

Pūku'i, M. 1983. *Ōlelo No eau: Hawaiian Proverbs and Poetical Sayings.* Honolulu: Bishop Museum Press.

Pūku'i, M., E. Haertig, and C. Lee. 1972. *Nānā I Ke Kumu.* Vol. 1. Hololulu: Hui Hanai.

Pūku'i, M., E. Haertig, C. Lee, and J. McDermott. 1979. *Nānā I Ke Kumu.* Vol. 2. Honolulu: Hui Hanai.

Rheingold, H. 1988. *They Have a Word for It: A Lighthearted Lexicon of Untranslatable Words and Phrases.* Los Angeles: Jeremy P. Tarcher.

Shook, E. V. 1983. Ho'oponopono: A Discussion Guide for Two Videotapes. Honolulu: University of Hawaii School of Social Work and Pacific Basin Family and Child Center.

———. 1985. *Ho'oponopono: Contemporary Uses of a Hawaiian Problem-Solving Process.* Honolulu: University of Hawaii Press.

Watson-Gegeo, K., and G. White. 1990. Disentangling Discourse. In *The Discourse of Disentangling: Conflict Discourse in Pacific Societies*, eds. K. Watson-Gegeo and G. White. Palo Alto: Stanford University Press.

Whitney, S. 1987. "I Would Always Take Care of My Net": Self-Esteem and the Assumptive World of Local Youth. *Hawai'i Community Education Forum* 1(1):7–13.

Select Bibliography

As befits a new and emergent field, the titles below run a gamut of disciplines—from classics in the field (Gluckman 1955; Boulding 1962) to work representing some of the newest perspectives (Starr and Collier 1989; Grimshaw 1990); from general and prescriptive statements (Raiffa 1982) to work deeply rooted in historical context and ethnographic specificities (Koch 1974; Moore 1986); from works dubious of the role of culture in conflict resolution (Burton 1979, 1990; Zartman and Berman 1982) to works essentially predicated on it (Geertz 1983; Rosen 1989). Such a bibliography, needless to say, always remains "select," incomplete and unfinished.

Abel, R., ed. 1982. *The Politics of Informal Justice: The American Experience*. New York: Academic.

Arno, A. 1985. Structural Communication and Control Communication: An Interactionist Perspective on Legal and Customary Procedures for Conflict Management. *American Anthropologist* 87(1):40–55.

Avruch, K., and P. W. Black. 1987. A "Generic" Theory of Conflict Resolution: A Critique. *Negotiation Journal* 3(1):87–96, 99–100.

———. 1990. Ideas of Human Nature in Contemporary Conflict Resolution Theory. *Negotiation Journal* 6(3):221–28.

———. 1991. The Culture Question and Conflict Resolution. *Peace and Change* 16(1):22–45.

Azar, E., and J. Burton, eds. 1986. *International Conflict Resolution: Theory and Practice*. Boulder: Lynne Reiner.

Bendahmane, D. B., and J. MacDonald, eds. 1986. *Perspectives on Negotiations: Four Case Studies and Interpretations*. Washington, D.C.: Foreign Service Institute, U.S. Department of State.

Bercovitch, J. 1984. *Social Conflict and Third Parties: Strategies of Conflict Resolution*. Boulder: Westview.

Binnendijk, H., ed. 1987. *National Negotiation Styles*. Washington, D.C.: Foreign Service Institute, U.S. Department of State.

Black, P. W., and K. Avruch. 1989. Some Issues in Thinking about Culture and the Resolution of Conflict. *Humanity and Society* 13(2):187–94.

Boehm, C. 1986. *Blood Revenge: The Enactment and Management of Conflict in Montenegro and Other Tribal Societies*. Philadelphia: University of Pennsylvania Press.

Bohannan, P., ed. 1967. *Law and Warfare: Studies in the Anthropology of Conflict*. Austin: University of Texas Press.

———. 1989 (1957). *Justice and Judgement among the Tiv*. Prospect Heights, Ill.: Waveland.

Bossy, J., ed. 1983. *Disputes and Settlements: Law and Human Relations in the West*. Cambridge: Cambridge University Press.

Boulding, K. E. 1962. *Conflict and Defense: A General Theory*. New York: Harper and Row.

Burton, J. W. 1969. *Conflict and Communication: The Use of Controlled Communication in International Relations*. London: Macmillan.

———. 1979. *Deviance, Terrorism and War*. New York: St. Martin's.

———. 1990. *Conflict: Resolution and Provention*. New York: St. Martin's.

Burton, J. W., and F. Dukes. 1990. *Conflict: Practices in Management, Settlement and Resolution*. New York: St. Martin's.

Carroll, R. 1988. *Cultural Misunderstandings: The French-American Experience*. Chicago: University of Chicago Press.

Cohen, R. 1990. *Culture and Conflict in Egyptian-Israeli Relations: A Dialogue of the Deaf*. Bloomington: Indiana University Press.

Comaroff, J., and S. Roberts. 1981. *Rules and Processes: The Cultural Logic of Dispute in an African Context*. Chicago: University of Chicago Press.

Dentan, R. 1968. *The Semai: A Nonviolent People*. New York: Holt, Rinehart and Winston.

Deutsch, M. 1973. *The Resolution of Conflict*. New Haven: Yale University Press.

Doob, L., ed. 1970. *Resolving Conflict in Africa*. New Haven: Yale University Press.

Druckman, D., A. Benton, F. Ali, and J. Bagur. 1976. Cultural Differences in Bargaining Behavior. *Journal of Conflict Resolution* 20(3):413–52.

Fisher, R., and W. Ury. 1981. *Getting to Yes*. Boston: Houghton Mifflin.

Foster, M. L., and R. A. Rubenstein, eds. 1986. *Peace and War: Cross-Cultural Perspectives*. New Brunswick: Transaction.

Geertz, C. 1983. Local Knowledge: Fact and Law in Comparative Perspective. In *Local Knowledge*. New York: Basic.

Gibbs, J. 1963. The Kpelle Moot. *Africa* 33:1–11.

Gluckman, M. 1955. *The Judicial Process among the Barotse of Northern Rhodesia*. Manchester: Manchester University Press.

Greenhouse, C. 1986. *Praying for Justice*. Ithaca, N.Y.: Cornell University Press.

Grimshaw, A. D., ed. 1990. *Conflict Talk: Sociolinguistic Investigations of Arguments in Conversations*. Cambridge: Cambridge University Press.

Gulliver, P. H. 1979. *Disputes and Negotiations: A Cross-Cultural Perspective*. Orlando: Academic.

Hamnett, I., ed. 1977. *Social Anthropology and Law*. New York: Academic.

Harrington, C. 1985. *Shadow Justice: The Ideology and Institutionalization of Alternatives to Court.* Westport, Conn.: Greenwood.

Hines, J. 1980. *Conflict and Conflict Management.* Athens: University of Georgia Press.

Howell, S., and R. Willis, eds. 1989. *Societies at Peace: Anthropological Perspectives.* New York: Routledge.

Humphreys, S. 1985. Law as Discourse. *History and Anthropology* 1:241–64.

Kelman, H., and S. Cohen. 1976. The Problem-Solving Workshop: A Social-Psychological Contribution to the Resolution of International Conflicts. *Journal of Peace Research* 13(2):79–90.

Kiefer, T. 1986 (1972). *The Tausug: Violence and Law in a Philippine Moslem Society.* Prospect Heights, Ill.: Waveland.

Koch, K-F. 1974. *War and Peace in Jalemo: The Management of Conflict in Highland New Guinea.* Cambridge: Harvard University Press.

Kochman, T. 1981. *Black and White Styles in Conflict.* Chicago: University of Chicago Press.

Kolb, D. 1983. *The Mediators.* Cambridge: MIT.

Merry, S. 1987. Disputing Without Culture. *Harvard Law Review* 100:2057–73.

———. 1990. *Getting Justice and Getting Even: Legal Consciousness among Working-Class Americans.* Chicago: University of Chicago Press.

Moore, C. 1986. *The Mediation Process.* San Francisco: Jossey Bass.

Moore, S. 1986. *Social Facts and Fabrications: "Customary" Law on Kilimanjaro, 1880–1980.* Chicago: University of Chicago Press.

Nader, L., ed. 1965. The Ethnography of Law. American Anthropologist 67(6), part 2 (Special Issue).

———. 1969. *Law in Culture and Society.* Chicago: Aldine.

Nader, L., and H. Todd, Jr., eds. 1978. *The Disputing Process—Law in Ten Societies.* New York: Columbia University Press.

Raiffa, H. 1982. *The Art and Science of Negotiation.* Cambridge: Harvard University Press.

Rosen, L. 1989. *The Anthropology of Justice: Law as Culture in Islamic Society.* Cambridge: Cambridge University Press.

Rubenstein, R. A., and M. L. Foster, eds. 1988. *The Social Dynamics of Peace and Conflict: Culture in International Security.* Boulder: Westview.

Sandole, D. J. D., and I. Sandole-Staroste, eds. 1987. *Conflict Management and Problem Solving: Interpersonal to International Applications.* New York: New York University Press.

Schelling, T. 1960. *The Strategy of Conflict.* Cambridge: Harvard University Press.

Shook, V. 1985. *Ho'oponopono: Contemporary Uses of a Hawaiian Problem-Solving Process.* Honolulu: University of Hawaii Press.

Starr, J., and J. Collier, eds. 1989. *History and Power in the Study of Law: New Directions in Legal Anthropology.* Ithaca, N.Y.: Cornell University Press.

de Waal, F. 1989. *Peacemaking among Primates.* Cambridge: Harvard University Press.

Watson-Gegeo, K., and G. White, eds. 1990. *Disentangling: Conflict Discourse in Pacific Societies.* Stanford: Stanford University Press.

Wehr, P. 1979. *Conflict Regulation.* Boulder: Westview.

Zartman, I., and M. Berman. 1982. *The Practical Negotiator.* New Haven: Yale University Press.

Index

Waite, Terry, 32
Wedge, Bryant: clinical approach to
  conflict resolution, 3; founding of
  Center for Conflict Analysis and
  Resolution, 2
Whiting, Arthur A., 26

Yarrow, C. H., 27

Zapotec culture: conciliation, 43 (*see
  also* Conflict resolution practice);
  conflict model, 43 (*see also* Conflict
  resolution theory; Law); harmony
  model, 8, 42, 44 (*see also* Conflict
  resolution theory); litigation, 42;
  social organization, 42; village law,
  42; violence, 42–43
Zero-sum games, 6, 33, 42, 66

About the Contributors

KEVIN AVRUCH is Professor of Anthropology and a member of the Faculty Advisory Board of the Institute for Conflict Analysis and Resolution, at George Mason University. He has published widely on ethnicity, politics, and religion in Israel and the Middle East and, with Peter W. Black, on culture and conflict resolution. He is the author of *Culture and Conflict Resolution* (USIP Press, 1998).

F. G. BAILEY taught anthropology at the University of California, San Diego. He specializes in the politics of small groups, particularly in formal organizations. His most recent book is *The Need for Enemies* (Cornell, 1998).

PETER W. BLACK is Professor of Anthropology and a member of the Faculty Advisory Board of the Institute for Conflict Analysis and Resolution, at George Mason University. He is a specialist on Oceania and has published numerous articles on religion, ethno-psychology, dispute behavior and, with Kevin Avruch, on culture and conflict resolution.

PETER JUST is Associate Professor of Anthropology at Williams College. Following extensive field research, his published work on the Dou Donggo has appeared in *American Ethnologist, Ethnology,* and *Ethos.* He is author of a monograph on Dou Donggo dispute settlement entitled *Dou Donggo Justice* (1998).

KAMIL KOZAN taught for several years in Turkey and Jordan. He is currently Associate Professor of Management at St. John Fisher College in Rochester, N.Y. His research interests include conflict management and cross-cultural issues in organizational behavior.

LEONARD KE'ALA KWAN is a Hawaiian language teacher at Kamehameha High School in Honolulu. He served five years as director of a counseling program which used Hawaiian cultural approaches such as *Ho'oponopono* in helping families resolve conflicts. He has a Master's Degree from the University of Hawaii at Mānoa.

JOHN PAUL LEDERACH is Professor of Sociology at Eastern Mennonite University, in Harrisonburg, Virginia. He worked and lived in Costa Rica from 1986–1988, where he did research, training, and mediation in the Central American region. He has written *Building Peace* (USIP Press, 1997).

LAURA NADER is Professor of Anthropology at the University of California, Berkeley. Her most recent book is *Naked Science* (Routledge, 1996).

JOSEPH A. SCIMECCA is Professor of Sociology at George Mason University. He is Chair of the Department of Sociology and Anthropology and formerly Director of the Center for Conflict Analysis and Resolution. His main areas of research are sociological theory, conflict resolution, and public policy. He is currently completing a book entitled *Counsel of the Wicked*.

E. VICTORIA SHOOK is Lecturer in Communication Studies at San Jose State University. She was formerly Assistant Director of the Program on Conflict Resolution at the University of Hawaii at Mānoa. She is the author of *Ho'oponopono: Contemporary Uses of a Hawaiian Problem-Solving Process* (Hawaii, 1985).

GEOFFREY M. WHITE is Senior Fellow, East-West Center, and a member of the graduate anthropology faculty of the University of Hawaii. His research on language, psychology and identity formation is published in numerous articles and several books, including *Identity Through History: Living Stories in a Solomon Islands Society* (1991), *Disentangling: Conflict Discourse in Pacific Societies* (1990, coedited), and *Person, Self and Experience, Exploring Pacific Ethnopsychologies* (1985, coedited).